**W9-BLF-985**

3660

Date Due

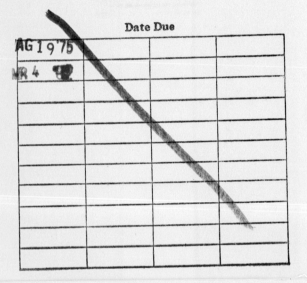

THE
MAN
FROM
GALILEE

THE MAN
FROM
GALILEE

A Life of Jesus

GEORGE M. LAMSA

DOUBLEDAY & COMPANY, INC.
Garden City, New York

Grateful acknowledgment is made to the A. J. Holman Company for permission to use material from *The Holy Bible from Ancient Eastern Manuscripts* by George M. Lamsa, published by A. J. Holman Company.

*This book is sincerely dedicated to
Mrs. Helen Buck Waggoner as a token
of my deep appreciation and gratitude
for her kind interest and generous help
in furthering the Aramaic work.*

*May the Lord God, our heavenly Father,
reward her abundantly.*

CONTENTS

Contents

INTRODUCTION

THIS VOLUME IS NOT JUST another life of Christ like hundreds of others which have been written by able men of all nationalities and religions. This is a book written by a native who was born and reared in that ancient Biblical culture where customs and manners remained unchanged from the time of the Patriarchs until the present day. The author also speaks Ancient Aramaic, the language which Jesus, His disciples and His followers spoke. This was the *lingua franca* and the literary tongue in the Near East and Palestine from the time of the patriarchs to the thirteenth century A.D. He understands the idioms, metaphors, and figurative speech just as Jesus' simple and unlearned disciples understood them. This is not all, the writer also grew up under the same difficulties and problems as Jesus, His disciples and the Jewish people did in those days.

Today, more than ever, people throughout the world are eager to know more about Jesus, His background and the forces which led Him to embark on His Messianic mission and which endeared Him to millions of people throughout the centuries.

Two thousand years have elapsed since Jesus of Nazareth walked on the shores of the lake of Galilee, recruited a few simple disciples and proclaimed himself as the Messiah. From the outset, He assured both the Jews and Gentiles of a better world order. An order wherein people of all races and colors would live in harmony, peace and tranquillity. Moreover, He shunned the decadent religious system with its rituals, ceremonials and animal sacrifices and supplanted it with a religion which was more practical and beneficial for mankind. Jesus admonished the Jewish people to return to the simple religion of the prophets and their forefathers.

Unfortunately, Christianity has not yet succeeded in changing the world. It has failed to bring understanding between nations and usher in the peaceful era which was predicted by the holy prophets. The strong nations still oppress the weak nations. Evil forces continue just as of yore. The lion still devours the lamb, the leopard the kid and the bear the sheep.

On the other hand, the crude instruments of war, the sword, spear and bow, which existed in Biblical days have been replaced by fearful, awesome weapons which can destroy the entire world.

Yet Jesus came to free those who were in bondage, to give hope to the hopeless, to lighten those who were heavily laden, to give sanity to the insane, to give healing to the sick, sight to the blind, spiritual food for the hungry and comfort to those who were mourning.

Today, millions of people have deserted Christianity seeking other ideologies. Many learned men even wonder if the Christ had come. Some still believe He is coming and others go on aimlessly and hopelessly trying to find the way.

Nevertheless, Christ has come. And the seed which He has sown is growing slowly. The leaders of the world, now more than ever, realize that Jesus' teaching is the answer for the ills of the world. This is because nothing has been left which mankind has not tried out, in order to solve world problems except the formula set forth by the man from Galilee.

Jesus, while studying the Law and the prophets, saw a new pattern for a new world order. A pattern which had never been tried before—a way (religion) which served mankind and which would usher in an era of peace and equality. A way wherein the nations of the world would have one measure for themselves, for their friends and for their enemies. For with the same measure they measure to others sooner or later would be measured back to them. Jesus knew that mankind, having been created in God's image and likeness has power to conquer evil forces, sin, sickness and death. All that men had to learn was the secret that God is a loving Father who seeks and cares for His children and that He is not a tyrant constantly in need of sacrifices and gift offerings. This inner knowledge of God made Jesus supreme over all other teachers of religions. Thus, He became a link between the religion of the Jews and the Gentile world, whereby to share God's divine promises which He had made to Jewish fathers with other races and people who were groping in darkness and seeking hard to find the living God, who is the Father of all people.

Centuries before Jesus' birth, the prophets of Israel in their quest for a new and better order, an order of peace and justice, foresaw a new realm, a universal state, embracing all races and cultures. They also found that Yehovah, their God, was the God of other races and peoples. And in their visions and dreams they had a glimpse of a perfect world order, wherein the weapons of war would be of no further use, except to be broken and made into plowshares and pruning hooks.

The Jews, hitherto, had looked upon religion objectively, in other words, the Living God was their God only and the Torah, the light of the world was given by God to them only. This is why they covered the Lamp of God (The Holy Bible) so that the Gentiles might not see the Light of God.

Centuries before, the Hebrew prophets and in particular the great prophet Isaiah had seen the perfect blueprint of this order. And they proclaimed it to dull and deaf ears of the priests and scribes in their day. Many of these prophets gave their lives declaring the reign of justice and happiness but they were unable to change the stubborn hearts of the priests and scribes who had made religion a business and were reluctant to exchange the old wine for the new.

These dedicated men of God gave up the hope of implementing the new order, but they saw hope in the future. After all, it takes time for a seed to sprout and grow. This is not all, in visions and dreams they saw that God would anoint and send a great prophet who would be equal to the hard task, the blessed Messiah (The Anointed One), the wonderful counselor, the Prince of Peace. In the sixteenth century B.C., Moses had assured the people of such a great prophet who would come in due time, a prophet greater than himself.

The new Prophet from Galilee had absorbed most of His early years in the deep study of the Law and the prophets, the men of God who had given their lives for the sake of truth so that the generations to come would live in peace and harmony.

Jesus' teaching is based on that of the prophets who acted as spokesmen for God. There is nothing in it which is alien to the Torah, the Bible, the Light of God. In other words, Jesus as the blessed Messiah had come to fulfill the Law and the prophets and to inaugurate the era of loving kindness and meekness. Moreover He found the key to the Scriptures whereby He unlocked the truths which were hidden from the eyes of the religious leaders of His day. He called on the people to clean the cup from within instead of from without, that is, to change their hearts. He told them that God was a forgiving Father ready to receive them when they changed their evil ways. During His time the Jewish religious men were busy writing commentaries upon commentaries trying to interpret the Law and the Holy Prophets. But instead they made them more complicated.

Jesus spoke with authority because He knew the Scriptures by heart and He could quote from them freely.

As we see from the following chapters in this book, the struggle was not between the Jewish people and Jesus but between Jesus and the Jewish religious authorities who had supplanted the truth of God with their own teaching and the traditions of the elders. Thousands of Jewish men and women followed Jesus and hailed Him as the promised Messiah and Savior of the world. These were the people to whom He had been sent. They were the people who carried the heavy burdens and bore harsh yokes. They were the ones who ministered to His needs and the needs of His disciples.

Jesus, from the outset, had assured the people that He had not come to weaken the law and the prophets, but rather to strengthen them and to put them into practice.

Apparently, it was hard for the Jewish authorities to reject man-made doctrines and dogmas which they had cherished for centuries. For example, it was hard for them to love those who they had been hating for centuries and to pray for those who had been persecuting them and putting heavy burdens upon them. It is sad to say that even today, after Jesus' Gospel has been translated in hundreds of languages and preached to untold numbers of people, His followers still find it difficult to love their enemies and to pray for those whom they have despised and to render good for evil.

Jesus' new teaching of meekness and non-resistance, like that of the prophets, was too alien to the priests and scribes. These leaders, like many Christian leaders of today were jealous of their teaching and high positions they occupied.

Jesus' teaching of meekness and loving kindness was not only hard for the Jewish leaders to accept, it had been difficult even for His disciples and followers to understand and put into action. Indeed it is hard to pray for our enemies and love those who hate us. It is difficult to believe that meekness would accomplish that which the sword and bow had failed to accomplish.

I have tried to be fair in this book. Fair to the Jews who for centuries had carried the Lamp of God amid much bloodshed and suffering, fair to the Gentiles because they lacked the Light of God, fair to the imperialists and oppressors because they did not know the way of God and believed in force.

May God our Heavenly Father bless all the readers of this volume and open their hearts to love Him with all their might and to love all the people of other races, colors and religions. I have avoided discussing theological and controversial doctrines. In this book I have portrayed Jesus of Nazareth as a man who knew our weaknesses and who shared our suffering, a neighbor who had sympathy and compassion upon those who had fallen and gone astray from the way of God. A healer who had mercy upon the sick and lepers. A great Savior ready to die for us that we may have an abundant and eternal life. I believe in Jesus' resurrection which is the greatest miracle in the world. He raised the dead and restored the sight of the blind. God had granted Him all power.

THE
MAN
FROM
GALILEE

I

JESUS
OF
NAZARETH

꧁ ꧂

NO GREATER MAN HAS EVER
walked upon this earth than Jesus of Nazareth. No
prophet, no seer, no philosopher has been more adored,
more worshiped or more loved than Jesus. Millions of
men and women through the centuries have prayed to
Him or have prayed to God in His name. Myriads of
souls have accepted Him as their Savior, have invoked
His name when in need of peace, health and consola-
tion. Kings and princes have removed their crowns and
placed them on the ground while they knelt before Him
in prayer.

And yet, Jesus was the meekest and most humble man
ever born of woman. He was more humble than the
lowliest peasant or fisherman in Galilee. The richest Son,
the King of kings, yet He was born in a cave partially

occupied by animals, those peaceful and harmless creatures of God that are so often enslaved and mistreated by
man.

We know little about Jesus, His background, His education or His friends. The Gospels are the only record we
have of His birth and life, and the little information
we have was collected by His disciples and faithful followers years after His death. Thus far, no new material
has been found, so except for the Holy Scriptures, we
have no source to turn to. All we know about the earthly
life of Jesus is based on a few episodes which are parts
of religious customs, ordinances and rituals which Jesus,
like all Jewish children, underwent. These customs are
still practiced in some parts of the world.

Why should we expect to know more about Him than
about His contemporaries—the boys with whom He
played, or the shepherds with whom He spent many
lonely hours watching sheep upon the hills, or the teachers who taught Him to read and write, or the leaders and
other dignitaries of His day? Today, there are thousands
of boys playing in the streets of American cities and
studying in schools. Someday they will become congress-
men, governors, the President, but we know nothing
about them because as yet they have contributed nothing
to our culture.

Jesus was divine, and the Spirit of God was upon Him
from His birth. But He was also the son of man and thus
was subject to time and space, to hunger and thirst, to
cold and heat. Luke tells us that He grew in wisdom and
understanding and that the grace of God was upon Him.
He was not alien to our world, but since He took on
flesh, He was part of it and a brother to His fellowmen.
But to Him, God was everything, and even as a child, He
had a tremendous understanding of God. To Him, God

was a Father who loved and cared for His children, who gave them gifts, and, like a good shepherd, led them from one pasture to another and was always near. Jesus' whole life was wrapped in the bosom of Judaism, and He remained loyal to the pure religion which God had revealed to Abraham and the prophets two thousand years before His birth.

The three great imperial powers which Daniel had seen in his vision—the Babylonian Empire, the image of gold; the Persian Empire, the image of silver; and the Grecian Empire, the image of brass—had come and gone. Now a new, even greater power was on the rise—the Roman Empire, the image of iron. A few decades before the birth of Jesus, Rome marched across Greece toward Mesopotamia and the Fertile Crescent, the lands known as the Cradle of Civilization. Syria and Egypt were soon to fall. The brief respite the Jews had had under the Maccabees was coming to an end, for Palestine, too, was in the path of the Romans.

In 67 B.C. three Roman generals, Julius Caesar, Octavius and Mark Anthony crossed the Aegean Sea on their way to conquer the Near East. These lands, weakened by racial and religious strife, could not withstand the onslaught. Palestine and Syria were to become the bastion of the Roman Empire because of their strategic positions, and Antioch and Damascus, with their wealth and manpower, were to become essential bases for the military operation against the Parthian Empire in the Euphrates Valley.

The main obstacle standing in the way of the Romans was Palestine. They had heard of the gallantry of the Hashmonians, and they knew that the Jews would fight to the death for the sacred heritage of their forefathers—their religion, their holy Temple in Jerusalem, and the treasure that lay in it. Therefore, they realized that they would have to come to an understanding with the Jews, an understanding that would not involve them in a long and costly struggle. Good fortune had, up to this time, been on the side of the Romans, and it did not fail them now. The Jews were fighting among themselves over the leadership and corruption of the High Priest. The antagonists were brothers, Hercanus and Aristobulus, princes of the decadent Hashmonian dynasty. Hercanus was the older, the rightful heir, but Aristobulus was stronger. The critical struggle demanded a strong man to lead the Jews.

In the household of the High Priest was a servant named Antipator, a subtle opportunist. Antipator sided with Hercanus and convinced him to take his case to the Roman generals in Antioch. Hercanus agreed and approached the Romans bearing gifts of gold and silver. Because of the bribe, the Romans decided in his favor and made him High Priest. When the Romans occupied Palestine, Hercanus was appointed an ethnarch to look after the Jewish affairs, and Antipator slowly established himself in power, becoming the liaison between the Romans and the High Priest. A Roman procurator was also appointed to establish and collect taxes and to see after other imperial interests.

The Hashmonian princes fought to regain their power, but in vain. Slowly but surely they submitted to King Herod, the son of Antipator, and became vassals of Rome. Mariamne, an Hashmonian princess, was given in marriage to Herod, who did everything he could to pacify the country, including the rebuilding of the Temple, a feat that took forty years. But his efforts were in vain; the Jews still hated him for his cruelty, and he lived in fear of his life. So great was this fear that the suspicious

Herod eventually had Mariamne executed and their two sons, Aristobulus and Antigonus, killed as well.

Such was the political and religious situation preceding the birth of Jesus of Nazareth and such were the events that heralded the destruction of the Jewish kingdom and the dispersion of the Jews from their homeland.

Assuredly, as a young man and a student in the synagogue, Jesus cherished the same hopes and aspirations that every Jew cherished: the coming of the Messiah, the Great Deliverer of Israel. At that time, all the people in Galilee and Judea prayed for the coming of the Great Leader, the only hope of Israel, the only one who could defeat imperial Rome and restore the kingdom of David.

These hopes for a brighter future were held dear by Jewish people throughout the land, and it was these hopes and the anticipation of the future that held them together in the midst of so much persecution and suffering. Indeed, without the faithful and divine promises of deliverance and restoration, the Jews would have been converted to paganism and assimilated by the stronger race that ruled over them, and the Lamp of God would have been extinguished. Then, too, the Jews hated and feared anything that was alien to the sacred heritage which had been entrusted to them and for which they had been called by God. Their Scriptures contained the truth, and they were guided by the moral law and the Light of God, the Holy Bible. Their religion was supreme; they did not need to borrow from the pagans.

It was divinely ordained that the Messiah Christ should come from an obscure place like Nazareth in Galilee, to be born and raised in a poor family. Most of the Hebrew prophets came from poor and obscure backgrounds. King Saul and King David were both shepherds chosen by God to become the shepherds of His people.

Jesus' mother, Mary, was a virgin chosen by God to give birth to the greatest of all prophets and seers. Joseph, who was known as His father, was a pious poor peasant who tilled his fields, kept a few sheep and once in a while worked as a carpenter fixing a broken plow or making a new door and key. For these jobs he received small gifts in payment—a few eggs, cheese, butter—whatever the people were able to give. He was so poor that when Jesus was dedicated to God, all Joseph could offer God was a pigeon, the offering that the poor and the destitute gave.

And yet his son was the richest man who ever lived.

2

HIS BIRTH
AND
CHILDHOOD

———❧❧ ❧❧———

THE APOSTLE MATTHEW SAYS, "The birth of Jesus Christ was in this manner. While Mary his mother was acquired for a price for Joseph, before they came together, she was found with child of the Holy Spirit." (1:18)

The institution of matrimony is different in Biblical lands from most of the rest of the world. Women are purchased for a price or dowry (*mahra*), and this price may be paid in money, sheep or in other possessions. When a man pays the price to the father of the bride, he takes the girl into his house and thus she becomes his wife. The prophet Hosea says one of the women he took as wife was bought for fifteen pieces of silver and an homer and a half (a bushel) of barley. When David married Saul's daughter Malchel, he had no money for her, so

Saul told him to kill several hundred Philistines. Jacob had to work for fourteen years to pay for his two wives. The price paid was dependent on the degree of nobility of the girl's family. This custom still prevails today, and the author has seen girls acquired in this manner. Marriages are arranged by parents or professional matchmakers, and often the bride and bridegroom have not seen each other before the actual marriage ceremony.

Now in the sixth month the angel Gabriel was sent from God to Galilee, to a city called Nazareth, To a virgin who was acquired for a price for a man named Joseph, of the house of David; and the name of the virgin was Mary. And the angel went in and said to her, Peace be to you, O full of grace; our Lord is with you, O blessed one among women. When she saw him, she was disturbed at his words, and wondered what kind of salutation this could be. And the angel said to her, Fear not, Mary; for you have found grace with God. For behold, you will conceive and give birth to a son, and you will call his name Jesus. . . . Then Mary said to the angel, How can this be, for no man has known me. The angel answered and said to her, The Holy Spirit will come, and the power of the Highest will rest upon you; therefore the one who is to be born of you is holy, and he will be called the Son of God. (Luke 1:26–31; 34–35)

Furthermore, the angel told Mary that Elizabeth, her cousin who was barren, had also conceived a child.

When Joseph, a simple and pious man from Nazareth, found that Mary was pregnant, he was horrified. He could not believe it, for he knew she had not been consummated and in Israel, where morality was strongly upheld, a woman who broke the moral law was stoned to death. Mary, however, assured him she was still a virgin and told him how Gabriel had come to her in a dream. Joseph immediately realized the townspeople would not believe the story of a dream, that soon the news of her pregnancy would spread and she would be accused of adultery and punished in accordance with the Mosaic Law. He therefore decided to send her back to her people without charging her, as would have been his right as the "wronged" husband. But before he could follow his plan, an angel of the Lord appeared to him in a dream and said, "O, Joseph, son of David, do not be afraid to take your wife Mary, because he that is to be born of her is of the Holy Spirit. She will give birth to a son, and you will call his name Jesus; for he shall save his people from their sins" (Matthew 1:20–21), and Joseph understood.

As Mary's time of delivery drew near, a decree went out from Caesar Augustus to take a census of all the people in his empire, probably for the purpose of levying new taxes on the already overburdened people. The decree required that each man return to his own city, so Joseph, and Mary heavy with child, returned to Bethlehem from Nazareth for their registration. And while they were in Bethlehem, Mary's days to deliver her child were fulfilled.

The Prince of Peace, whose birth had been heralded by prophets of old, opened His eyes in a cave devoid of carpets, chairs, beds and other comforts of this earthly life, and wherein the animals also dwelt. Yet it was cleaner and more peaceful than many of the places in Jerusalem and Rome where conspiracies and wars were conceived and carried out. Located outside the town of Bethlehem, where centuries before King David had lodged when he was a fugitive from King Saul, the humble cave was a proper place for the birth of a great Savior who was destined to change pride to humility, hatred to love, greed to sharing, and force to meekness. A temple not built by the hands of man, it became the cradle of a simple, natural, universal religion.

That night there were shepherds in the hills watching their flocks. Suddenly they heard unusual melodies sung by angels, and they were frightened. But an angel said to them, "Do not be afraid; for behold, I bring you glad tidings of great joy, which will be to all the world. For this day is born to you in the city of David, a Savior, who is Christ the Lord," and the angel gave the shepherds a sign to find the newborn babe. Suddenly, the silence of the night was broken as though a great conqueror was entering Jerusalem, and there were many angels singing and praising God, saying "Glory to God in the highest, and on earth peace and good hope for men."

At the same time a group of wise men from Chaldea arrived in Jerusalem. These men were astrologers and counselors to the kings, the descendants of savants who had made a thorough study of the stars and who had discovered the solar calendar. They were known as Magi, and they had seen an unusual and brilliant star never before seen. The founder of their religion, Zoroaster, like Moses, had predicted the coming of a great Savior, and the Magi had followed the star to Bethlehem. When King Herod heard that the Magi had been asking for the baby, he trembled with fear, for he thought a new king had been born who would try to usurp his kingdom. He immediately summoned the Jewish council and asked them where the birth had taken place, and they replied, "In Bethlehem of Judah, for thus it is written in the book of the prophet: Even you, Bethlehem of Judah, you are not insignificant in the eyes of the kings of Judah, for from you shall come out a king, who will shepherd my people Israel." (Matthew 2:5–6)

Then Herod called the Magi to him and instructed them to find out all they could about the baby and give him the information so he could worship Him too. So the Magi followed the star to the cave, where they found the baby and worshiped Him, offering Him gifts of gold, frankincense and myrrh. When they were ready to return to Herod, however, they were warned in a vision not to tell him of their discovery, so they left for their own country, taking another road probably over the desert to Damascus, then by the Euphrates River to Babylon or Agbatana, the capital of the Parthian Empire.

When Herod learned of their departure, he became enraged and in his anger, he issued an order that all male children up to two years of age were to be put to death, for he hoped in this way to do away with the child whom he considered a threat to his throne. Before the soldiers could carry out their orders and murder the infant Jesus, however, an angel appeared to Joseph, warning him of the danger and telling him to take Mary and their son to Egypt. And so they fled from Bethlehem, Mary riding on a donkey, through the treacherous Sinai desert to Egypt where they remained until the death of Herod made it safe for them to return once again to their homeland, Galilee.

When Jesus was forty days old, Mary and Joseph took Him to Jerusalem to be dedicated and redeemed. Since women were considered unclean after giving birth until they were purified forty days later, Mary at this time was purified in accordance with the Mosaic ordinance, an ordinance still obeyed by Eastern Christians. The priest who was to bless the most holy child did not know that the little babe whom Mary held in her arms was the very prophet of whom Moses had written fifteen hundred years before, "The Lord your God will raise up to you a prophet like me from the midst of you, of your brethren; to him you shall hearken." (Deuteronomy 18:15) The religious authorities did not know that this child was the promised Messiah by whom all the people of the earth would be blessed and who would become a light to the Gentiles and a hope to His people, Israel.

Like the other poor boys of Nazareth, Jesus played in the streets of the town, herded sheep in the hills, worked in the fields and traded in the marketplace. Sometimes He walked in the countryside carrying a sling made by His mother, His bow on His arm and a few arrows in a small quiver. And like the other boys, He rode asses. In His adult years, He was so expert that when He entered Jerusalem, He commanded His disciples to bring a she ass and her colt. Jesus rode upon the unbroken colt, and the colt walked as though it had been trained. On special occasion, He went to the hills with His friends where they cooked and danced, much as the young people do today.

When Jesus was twelve years of age, Mary and Joseph again took Him to Jerusalem—this time to be confirmed according to the Jewish ritual called *Bar-Mitzvah*, the most important event in the life of a Jewish boy. On their way to Jerusalem, the pilgrims passed some of the most historic sites connected with their history—Mount Gilboa where King Saul and his sons had been slain in battle, and Mount Tabor where Deborah had triumphed over the armies of King Nabin and his general, Sisera, on the plains of Kishon. These ancient memories became vivid, and the past and the present joined hands, especially in the minds of the young Jews who had studied about them at the small synagogue schools.

The day of *Bar-Mitzvah* was a day of joy for Joseph,

Mary and their boy, Jesus. The parents were proud to see their son standing at the Temple with the other boys from Jerusalem to be examined by the learned rabbis, scribes and priests who heard them recite the Law and the prophets and who asked them questions. It was a day of dedication, a day when all Jewish males stood before the Lord their God and promised to keep His Law and uphold His commandments, and it was this solemn dedication that enabled the Jewish people to preserve their religion and the Light of God amid many trials, persecutions and sufferings.

And it was a day of joy for the boys as well. For years they had looked forward to it, to seeing the revered Temple with its large stones, its beautiful columns, and its golden altars, and to walking in the streets of the Holy City where King David, Solomon and the prophets had walked. It was a day when both parents and children reaffirmed the Messianic hopes, the hopes of deliverance.

Jesus excelled at *Mitzvah* and caused the rabbis and learned scribes to wonder at His vast knowledge, for they did not know that the Spirit of the Lord and His grace had been upon Him while He was growing in wisdom and understanding. At this early age He was so familiar with the Scriptures, the Law and the prophets that He spoke with authority and answered correctly all the questions put to Him.

It was following these sacred rites that the boy Jesus was lost in the Temple. During the feasts, the historic city was crowded with pilgrims from all over the world. Both Jewish and foreign merchants brought their goods to sell, and the narrow, crooked streets of Jerusalem were choked with people prodding their heavily laden animals and at times pushing and cursing one another, even as they do today.

When the religious rites were over, Mary and Joseph left the Temple grounds and, like hundreds of other pilgrims, hurried to the marketplace to buy provisions for their long journey home to Nazareth. Parents were afraid to take their children with them through the crowded streets, for they might be lost or hurt, so before they left the Temple, Mary and Joseph instructed Jesus to wait for them at the Temple grounds where the country people usually gathered and where caravans were announced.

But when they returned from the marketplace, they found, to their surprise, that the young people had already departed. On feast days only, the boys and girls are permitted to walk a quarter of a mile or so ahead of their parents, singing, laughing and, at times, dancing. Joseph and Mary thought that Jesus had gone on with the young people, so they left the city. When they caught up with the young people, however, they found that Jesus was not with the other boys and girls, so they hastily returned to Jerusalem, for they feared that He was lost in the crowded city among the thousands of foreigners. Oh, what anxious hours they spent and what fears clouded their minds!

They stopped strangers and asked if they had seen their son, but in vain. When they reached the city, they hastened to the marketplace, for they thought that Jesus might be there. But they failed to find Him, so they hurriedly returned to the Temple grounds, to the outer court where they had left Him. He was nowhere in sight, and they questioned merchants, strangers, and the Temple attendants to see if they could help. And when all their efforts bore no fruit, they entered the Temple itself and went straight to the place where the dedication ceremonies had been held.

There Mary saw Jesus debating with the learned men,

and for a moment she forgot that she and Joseph had
been searching for Him. She stood shaking her head in
wonder and admiration. And when she could no longer
control herself, she rushed toward Him. In her excite-
ment and relief, she forgot that she was a woman and
that, in accordance with custom, she must know her place
in the House of God. When Jesus saw her, He left the
other boys and ran to her, for He realized that she and
Joseph had been searching for Him, and they embraced. Then Mary tried to scold Him and said, "Son,
why have you done this to me? Your father and I have
been sorrowfully searching for you."

Jesus saw that His parents were weary from their anxiety and search, and He said gently in Aramaic, the language of the people, "Why were you looking for me? Did
you not know that I would be in my Father's house?"
And then He added, "You told me to stay here until
you returned from the marketplace, and I waited for you
in the courtyard with the others, but when you failed to
come, I entered into the temple to learn and to share my
knowledge."

Then the family, united again, hurried to catch up with
the last caravan that had left Jerusalem for the north, for
despite the presence of the imperial and military outposts,
the roads, infested with robbers, bandits and revolutionaries, were dangerous, and they did not want to travel
alone.

3

THE BACKGROUND
FOR HIS
TEACHING

JESUS MUST HAVE SPENT CON-
siderable time tending the sheep, God's lovely, faithful
and harmless creatures. He was so familiar with the duties of a good shepherd that He said of Himself, "I am
the Good Shepherd." (John 10) It was among those hills
where He watched the sheep that He came close to nature and learned its secret. It was here that He saw
flowers, clothed in glory and majesty, springing from the
ground and the birds caring for their young. They in-
spired Him and revealed to Him God's abundant love
and His divine care for His children.

Sheep-raising was a humble and honest occupation
which in Biblical times produced many judges, prophets,
kings, and spiritual leaders, for there is no occupation in
the world that gives man a better or clearer concept of

God than the pastoral life. The good shepherd never discriminates between his own sheep and those of his neighbors. He searches for a sheep when it is lost whether it is his own or his enemy's, and he binds its wounds when it is injured.

Jesus must also have studied the plant life and the soil because in His parable of the seed and the soil, He reveals His familiarity with the soil and the mysterious growth of the seed. The carpenter shapes lifeless objects so they may be used by men, but the shepherd deals with living creatures from which he learns about God's Fatherly care.

There is no mention in the Gospels that Jesus ever worked as a carpenter. Even though He was known as the son of the village carpenter, He evidently knew nothing about the occupation, for in His teaching He never mentions a single tool used by a carpenter or used in a carpenter's shop. Beds, chairs, chests and tables were unknown until relatively recent years, and there was little for a carpenter to do to make a living. Moreover, in the East articles were made to last, to be handed down from one generation to the next. They seldom needed repairs.

All of Jesus' teaching, like that of the prophets before Him, was drawn from the most important aspects of life. In the marketplace He observed the dishonest merchants measuring goods with short and long measures. In some shops there were two men, one with long arms and one with short arms. The man with long arms bought cloth for the shop; the man with short arms sold it to the customer. Both, of course, claimed that the length of their arm was a yard. Jesus said, "With the same measure with which you measure, it will be measured to you." (Matthew 7:2) He also noticed that some used diverse weights and crooked balances, although the Scriptures warn against this practice.

In the East, those who defraud are defrauded; those who cheat are cheated; but those who measure honestly in turn receive honest measures; and those who give, receive. In other words, the people reap what they have sown. This is an immutable law, the law of compensation. It can never be altered.

Jesus must also have seen one servant working for two masters, loving one master and hating the other, for He later said, "No man can serve two masters; for either he will hate the one and like the other; or he will honor one and despise the other. You cannot serve God and mammon (wealth)." (Matthew 6:24)

In Jesus' day, the religious and political problems were studied and debated at the synagogues, in courtyards, on street corners—even in the caravans—and Jesus must have taken part in these discussions.

He expounded the Law and the prophets, pointing out some of the passages in the books of the prophets who had predicted these harsh and hopeless days because their forefathers had refused to listen to the voices of the men of God. They had worshiped, instead, alien gods and had adopted pagan customs and ordinances. They had exchanged truth for error, light for darkness, and the things of the Spirit for the things of the flesh, and now they were reaping what they had sown, and gathering what they had scattered.

Then, too, about four hundred years had elapsed since the last of the Jewish prophets, Malachi, had passed away. The word of God was especially precious, for during those four centuries there had been no prophets, no seers, and no spiritual leaders to guide the people. Dur-

ing this period the hopes for the restoration of the Jewish kingdom were low. The Jews, like many other minor races, were caught between two great imperial powers, the Roman and the Parthian empires, and these two great rivals were fighting for world supremacy. The leaders of the small nations had been shorn of power, reduced to slavery, and, burdened with high taxes and tributes, they usually leaned toward the stronger nation so their lives would be easier. But sometimes the fortunes of war suddenly changed, and the people suffered the consequences.

Many new philosophies and ideologies appeared. Neoplatonism had spread beyond the confines of Greece and was prevalent in Egypt, Syria and even in Palestine. In the East, there was the great religion of Zoroaster, presided over by two gods, Hormizd, the god of light, and Ahriman, the god of darkness. But the most powerful religion in the Roman Empire, the one that had been adopted by the Imperial Army, was Mithra, an offshoot of Zoroastrianism.

In Palestine there were three great religious and political parties: the Pharisees, the most ardent and articulate party, strictly Jewish in all its aspects, loyal to the tenets of long-established Judaic teachings and traditions, their sole objective was to free the land and restore the kingdom of David; the Sadducees, the righteous ones, who had succumbed to the Roman rule; and the third party was made up of the learned scribes, the interpreters of the Law and the prophets, and the teachers of the people.

Jesus came into the world with something dynamic, practical, but disturbing to the minds of His teachers. He saw that the only hope for the salvation of mankind, the only hope for a lasting peace, was a universal re-

ligion as envisioned by the Jewish prophets. And to prove
that God's plan was a universal plan and that God was
God of all nations, He quoted the Scriptures. When hundreds of Jews in Israel were suffering from leprosy, He
pointed out how Naaman, a Syrian pagan, had been
healed. He told the people about the prophet Elijah who,
during a severe famine, was fed by a Syrian widow.

But the people were so confused that they could not
recognize Jesus as the new Prophet from Nazareth in
Galilee. They did not know that He had gone straight to
the source of Judaism, to the fountain of living water
found in the teachings of the prophets—to the Holy Bible.
Although He must have been obedient to His earthly
teachers, His whole life was captured by the Holy Scriptures, by the words of the prophets, for His mind delved
deeper into the Scriptures, and His concept of God was
therefore different from that of His contemporaries. In
the Holy Bible Jesus found the remedies for the ills of
His people and for the world. He found God was not a
tyrant, but a Good Shepherd caring for all people without
discrimination. The God of the Jews was the God of the
world.

This new concept of the God of Israel was contrary to
the elders who believed Judaism to be the center of the
universe with the Gentile and pagan nations like planets
and stars around it. They had forgotten that their forefathers had been called by God to enlighten the world
and to become a blessing to the Gentiles. So, invariably,
while He was at school, Jesus disagreed with the religious
authorities and even condemned some of the rigid observances of the Law.

It is evident from the Scriptures and from His teachings, however, that He was brought up strictly in the
Jewish religion and was trained at the synagogue in

Nazareth where He received the coveted title of Rabbi, "My Great One" or "My Teacher."

And it was at the synagogue that He declared Himself to be the Messiah.

4

JESUS
REACHES
MANHOOD

As we have said, most of
Jesus' life before He declared Himself to be the Messiah
at the synagogue in Nazareth was spent quietly in town
or in the fields. Nevertheless, He continued his discourses
on religion with whomever He met in the streets or in the
country. In the East, one does not have to enter a semi-
nary or a monastery in order to become a teacher of religion. Most of the religious education is obtained by listening to the debates of the elders and conversing with
friends.

For years Jesus had been studying and examining the
Scriptures and seeking the truth. Finally, in the synagogue of the small, obscure town of Nazareth in Galilee,
He found the Pearl of Great Price inscribed upon old
parchment scrolls stored in the vault of the synagogue.

He found the lost key to the Scriptures which would un-
lock their mysteries and show the way to the Kingdom of
Heaven.

To find a pearl of great price does not always mean
immediate happiness. It may mean misery and tribulation, for one has to work hard to prove its validity. It must
be examined by experts and declared genuine. The value
of the Pearl which Jesus found was not recognized because the people had never seen such a gem. As shrewd
merchants are the only ones who can pass judgment on a
pearl, so the only ones who could pass judgment on the
Truth which Jesus had found were the learned men and
the religious authorities.

Jesus knew that the Truth that He had found in the
Holy Scriptures would work only if it were put into practice. But the difficulty came in persuading the religious
leaders that what He had discovered was the Truth. How
could He turn the people from hate to love? How could
He convince them to pray for their persecutors? How
could He prove to the people that love and meekness were
the greatest weapons against war?

All the learned Jews throughout Judea and Galilee were
constantly examining the Scriptures, trying to find ways
whereby they could escape their captivity. The people
wondered why the great rabbis, the graduates of higher
schools of learning, did not find the truths which Jesus
claimed He had found. This question is still asked today,
for people rely on the discoveries made by the accepted
authorities, not by young and unknown teachers of religion.

The elders wondered why the mantle of the Messiah
should fall on a Galilean rabbi. They believed the Messiah would come from Judea, from Bethlehem, the town
of David. The Messiah was to be greater than David, for

He must defeat imperial Rome and free God's enslaved people. Galilee had never produced a prophet or a seer. Nicodemus, a member of the council, who had spoken for a Galilean Messiah, was rebuked by the Pharisees and scribes: "Art thou also of Galilee? Search and see, for out of Galilee ariseth no prophet." They said this because Galilee was inhabited by Gentiles.

Not many years before, a great leader named Toda had appeared. Thousands of men had rallied behind him, and some even acclaimed him as the long-awaited Messiah Christ. But he had been defeated by the Romans in the battlefield, and his followers had been destroyed.

When Jesus reached the longed-for age of thirty, when He became a man, He sat in the council with rabbis, statesmen and counselors. After all, He Himself was a rabbi, a brilliant student of religion who was well versed in the Law and the prophets. Moreover, He was familiar with the Jews' struggle to keep their faith and to restore the kingdom of David.

The main topic for discussion in the council was the Roman occupation and the cruel King Herod, for the Romans had come to stay. Their occupation, however, was different from that of other great powers which had occupied Palestine. Those previous conquerors had come for the sole purpose of plundering the land, stealing the silver and gold, and then leaving. Remembering this, the Jewish leaders lavished large sums of Temple gold and silver upon the Roman generals and procurators in the hope of ridding the country of King Herod. But when one group of high Roman officials became rich through bribes, they left and were replaced by another hungry group, and so it continued throughout the Roman rule over Palestine. Herod was policing the country for the Romans, and all attempts toward freedom were frustrated by him and by the Roman legions who stood ready to carry out his orders.

Galilee was near the gateway to the East—Antioch, where the Roman proconsul lived and where were kept thousands of Roman soldiers, great stores of food, arms and other military supplies. For a long time the Romans had coveted the Fertile Crescent valley with its rich grain and cotton fields and skilled artisans. These lands supplied the markets of the world with goods woven in Nineveh, Babylon and Damascus—copper and tinware, swords, knives, gold and silver. The fame of this land had spread over Europe when, a few centuries before, it had been conquered by Alexander the Great and his Macedonian army. Finally, after a long struggle, the Persians had succeeded in overthrowing the Grecian rule and now the Parthians, the successors to the Persians, were defending these rich and strategic provinces.

Many times Jesus had stood in the streets of Nazareth and watched the Roman legionaries, laden down with military equipment, march through Nazareth on their way to Syria and Antioch. Jesus felt compassion for these foreign soldiers whom His people despised. He pitied them when He saw them bending under their heavy loads and begging for water because He knew that they did not realize what they were doing, that just as they were marching in the streets of an alien people, so other soldiers would march in the streets of their own cities. They did not know that he who takes the sword, sooner or later perishes by the sword. He offered to help them, but when they heard the strange words of comfort and when they looked into His eyes that shone like sapphires exposed to the sun, they refused His offer. Never-

theless, overcome with His kindness, they felt the presence of a holy man and were refreshed.

Sometimes He met bandits and other outlaws who hid
in caves and robbed wayfarers to obtain clothing and
food. Jesus saw the good in these men, too, for He knew
they were the children of God who had gone astray.
When they asked Him for His coat, instead of resisting,
He quietly offered His shirt too. His gentle words fell on
the ears of the rough bandits as the gentle rain falls upon
the tender grass, and they kept talking to Him and drinking from the new fountain of life which He offered to
them.

Jesus had drunk from both the bitter and the sweet
cups of life. His first challenge was to know Himself, for
when one knows oneself and examines one's own problems, then one can understand the heart and feelings of
others and help them to solve their problems. All men
have the same aspirations and desires. They all want to
enjoy life and to have abundant material possessions, but
some, no matter how hard they try, fail. When one
method fails, they try another and sometimes they go
astray, thinking they have found a shorter way to success and happiness.

Thus it was through Jesus' own wide experiences that
He found the answer for all world problems and human
ills. Because of His contacts with and concern for all
classes of people, He became honored as the greatest
teacher of all times and the greatest physician of human
bodies and souls.

At the council meetings, Jesus shared some of the things
He had learned from the prophets and from the school
of human experience. But before the learned men could
grasp them, they had to be taught again as they had
been taught in the days of the prophets. They had to re-

pent to be born again, that is to become like children and start all over, but Jesus knew they would reject the truths just as their forefathers had rejected the prophets. Moses had learned this the hard way in a treacherous desert. When his people had been hungry, they demanded bread; when they were well fed, they began to quarrel among themselves and to revolt against God just as they do today. No matter how much bread people eat, they are dissatisfied without the basic truths of life. When they come to know God, they are always free.

Even though there was nothing in Jesus' teaching that was contrary to the Scriptures, the elders at the synagogue would not listen. They began to suspect Him because instead of blaming their enemies, He blamed them for their difficulties, particularly their leaders, the Pharisees, the scribes and the Sadducees. They had broken God's commandments.

But many people felt that the teachings of Jesus, based on love and nonresistance, might offer some hope for freedom. If this teaching could not be preached in the synagogue, it could be preached on the street corners, in the marketplaces, even upon the housetops.

And so the seeds for the new teaching were to be sown again, and the people were to be taught to be born again, to become like little children.

5

JOHN
THE
BAPTIST

ONE DAY IN MAY A CARAVAN
on its way from Jerusalem to Tiberias arrived at Nazareth.
It was sunset, and the laborers were returning from the
fields. The caravan halted by a well, and the caravaneers
alighted to rest and to give water to the donkeys. Townspeople hurried to the well, and the women who had gone
to fetch water laid their jars on the ground and eagerly
awaited the news from Jerusalem. Hitherto, the news
from the Holy City had been discouraging: Some time
before, Pilate, the Roman governor of Judea, had put to
death many Galilean pilgrims to Jerusalem, and now the
people, as they waited, were tense.

But this time the news was good. The Lord God had
again remembered His people and after four hundred
years had sent them a prophet: John, the son of Zachariah

the priest and cousin to Jesus. Even now, John was at the River Jordan announcing the coming of the Kingdom of Heaven and calling on the people to be baptized and to repent of their sins.

The news was received with jubilation. The people felt that God had at last remembered His covenant with His faithful servant Abraham and His promises to David. He had sent another prophet to admonish His people, to call them to repentance and to rebuke them for their sins. The leader of the caravan told them that many Pharisees, scribes and other Jewish leaders had gone to Jordan to see John and that some of the people believed that he was the Messiah.

While the leader was talking, Jesus had left the synagogue and as He approached the well, He saw the crowd and the caravan. The people made way for Him, and when the caravan leader saw Him, he realized He was a rabbi and one of the respected citizens, and he rose to salute Him. Jesus asked him to continue with his news, but before he could start, a woman filled a pitcher with water, drew near and handed it to the leader. When he had quenched his thirst, he began to speak again.

"Truly, truly, I say to you, this man John, the son of the priest, has aroused the people and captured their hearts. Why, everybody is talking about him. On the temple grounds, in the streets, and in the public places all you hear is about the new prophet. Aye, even the stubborn Pharisees and scribes have been discussing him. And there has been a rumor that John has been discussed at the Sanhedrin."

Then he added, "Before we left the city, we heard that a prominent delegation of Pharisees and scribes was on its way to the River Jordon, where the new prophet has been preaching baptism and calling on the people to repent and turn to God, for the Kingdom of Heaven, the universal state proclaimed by Isaiah, is at hand."

As he spoke, the caravan leader shook his head in wonder, and the townspeople looked at him with awe. They were proud of their own humble and meek rabbi, Jesus, who had been teaching the same doctrine, imploring the people to stop relying on their leaders but to repent and turn to God. For His part, Jesus was happy that His cousin had at last seen the Light of God and the salvation of his harassed people.

When darkness had covered the land and the brilliant stars appeared in the clear Galilean sky, the crowd disbursed, and Jesus, too, left. The tired travelers lay down on the ground so they might start early in the morning for Tiberias.

On the following Sabbath, the chief of the synagogue in Nazareth surprised the people by reading a letter from a rabbi in Jerusalem. The letter confirmed the good news that the caravan leader had told them, and the rabbi further stated that the authorities of Jerusalem were pleased with John's conduct since he did not condemn the Romans, but placed the blame for their unhappy situation on the heads of the people themselves. He went on to say that some people believed that John was Elijah or one of the other great prophets who had returned to guide them, and some even ventured to say that he was Messiah Christ Himself.

As was His custom, Jesus was seated in the first row in the synagogue, and when the chief of the synagogue stepped down, Jesus rose and read the lesson from one of the prophets. Everybody watched Him carefully, for they hoped that He might tell them His reaction to John, but He held His peace. The time had not come.

A short time later another caravan came to Nazareth

and since it was on its way to Judea, Jesus decided to join it and go to see John, for He could wait no longer. It was late spring; the trees had blossomed and the tender branches were loaded with young fruit. The vineyards were green, and the air was noisy with the singing of birds. It was spring in the life of Jesus too. Already He had scattered some of the seeds of His teaching in the town, out in the country, and in the synagogue. Now His summer was near, and the fields were getting white and ready for the reapers.

When Jesus came to the place where John was preaching, He stood with the crowd and watched His cousin baptizing and calling on the people to repent. The crowds were different from the peasants in Galilee. There were artisans, merchants, soldiers, government officials, even Pharisees, Sadducees and scribes, and among them were some of the educated Jews who were convinced that John was one of the great prophets come back to lead the people out of chaos.

Jesus smiled when John daringly denounced some of the people, saying, "Oh, you offspring of scorpions. Who has warned you of the impending disaster which is to befall you? Who has told you to repent?" (When a scorpion is conceived, the father dies, and when the offspring are born, the mother dies, so they have neither father nor mother to warn them of danger. The Jews, likewise, were without prophets, and John wondered who had warned them and admonished them to come to him.)

John told the people to repent and like a good tree, to produce good fruit; otherwise, the ax was poised to cut the trunk for use as fuel. (In the East, any tree which does not bear fruit is used for fuel.) He also warned them not to think that just because they were descended from Abraham, they would be spared.

When Jesus saw the people responding to the exhortations and going forward to be baptized, He, too, followed. When the Baptizer saw Him, he hurried to Him, saying, "*Shalom Eleco Eshoo.*" Jesus responded, "*Shalam Eleco Yokhonan,*" and they embraced and kissed each other on the cheek as Easterners do.

The people stood patiently waiting, for John was so overcome at seeing Jesus again that for a moment he forgot what he was doing. Probably they had not seen each other for several years and had news of each other only by means of the caravans.

"Have you been standing here for a long time?" asked John.

"I have been here in the crowd for some time," replied Jesus with a smile.

"Why didn't you come straight to me so that I could introduce you to the people?"

But when Jesus went forward to be baptized, John's attitude toward Him changed, and he exclaimed, "I am not worthy even to loosen the strings of your shoes. I baptize you? Oh no. You should baptize me! No! No! I will not do it. You are greater than I. I am nothing in comparison to you."

Jesus replied softly so the crowd would not hear, "Let us not argue. Baptize me. Let everything be fulfilled in order, and we will discuss things later," for He was not interested in formalities. His main concern was the truth and the new teaching—that the greater should act as servant.

Then Jesus came from Galilee to the Jordan to John, to be baptized by him. But John tried to stop Him, saying, "I need to be baptized by you, and yet have you come to me?" But Jesus answered and said to him, Permit it now, for this

is necessary for us so that all righteousness may be fulfilled;
and then he permitted Him. (Matthew 3:13–15)

Then John stood upon a hillock and lifting high his
hands, cried, "Here is the Lamb of God who has come to
save the world. I am baptizing you [pointing to the peo-
ple] with water, but He will baptize you with the Holy
Spirit. I am washing your bodies to become the temples
of the Holy Spirit, but He will cleanse your sins and
save your souls."

The crowd was amazed to hear the prophet John paying homage to a stranger from Nazareth. They had come
to see one prophet, but now it seemed they had found
two, and the last one greater than the first. None of them
had ever seen or heard of Jesus, yet here at the River
Jordan these pilgrims, who had left their work and
walked long distances to see the new prophet John, were
witnessing the birth of a new religion, a new Judaism
devoid of temple and priesthood. Here they were seeing
a greater prophet than all the prophets who had come
before. Here they were witnessing a sinless man lowering
Himself to be baptized by a sinner.

And so John baptized Jesus just as he had baptized
hundreds of other men and women. But as he baptized
Him, he saw what another human eye could not see: The
Spirit of the Lord like a dove alighting upon Jesus. (The
dove is the symbol of purity and peace and the bird that
brought the good news to Noah that the flood was re-
ceding. Thus, the pure, holy, formless Spirit of God was
momentarily manifested in physical form.) During this
moment of ecstacy, He heard a voice from heaven, un-
heard by anyone else, saying, "This is my beloved Son,
with whom I am pleased."

When Jesus was baptized, He immediately went up out
of the water; and the Heavens were opened to Him, and
He saw the Spirit of God descending like a dove, and
coming upon Him; and behold, a voice from heaven which
said, This is my beloved Son, with whom I am pleased.
(Matthew 3:16–17)

John remembered the words of his mother, Elizabeth,
who years before had told him the story of Jesus' con-
ception and birth, of how Mary had been visited by the
Angel Gabriel, who had told her that what was conceived by her was so great and so holy that He would be
called the Son of the Most High God and that He would
become the Savior of the world.

When John had finished baptizing, a group of Pharisees,
Sadducees and scribes arrived from Jerusalem. They had
been sent by the religious authorities to find out more
about the teaching of John and by what authority he
taught, although they did not feel that he was dangerous.

"Who are you?" asked a prominent Sadducee. "Are
you a prophet or are you the Messiah Christ?"

In a firm voice, John replied, "I am not the Christ."

"What, then, are you? Are you Elijah?"

John replied emphatically, "I am not."

Then they said to him, "Who are you anyway, so that
we may give an answer to those who have sent us? What
do you say concerning yourself?"

John replied meekly, bowing his head and looking at
the ground, "I am the voice of one crying in the wilderness, preparing the way of the Lord, making the paths of
our God straight in the plain. Let all the valleys be filled
up and all the mountains and hills be levelled; let the
crooked places be made straight and the rough places like
a plain; let all flesh see that salvation of the Lord [which

means, cleanse the religion of the Lord, remove the false doctrines which are an obstacle in the paths of those who want to return to the true religion of the Lord]. Let all injustices be removed; all the proud religious authorities become humble and meek; so that their light and the truth of God may shine upon all races and people in the world."

Then one of the Pharisees spoke: "Why, then, do you baptize if you are not the Christ nor Elijah nor a prophet?"

John answered, "I baptize with water; but among you stands One who comes after me. He is ahead of me, the One, even the strings of whose shoes I am not good enough to untie."

John was looking at Jesus, who stood in the crowd, His eyes closed as though meditating on John's words.

Then the people who had been overcome with his words said to him, "What, then, shall we do; how can we prepare ourselves to become the citizens of the Kingdom of Heaven?"

And John replied, "He who has two shirts, let him give one to him who has none; and he who has food, let him do likewise." And to the tax collectors, he said, "Do not exact anything more than what is commanded from you to exact," and he admonished the soldiers not to molest the people and not to misuse their power. He told them that their wages were enough, for in the East soldiers can rob the people, collect bribes from them or imprison them.

By the second day, the fame of Jesus had spread not only among the people, but among John's own disciples, for when John was standing with two of his disciples, Andrew and Simon Peter, he looked at Jesus as He was walking and remarked, "Behold the Lamb of God." Andrew turned to Simon Peter and said, "We have found the Christ," and both went after Jesus.

Up to this time, Jesus had said very little of His Messiahship or of the dangerous missions on which He was soon to embark. John the Baptist had been the one who had fearlessly spoken the truth and had told the people what the Lord God had revealed to him—the identity of the Man from Nazareth. A true prophet of God, he was not interested in power and honor. His main concerns were the Jewish religion and the welfare of his people, and so Jesus embarked upon His mission with no rival.

6

MESSIAH
CHRIST

WITH JOHN THE BAPTIST'S proclamation that He was the Everlasting Messiah, the Prince of Peace, the long-waited Savior of His people, Jesus knew that He must act. Talking would not solve the Jews' problems. He had to reveal the secret first to the people at the synagogue where He had been teaching; He had to tell His own family; and finally, He had to tell the people. The time had come when He must either confirm or deny what John had said.

He knew His course would not be easy. Although He knew that He was the promised Messiah, the Man for whom Israel had waited so long, he also knew that the people were slow to understand and slower still to change from their old beliefs to new. He knew they were expecting a powerful, militaristic Messiah Christ, one who could defeat their enemies in battle and cause all nations to live together in peace, so the people could forge their swords and daggers into plowshares and pruning hooks. He knew they would be reluctant to follow a poor and obscure Galilean peasant, a man of whose background the high priests and scribes knew nothing, a leader without an army and military supplies. Too often had they been deceived by disloyal and corrupt religious leaders. If they had not listened before to men who claimed they were prophets of God, why should they now listen to a simple young man who had been raised far away in Galilee, a meek man who would not even break a bruised reed? Jesus' greatest task lay in finding a way to convince His people that He was the promised Messiah, the Christ.

He was led by the Holy Spirit to the desert, far from the noise and turbulence of the world, to examine Himself and to test His strength for the great mission that lay ahead. When man is alone and praying, he becomes one with God, and God answers his prayers.

Moses before Him had fasted and prayed for forty days and forty nights in the wilderness so that he might hear the small voice of God, and from God receive the Ten Commandments. So, too, had Elijah who, in the darkest hour of Israel, went to Mount Horeb, the desolate mountain in Sinai, to find the answer to Israel's trials under the reign of wicked kings of Israel and the spread of Baal worship in Israel and Judah.

The Lord God had revealed everything to Jesus. He had heard Him saying, "This is my beloved Son, with whom I am pleased." He had seen His portrait as Messiah in the writings of the prophets that He had studied so thoroughly. But how could He prove to the people that this voice came from God without performing some miracles and showing one or two great signs? Sixteen centuries before, the Israelites had demanded that Moses show them a miracle that they might believe he was sent by God. Eight centuries before, Isaiah had faced the same difficulty when he told the people that Messiah Christ would have to suffer in order to change force and hatred to meekness and love. The king and the people were unable to understand him. Eyes they had, but they could not see. Ears they had, but they could not hear. They had no spiritual understanding, nor were they willing to repent and return to God to find comfort and healing. And Isaiah had been killed during the reign of Mannasseh because of his teaching. Could the leaders now see that which Jesus had seen and hear that which He had heard in the silence of the Jordan valley?

The desert to which Jesus retired was somewhat desolate and devoid of trees and shrubs, but God's glory and His Eminence were manifested everywhere. At night one could see myriads of stars and feel harmony and divine order, and in the silence one could easily talk with the angels, the messengers of God. The long fasting and prayer would help Him transcend the material world and live in the realm of heaven. Here would His strength and endurance be tested, for the physical and spiritual forces would clash. But in this uninhabited land, the soul would triumph over the body, and truth would conquer error.

Matthew tells us:

He fasted forty days and forty nights; but at last He was hungry. And the tempter [the doubtful opposition, the leader of the people] drew near and said to Him, If you are the Son of God, command these stones to become bread. But He answered, saying, It is written that it is not by bread alone that man can live, but by every word which proceeds from the mouth of God. Then the adversary took Him to the holy city, and he made Him to stand on the pinnacle of the temple. And he said to Him, If you are the Son of God, throw yourself down; for it is written that He will command His angels concerning you, and they will bear you up on their hands so that even your foot may not strike a stone. Jesus said to him, Again it is written that you shall not tempt the Lord your God. Again the adversary took Him to a very high mountain, and he showed Him all the kingdoms of the world and their glory. And he said to Him, All of these I will give to you, if you will fall down and worship me. Then Jesus said to him, Get away, Satan, for it is written, You shall worship the Lord your God, and Him only shall you serve. Then the adversary left Him alone; and behold, angels drew near and ministered to Him. (Matthew 4:2–11)

All these temptations were images in Jesus' mind of the things He was going to face.

Only the leaders who fed, clothed and protected the people were revered, and Jesus knew that after He declared Himself to be the Messiah, thousands of hungry people would come to Him to relieve their hunger. How could He feed them? The answer came to Him when the forty days of fasting were over, and His weakened body craved food. He looked around Him and saw round stones, hot in the sun, that resembled Syrian and Palestinian bread. He wished, in His hunger, that He might have a loaf or two of that delicious bread so He could eat and be satisfied. And then He realized that being the blessed Messiah, the Son of the Living God, He could change those hot stones into bread. The Jews were sure that the Messiah could perform any kind of miracle re-

gardless of whether it was contrary to the law of God or
not.

But Jesus had heard the people discussing the miracles
and reciting tales of magicians who had turned their
staffs into serpents and stones into bread. He knew such
magical acts were false and therefore forbidden by the
Mosaic Law because they were contrary to the laws of
God. When the wandering Israelites in the desert were
hungry for bread, God did not change stones into loaves
of bread, but He led the people to the areas where manna
—the delicious bread that falls in the stillness of the
night—fell. And when they were thirsty, He showed them
where the wells were hidden.

Jesus knew that God's laws were from everlasting to
everlasting, and that any attempt to change them would
be to tempt God. To have faith in God is greater than all
the miracles and wonders in the world, and He knew
that faith was what the people needed most.

When the devil, the adversary, had carried Jesus to one
of the highest summits of His imagination, other earthly
thoughts crept into His young mind—thoughts of power,
grandeur, wealth and prominence.

*How would it be if I went to Jerusalem and in the mid-
dle of the day, when the streets are choked with people,
climb to the pinnacle of the Temple and stand there for
a while and then call to them to watch me jump? Would
not the whole city rally behind me and acclaim me as
their Messiah? Would not the scribes examine the Scriptures and find out that I was caught in the arms of the
angels so I would not fall?*

But the Spirit of the Lord said to Him, "No, it cannot
be done, for it is contrary to the law of God, and it was
written you shall not tempt the Lord your God."

No one has ever accomplished his objective by tempting God and breaking His laws. If a man should be able to perform such a trick, the people would say he was a master magician, and Moses had condemned the magicians, the soothsayers, and the sorcerers who had deceived the people centuries before.

The inner voice said to Jesus, "You must change the people's hearts and their attitude towards their God."

The adversary made his last attempt. He took Jesus to the highest of all peaks in human aspiration—wealth, power and glory. And there he lifted the mental curtain and showed Him all the kingdoms of the world with their glory and majesty and said to Him: "I will give you all these kingdoms and all this glory, and all that is therein, if you will do just one thing—bow down to me and worship me." This, indeed, was a generous offer for those who seek the material wealth of the world.

For Jesus had had a thought in His human mind that the priests and Temple authorities would certainly welcome such a brilliant and promising young men whom God had endowed with power, wisdom and understanding if He would bow to the high priests and take orders from the council members.

But again, the inner voice reminded Him, "It is written you shall worship the Lord your God and Him only shall you serve." That is, you must listen and obey only the voice of God and not bow to any man.

Thousands of men and women have sold themselves for the sake of honor, glory and other material rewards, and have sacrificed the truth. For these faults, they have deprived humanity of their gifts and contributions. And where are the golden and jeweled swords, the coveted medals and honors which have been bestowed upon them? Forgotten.

Finally, Jesus triumphed against the material world

and all the alluring prizes it offers to those who forsake God. All men are created equal in God's sight. Why, then, should one person worship another—a human being like himself?

Shortly before, John the Baptist had introduced Jesus to the people by the River Jordan. He had testified that he had seen the Spirit of the Lord descend from heaven and rest upon Him. But John's words were already forgotten by most of the people, so who would dare to introduce Him at Jerusalem and in Nazareth? Who would dare to speak of the son of a humble carpenter as the Blessed Messiah? Jesus decided in the arid Judean desert that *He* would proclaim Himself the Messiah Christ.

There is nothing more difficult for a man to do than to introduce himself and tell the people how great, how holy, how honored he is. But when the right time came, Jesus would do it. He would read from the Scriptures, from the scroll of the prophet Isaiah, and then leave it to the people to reject or to accept Him. For had not Isaiah said,

The land of Zebulun and the land of Naphtali have rejoiced; the mighty dominion, the way by the sea, the country beyond the River Jordan, and Galilee of the Gentiles have rejoiced. The people who walked in darkness have seen a great light; those who dwelt in the land of the shadow of death, upon them has the light shined? (Isaiah 9:1–2)

At last Jesus emerged victorious. The truth had triumphed over error, and He was ready to return to His own country to face His relatives, the leaders of the synagogue, and His people.

The news of John's proclamation that Jesus was the

promised Messiah spread through Galilee and Judea and dismayed those who believed John to be the Messiah. But some of the people who had seen Jesus and heard Him speak were delighted with the news, although others ridiculed Him.

The leaders of the synagogue did not understand nor could they fathom John's actions and motives. They and the people of the town were eager for Jesus' return.

But Jesus stopped in the prosperous town of Capernaum to teach in the synagogue there. Unlike the scribes and the Pharisees, He taught with authority, for He knew the Scriptures well and could back up what He was teaching. Everyone praised Him and admired His teaching, for no one had taught this way before. Yet Jesus only echoed what had been said by the prophets centuries before: peace and light, like air, sun and water, are universal and essential to life, and they must be shared with all peoples of the world.

After Jesus had spent some time in Capernaum, He went on to Nazareth. On the Sabbath, as was the custom, He entered the synagogue and, placing the shawl upon His shoulders, stood up to read from the scroll of Isaiah:

> The Spirit of the Lord is upon Me; because of this He has anointed Me to preach good tidings to the poor; and He has sent Me to heal the brokenhearted, and to proclaim release to the captives and sight to the blind; to strengthen with forgiveness those who are bruised; and to preach the acceptable year of the Lord. (Luke 4:18–19)

Then He rolled up the scroll, gave it to the attendant and sat down. The people watched Him closely, for they were eager to hear about His trip to Judea, what He thought about John the Baptist, and about the new reformation. But Jesus, instead of talking about John, went right to the Scriptures and said to them, "Today this Scripture is fulfilled in your ears," and the people were amazed by the words of grace which He spoke. They asked, "Is not this man the son of Joseph?" And Jesus answered them by saying:

You might probably tell me this proverb, Physician, heal yourself; and all that we heard you did in Capernaum, do also here in your own city. Truly, I say to you, No prophet is acceptable in his own city. For truly I say to you, There were many widows in Israel in the days of the prophet Elijah when heaven was closed for three years and six months and there was a great famine throughout the land; Yet Elijah was not sent to one of them, but to Zarephath of Sidon, to a widow. And there were many lepers in Israel in the days of the prophet Elisha, and yet not one of them was cleansed except Naaman the Aramean. (Luke 4:21–27)

When the people heard Him commending the much-hated Syrians more than themselves, the chosen people of God, they became angry. At first, when He had begun to read, the people had not understood what He was trying to tell them. The passage was familiar and needed no further explanation, but they did not realize that He was referring to Himself. As soon as He read the words, "Today the Spirit of the Lord is upon Me," however, the leaders of the congregation became enraged. Rising up, they took Him forcibly from the synagogue.

If it had not been the Sabbath, the people, in accordance with the Law of Moses, would have stoned Him to death, but such an act would constitute the breaking of the Sabbath, so they decided to take Him to the top of a mountain and push Him off. But when they reached the top, no one dared push Him, for that, too, would break the Sabbath. While they were arguing among themselves, trying to find a way to put Him to death without breaking the Holy Day, Jesus escaped. By the time they had stopped their bickering, He was on His way to Capernaum where He had some supporters and a few disciples.

The religious authorities in Nazareth were not sorry to see Him go. Many of them felt He was strange, perhaps even insane, for, after all, He was only a country rabbi and a peasant. His own relatives, with the exception of Mary, His mother, were ashamed of Him and felt they would rather lose Him than be ousted from the synagogue. Like the others, they could no longer share His new teaching and His attacks against the religious authorities whom they revered and yet feared.

Galilee was a fertile field for reforming Judaism. It was far from Jerusalem, the center of the Jewish religion, the Temple and the fanatical religious authorities, and it was close to the Gentile lands of Syria and Lebanon. The people were different from those in Judea—seeking change and ready for it, for they came from many races and cultures. Many of them were the descendants of the people whom the kings of Assyria had brought from the other side of the Euphrates River and had settled in the land formerly inhabited by the ten tribes of Israel.

The forefathers of the Galileans had accepted the God of Israel, but they also continued to worship their own pagan gods. While they kept the Law of Moses, they did not observe some of the ordinances which arose from the Jewish racial traditions. More liberal than the Jews in the South, they did not wash their hands before they ate. They did not wash everything they bought at the marketplace, nor were they strict in their observance of the Sabbath. Moreover, they spoke Aramaic, the Northern dialect, while the Jews spoke the Chaldean or the Southern dialect.

With more religious freedom in Galilee than in Judea, it was easier for Jesus to plant the seeds of the universal religion there around the beautiful lake of Galilee, the symbol of life in that arid land.

Jesus expected some opposition to His teaching from the leaders of the Jewish religion in Galilee. But He was not afraid of opposition or even persecution, for He knew that persecution would help spread His teaching, and opposition is the life of a new movement.

7

THE DEATH
OF
JOHN THE BAPTIST

AFTER THE DEATH OF KING
Herod the Great, his kingdom had been divided among
his sons. Archelius, his son by his Samaritan wife Maltasy,
became king of Judea, the most important section of the
kingdom; Herod Antiphas received Galilee, the next most
important part; and Philip became tetrarch of Abilene,
consisting of Ituraea, Trachonies, and Lysanies. All three
sons were just as cruel as had been their father.

Philip died and Archelius, having become even more
villainous than Herod the Great, was finally exiled to
Austria, leaving Herod Antiphas king of Galilee, Judea
and Abilene. Pontius Pilate was appointed the governor
of Judea, and the High Priest was made the ethnarch.

Gradually, the Romans, in their never-ending quest for
more land and power, annexed all of Palestine, and Herod

Antiphas became answerable to the Roman authorities. Although his capital was at Tiberias, the beautiful town Herod the Great had built in honor of the Emperor Tiberius Caesar, he spent considerable time in Rome and Caesarea playing politics and handing out bribes in attempts to maintain his weak position as king of Galilee. Tiberias was built on the slope of a high mountain and faced the lake of Galilee. It had many orchards, vineyards, marble palaces, and other scenic beauties in addition to hot baths which the Roman officials often visited. While they were in Tiberias, they were entertained lavishly by the tetrarch.

Although Herod Antiphas was nominally Jewish, in order to please his Roman masters and win their favors, he introduced many pagan customs into his kingdom and had even placed some pagan images in his palace. Like the Romans, he cared nothing for the welfare of the Jews nor for their religion and, in fact, both the Romans and Herod hated the Jewish religious authorities who watched over their people and sometimes took their complaints to Rome. Herod did everything in his power to crush the Jews, taxing them heavily so as to be able to bribe the Romans and thus remain king over the Jews.

King Herod Antiphas had already had an unhappy encounter with John the Baptist. John had been preaching in the small towns along the River Jordan and the news of his preaching had been brought by his disciples into Galilee. Jews from all walks of life had been flocking to him, some of them looking on him as a great prophet whom God had sent to deliver His people from the Romans and return them to God.

When Philip, the brother of Herod Antiphas, had died, Herod wanted to marry Philip's widow, the beautiful Herodia, the daughter of his half brother, Aristobulus, who had been executed by Herod the Great. The Jewish law permits a man to marry his brother's wife, providing the deceased had left no heirs. Philip and Herodia, however, had had a daughter, Bozia. But this did not stop Herod Antiphas. He felt safe in breaking the law, for who would dare prevent a king marrying a woman with whom he had fallen in love?

John the Baptist was preaching near Tiberias at this time, and in his discourses, he did what the rabbis and scribes had not dared to do: He denounced the king and queen as adulterers who had broken the Law of Moses and were living in sin. Herodia, he said, was nothing more nor less than a harlot.

At first the king restrained his anger, for he feared that if he punished the popular Baptist, the people might revolt. Then, too, he was fearful for his shaky rule over the turbulent Galilee. He knew the Romans were seeking a chance to depose him and exile him as they had exiled his brother Archelius. The Roman proconsuls were tired of native upstarts who lived so extravagantly at the expense of their subjects and who gave the Romans so many headaches. All Palestine had to become completely Roman like Antioch and Celecia.

So Herod held his peace and acted as though he had not heard the denunciation by the prophet. After all, he was the king, and if he waited, sooner or later he would have a chance to avenge the honor of his beautiful queen.

And John the Baptist continued his attacks against the royal couple. Finally, Herod felt the time had come when he must act, so he had John arrested and imprisoned in the fortress of Makorus. Most of John's followers deserted him, and only a few of his close disciples, most of them in hiding for fear of persecution, remained loyal to him. Dark clouds of anxiety gathered over Galilee, for the news of John's arrest and detention spread rapidly through the land. Even the man he had proclaimed Messiah Christ could not save him, for He Himself was in danger of arrest.

Makorus was an ancient prison haunted by the spirits of men who had been tortured and executed within its depths. The glorious spring of John's life had come and gone, but there is always another spring when nature is again clothed with color and hope. He spent many months of suffering in the dreary and damp fortress, and during his long and lonely hours in the dark cell, he thought of Jesus of Nazareth. Suffering and agony brought doubts, and he wondered if the man he had met at the Jordan River was really the Messiah and if the voice he had heard was really a voice from Heaven.

In ancient lands, prisoners are fed by their relatives and friends, and so it was that when some of John's disciples, risking arrest, came to visit him and bring him food, he sent two of them to find Jesus and to ask Him whether He really was Messiah Christ. In John's eyes, Jesus had accomplished little, and nothing of importance. True, He had been preaching, but nothing had happened to arouse the interest of the religious authorities or to change conditions. There had been no mass conversions, no changes in the government. Jesus had been preaching and healing and calling on the people to repent, but it was not enough. John needed action to be convinced. Many Hebrew prophets and reformers had performed miracles, had healed the sick and raised the dead, but they had not been able to deliver their people from foreign oppressors. The Messiah Christ was to succeed where others had failed. So, as his disciples were leaving his cell, John looked at them and said sadly, "Yes, ask Him if He is the Messiah Christ."

Jesus had heard of John's imprisonment and had carefully avoided arrest by moving from one place to another. He seems to have taken the news calmly, for He continued to preach as though nothing had happened, although John's followers and the nationalistic Jews had held a demonstration in protest against John's arrest. The protests had been futile; indeed, they had made the situation worse. Jesus Himself had not even raised His voice, and John was embittered.

John's disciples brought his message to Jesus while He was preaching in Capernaum. They described his imprisonment, his suffering, and how he and many of his followers expected Jesus to rally the people and protest to the king.

Jesus listened quietly, His head bowed, His eyes on the ground. When they were through, He raised his eyes and looked at them and said, "What could I have done, and what can I do now? Have I an army to support a protest to the king or to the Romans? Would the people stand behind me? I am also like John, a voice crying in the wilderness, but who would hear me and rally behind me?"

Then He added, "John acted unwisely when he denounced the king and called the queen a harlot. There are many evil men like Herod in this land, and many harlots like Herodia. As a matter of fact, those who pretend to be religious and shepherds of the people are worse. It was they who sold the people to Herod and to the Romans for material gain, glory and worldly power. No one can accomplish anything by attacking people's characters, especially the characters of those who rule over us. Had the people been good, their rulers would have been good, too. Did not the prophets tell us that? What did Elijah and Elisha gain by attacking King Ahab and his wife Jezebel? They were driven into the mountains and the desert, and the people were left like sheep without a shepherd. John's denunciation of the king and queen has put him in a position where no one can help him. He should have prayed for them. He should have followed our teaching—the way of meekness, forgiveness and love. Hatred produces hatred, and force needs more than force to crush it."

When Jesus had finished, He folded His arms across His chest and said quietly, "Tell John I have been fulfilling my mission. I have been preaching and spreading the good news of the coming of the Kingdom of Heaven. I have been doing what he was doing some time ago in the towns in Judea and by the River Jordan. I have been sowing seeds for a new order—a new religion which will embrace all nations of the world, but it will take time for the seeds to spring up, grow and mature. Tell John, too, that the sick are healed, the lepers cleansed, the lame walk, the blind see, and the dead are raised. I have done all the things which the Christ is expected to do. What else can I do to prove to him that I am the Messiah Christ and no one else is coming?"

When Jesus had dismissed the messengers, He turned to His disciples and said sternly, "No one born of a woman is greater than John, and yet, the least person in the Kingdom of Heaven is greater than John." And as He prophesied, a few years after the Resurrection, even the least disciples had become more important and had more understanding than John the Baptist and the prophets who had preceded him. Millions of men and women have invoked the names of Peter, James and John, those followers of Christ who had once been unknown fishermen. The new order did indeed become greater and more important than the old.

On Herod's birthday, the king invited many guests—officers of the Roman legions and high government dignitaries—to a lavish banquet in celebration. After the feasting there was dancing by beautiful, scantily clad dancing girls, and when they had left the royal presence, the young daughter of Herodia from her late husband, Philip, rose to take her turn. Herod was exceedingly pleased and as a reward swore that he would give her anything she wished, even half his kingdom if she wanted it. But the girl had been well coached by her mother. Lowering her eyes to the floor as though hesitant to ask, she said firmly to her stepfather, "Give me, right here and now in this banquet hall, on a tray, the head of John the Baptist."

The king, who had not intended to put John to death, was cornered like a lion surrounded by hunters. But he had given his word before his guests, and he could not take it back. He commanded that the head of the prophet be given to her.

John the Baptist was beheaded in the prison, and his head, on a silver tray, brought to the banquet hall and presented to the girl. With trembling hands, she accepted it, and going to her mother, handed it to her. Thus did Herodia have her revenge.

When John's disciples heard of the execution, they went to the prison, removed the body and buried it. Then they went to Jesus to tell Him what had happened. Jesus realized immediately that His own life was in danger. Herod's palace was but a few miles from Capernaum, and if he could execute John, how easily could he put Jesus to death to please His enemies and thus reconcile himself with the religious authorities over the execution of John. Nevertheless, He continued His preaching and healing, for John's death had served to unite both his and

Jesus' disciples and had aroused the people's feelings against the king and the religious authorities.

The ministry of John the Baptist had come to an end. But the echoes of his voice were still heard through another voice—the voice of Jesus, the man whom John had acclaimed Messiah Christ.

8

THE WEDDING
AT CANA

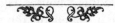

A FEW WEEKS AFTER JESUS had returned to Nazareth from Capernaum, Mary told Him that she had had word that one of their relatives in Cana, a town not far from Nazareth, was to be married and since she and other members of the family were going, she asked Jesus if He, too, would like to go.

He agreed because it was an ancient and sacred custom that relatives and close friends participate in the wedding feast and share the happiness of the newlyweds. Even strangers came to offer their blessings and bestow gifts. Friends and relatives often traveled two or three days to attend the wedding feast and they looked forward to hearing the music of drums and tambourines and to watching the dancers.

Accompanying Jesus and His family to the wedding at

Cana were a few young men who had heard John the Baptist proclaim Jesus the Messiah and who believed in Him despite His humble position.

As they neared Cana, they could hear the music, and when they entered the town, they found that the townspeople had already begun the wedding ceremonies and women dressed in colorful clothing were already dancing at the door of the wedding house. The house itself was filled with guests, each seated on the floor according to his social position. The prominent men were sitting on cushions in the center of the room; the ones of lesser prominence were on the floor closer to the door. Women, musicians and the servants were seated near the door, too. All the guests began eating and drinking toasts to the newlyweds and to the more prominent guests.

Although Easterners seldom drink and but moderately when they do, at wedding feasts they drink until they are drunk, for they feel that the more they drink, the more they honor the bride and groom. Religious men, who generally do not drink, toast the bridal couple with water. The food for wedding feasts was prepared by the women of the town and brought to the wedding house on trays. While the people were eating, the more prominent guests gave money to the servants to go out and purchase wine. They did this in accordance with their social standing, and each person waited until his turn came so as not to embarrass guests who were seated on the cushions. When a man's turn came, he poured wine into a cup or bowl and gave it to the other guests, mentioning as he did so, the name of the guest who paid for it. Because of this custom, which sometimes continued for hours, many happy weddings ended in tragedy when the guests had too much to drink, insulted or even stabbed each other.

The prophet Habakkuk says, "Woe to him who makes

his neighbors drink the dregs of fury, and makes them drunk that he may look on their nakedness." (Habakkuk 2:15) This is because a drunken man may expose his nakedness and shame.

The prophet Isaiah also condemned drunkenness, saying, "But these also have erred with wine, and with strong drink are gone astray; the priests and the prophets have erred with strong drink, they are overcome with wine, they stagger with strong drink." (Isaiah 28:7)

Before Jesus' turn to offer wine to the guests came, Mary rose from her place by the door and went to Him. Thinking that He had forgotten to do His part to make the wedding feast merry, she told Him that the wine was decreasing and that the guests were clamoring for more.

But Jesus said to her, "Woman, My turn to entertain has not yet come, when it comes I will do My part." (In Aramaic, the word meaning *turn* also means *time*.)

Jesus, because He had studied the Scriptures so carefully, knew drunkenness was not only unwise, but was condemned. When He had finished speaking to His mother, He looked toward the door and saw six stone jars, each of which could hold several gallons of water. He said to the servants, "Fill the jars with water," and when they had done so, He told them, "Draw out now and bring it to the chief of the feast."

According to custom, the most important guest at a wedding feast drinks first and commends those who have provided the drink. Thus, the chief guest drank of the water that had become wine—the best wine he had ever drunk—and then he said to the bridegroom, "Every man at first brings the best wine until the guests are drunk, and when they are well drunk, then he gives them weak wine for they would not know the difference, but you have kept the best wine until now."

In Aramaic, the term *wine* also means *teaching, joy* and *inspiration,* and the wine that Jesus offered was spiritual wine. The earth was not its mother, the air was not its father; it was not nourished by the warmth of the sun, nor was it watered by the springs; it was the spiritual wine which only God could make, the best wine that opened the eyes of the guests so that they recognized the presence of Jesus. The guests who had been clamoring for more wine were satisfied. Religious men never give strong drink during the wedding feasts. They give water or other refreshment.

After the family had returned to Nazareth from the wedding, Jesus once more left for Capernaum, and there He taught in the synagogue on the Sabbath. People were amazed at His teaching, for He knew the Scriptures by heart and could teach with the power of the Holy Spirit and with authority. In addition, he performed many miracles.

One Sabbath as He was preaching in the synagogue, a man, who was insane and could not control himself, cried out, "Leave us alone. What have we in common, Jesus of Nazareth? Have you come to destroy us [that is, destroy our religion]? I know who you are, Holy One of God." But Jesus rebuked him and told him to be still. Then He cast out the evil thoughts that had possessed him, and restored his mind. The people in the synagogue were amazed at this power that Jesus had over evil spirits, and His fame spread through Capernaum.

And on another day as He left the synagogue, He went to the house of Simon Peter, whose mother-in-law was suffering from a severe fever. Simon begged Jesus to heal her, and Jesus rebuked the fever so that she was cured.

But many people in towns around the lake of Galilee did not believe in Him and ridiculed His miracles. Soon towns like Capernaum and Bethseida turned against Him so He could no longer perform miracles. But His teaching took root in the cities, and even those who resisted and mocked Him helped to spread His teaching by their opposition. The religious authorities of Galilee were friendly to Him, however, and some even sought healing at His hand. Even the chief of one of the synagogues asked Him to raise his daughter from the dead, and others brought their children to be healed and blessed by Him.

His work was like that of a sower who scatters the seed on the ground. Some of it falls in good soil and brings abundant fruit while some falls by the wayside and is eaten by the birds.

One of the most difficult obstacles that Jesus had to overcome was the old Jewish concept of the coming of the Messianic Kingdom. For centuries the Jews had been taught that the world would suddenly change with no effort on their part. Good would triumph over evil; the rich would share their wealth with the poor; the sinners would become saints; dishonest men would become honest; hate would change to love; and the weapons of war would become the weapons of peace.

To destroy these false beliefs that had taken root in the hearts and minds of the people, Jesus had to speak in simple parables based on things with which the people were familiar and which they could therefore easily understand. He was to sow the new seeds of the new teaching, so He related the parable of the sower and the seed. Most of the people who came to hear Him had seen the sower scattering his seed with faith that the seed that he sowed after feeding his family would in time germinate, grow and multiply. But Jesus also wanted the people to understand that not all of the seed which is thus scattered falls into good ground. Some falls on rocky ground, some dries up, some falls among thorns and briars that choke it. Still other seed falls by the wayside where it is eaten by birds.

But even this simple parable had to be explained:

Now listen to the parable of the seed. Whoever hears the word of the kingdom and does not understand it, the evil one comes and snatches away the word which has been sown in his heart. This is that which was sown on the roadside. That which was sown upon the rock, this is he who hears the word, and immediately accepts it with joy; but it has no root in him, except for a while; and when trouble or persecution comes because of the word, he immediately stumbles. That which was sown among thistles, this is he who hears the word, but worldly thoughts and the deception caused by riches choke the word, and it becomes fruitless. That which was sown upon good soil, this is he who hears my word and understands it, so he bears fruit and produces some one hundredfold and some sixty and some thirty. (Matthew 13:18–23)

Jesus wanted the people to know that some of them would follow Him readily, but, not understanding His teaching, would become disappointed and leave Him, just as seeds which fall upon rocks germinate quickly, but also dry quickly. Others would gladly accept His teaching, but their worries and cares would cause them to reject it as briars choke out wheat. But some of His teachings would find their way into the hearts of sincere men and women to produce abundant fruit and multiply.

In another parable, Jesus likened the Kingdom of Heaven to a grain of mustard seed:

> The kingdom of heaven is like a grain of mustard seed, which a man took and sowed in his field. It is the smallest of all seeds; but when it is grown, it is larger than all of the herbs; and it becomes a tree, so that the birds of the air come and nest in its branches. (Matthew 13:31–32)

Jesus wanted the people to know that there would be good and evil even in the Kingdom of Heaven, so He related the parable of the wheat and the tares:

> The kingdom of heaven is like a man who sowed good seed in his field. And when men slept, his enemy came, sowed tares among the wheat, and went away. But when the blade sprang up and bore fruit, then the tares also appeared. So the servants of the landowner came and said to him, Our Lord, behold, did you not sow good seed in your field; whence did the tares come into it? He said to them, An enemy did this. His servants then said to him, Do you want us to go and pull them out? But he said to them, It might happen that while you were pulling out the tares, you might uproot with them also the wheat. Let them both grow together until the harvest; and at the harvest season, I will say to the reapers, Pick out first the tares, and bind them into bundles to be burned; but gather the wheat into my barns. (Matthew 13:24–30)

Tares are weeds that worry farmers because they resemble green peas and when they are left in the grain, they spoil the taste of the bread. When the wheat is harvested, therefore, the tares are separated and burned.

Until the Kingdom of Heaven becomes the Kingdom of

God, evil and good will flourish side by side because it would be difficult to remove evil without destroying some of the good, just as it would be hard to pull out tares without destroying some of the precious wheat.

The characteristics of the Kingdom of Heaven as taught by the ancient Hebrew prophets were different from those taught by the Jewish elders and in the rabbinical schools. According to Jesus, the Kingdom was to come gradually and evil was to be eradicated slowly. The people would have to repent and search in order to find it, for it must be acquired through patience and hard labor, but when people finally do find it, they give up everything to possess it.

Jesus related another parable about a man who searched for a pearl of great price. When he found it, he sold some of his possessions in order to purchase it. The pearl became his dearest possession, for he could easily hide it in his garments. But his other possessions that he could not hide could be stolen by thieves or confiscated by corrupt government officials.

Truth is like a pearl of great price. A man may lose everything in this world, but no one can take his religion from him.

9

THE
KINGDOM
OF
HEAVEN

❦

THE LONG-AWAITED KINGDOM
of Heaven was near. But how near? Although there was
no question about its eventual coming, no one knew when
it would take place. All Jews saw the need for the restoration of the Davidic kingdom and the triumph of
justice, and while most of them expected it to come soon,
they made no effort to bring it about. They did not realize it would start with an individual. All who came to
hear Jesus and, before Him, John the Baptist shared this
Jewish belief.

The Jews are a patient people. Abraham's descendants
had waited more than four hundred years before they
inherited the land of Canaan, but now things were different. Rome was gradually extinguishing the Lamp of
God, patience was running out, and the people were los-

ing their hope. Jesus felt the expectation for the Kingdom in the words and the hearts of the people who sat at His feet. He realized they expected a sudden change, for He, too, had once cherished these Messianic hopes. But now He had to change this belief and make them understand that human hearts cannot be changed overnight.

As the crowd by the lake of Galilee waited, Jesus spoke to them, saying, "The kingdom of heaven is like a grain of mustard seed which has been sown in the ground. It takes a long time to germinate, sprout, become a plant and produce other seeds. Or, like the leaven which is hidden in the meal, it takes time to permeate the whole meal." But the people still did not understand the spiritual implication or why the God of Israel who had created the world in six days, and who had performed so many miracles in the past, could not change the world quickly. Nor did they understand that everyone who paid his tithes, presented his offerings, and fulfilled his vows was not automatically an heir of the Kingdom. They did not realize that they had to search their own hearts, for, like a valuable pearl that is hidden in a field, no one else could find it for them, but they themselves.

Jesus reminded them that just as good fish and bad fish are caught in a net, so will there be good men and evil men in the Kingdom of Heaven, for how can evil be destroyed without destroying some good with it? But He also showed them that God has patience and mercy even upon the wicked because they, too, are His children. He will not destroy them, but they will ultimately destroy themselves.

The people had to be constantly alert like the wise virgins who, not knowing when the bridegroom was coming, purchased extra oil to keep their lamps burning so that they would be permitted to enter the wedding house to share the bridal festivities.

Jesus cited many other parables to describe the Kingdom of Heaven to His people, and the people listened and were amazed. Every parable was aimed like an arrow at a target; every one of them was cited to change the incorrect concept about the Kingdom of Heaven and the reign of God.

One of the most difficult of the Jewish beliefs that had to be changed was the priests' concept of the God of Israel as a God of wrath and vengeance, a God constantly in need of sacrifices and offerings to be appeased, a God who depended on His people more than the people depended on Him. This belief was deeply rooted in the people, but Jesus was a courageous teacher who never compromised. Like Isaiah and Jeremiah, He spared no words in condemning the false doctrines which the priests, Pharisees and scribes considered sacred and had used to supplant the truth of God.

To prove that the God of Israel was a loving Father and a generous giver, Jesus composed another parable, this one concerning the shepherd who would leave all his sheep in the field and go into the hills to search for one lost animal and who rejoiced when it was found. His listeners were all familiar with the shepherd and his sheep, so they understood that Jesus was trying to persuade them that God's love toward His children is even greater than that of a shepherd and that He rejoices when a sinner repents and returns to Him.

Thus did Jesus try to impart to the people some of the characteristics of the Kingdom of Heaven for which they had waited so long and so patiently. As yeast slowly leavens bread, so was His teaching to leaven the world.

The Prophet from Nazareth had been healing all kinds

of diseases, even restoring to mental health those who had lost their sanity. These deeds were sufficient evidence for those who were sincerely seeking the Messiah, and they were convinced that they had found the man who could save them. They rallied to Him, but the more popular He became, the more the Pharisees and the scribes envied, hated and mistrusted Him because He directed His attacks only against the religious authorities whom He called hypocrites and blind guides leading the blind, for they were responsible for the misfortunes that had befallen the people.

Had Jesus, like John, denounced the king and queen and the Romans, He might have received some sympathy from the religious leaders, but He placed all the guilt at the doors of the high priests, the scribes and the Pharisees who were able to read the Scriptures and therefore knew the truth. It was their evil acts and unfaithfulness to the Law that had led the Romans to occupy the country; it was they who did not want to repent and enter the Kingdom, who stood at the door to prevent those who would enter; it was they who taught the Law and the prophets and asked the people to obey the Law that they themselves did not obey; it was they who placed the heavy burdens on the people and would not even stretch forth their hands to help them. It was they who did not practice what they preached.

Jesus realized that if He could succeed in reforming His own people and bring them to the way of God, their light would shine upon the Gentiles and the pagans, and they, too, would return to God. But the greatest obstacles He faced were the priesthood, the temple complex, and the religious organization. These groups were not interested in reform. They were satisfied with the existing corrupt and unjust order. Their positions were secure, and they were happy and content. Why should they change to something new and uncertain?

Then the majority of the people who had previously welcomed Him with open arms became suspicious of His motives and His teaching. He no longer was able to speak in the synagogues and marketplaces, and He was forced to become secretive in His movements. He began to travel and to preach wherever He found listeners. Even Herod and the religious authorities began to be worried, for they did not understand what He was trying to do.

Jesus, like the ancient Hebrew prophets, had heralded the coming of the Kingdom of Heaven and, like John the Baptist, had called on the people to repent. They all knew that someday the reign of God would be established upon the earth, for thus had they been taught, but centuries had passed and nothing had happened. The mighty were still mighty; the weak were still weak; the stronger still devoured the weak; evil still prevailed. So the people ignored Jesus and carried on with their daily lives.

So Jesus embarked on His mission to challenge the forces of evil, to reform not only His own people, but the world, and to accomplish this mission, He found from His study of the Scriptures a new way. If war results in more war, if hatred produces more hatred, if force results in force, He would use the dormant strength that lies in meekness.

Aware of the constantly changing world, He founded a new spiritual and lasting order. If a man is to change the world and the hearts of his fellowmen, he has to change his own heart first, his own way of life, and this change can be accomplished only by the armor of the Spirit—love, meekness and kindness.

Hitherto, these forces had lain hidden from the eyes of

men. Philosophers and prophets, convinced they would not work, had dared not advocate them, for they thought that force and fear were the shortest ways to reach the summit of human aspiration and fulfill all human desires. Only Jesus and the Holy Prophets knew the truth.

And to spread this truth, Jesus chose His disciples or students from among the simplest of men—the peasants, the fishermen, and those who had fallen but who wanted another chance. These were the men who would succeed Him and carry on His work after His death.

He chose twelve, a holy number since there are twelve signs of the zodiac, twelve months of the year, and twelve sons of Jacob. Thus, every disciple was symbolic of a tribe of Israel.

In the old days when schools were rare and education was in its infancy, the students lived with their teacher, eating and traveling with him, and learning from personal experience. So had Moses trained Joshua, who accompanied him on many of his journeys and later became his successor. And so had the prophet Elijah trained Elisha, a farmer. At that time, students were often called servants because they also ministered to their teacher and ran errands for him. Not only did they hear their master teach and admonish the people, but they also saw him perform miracles. This school of experience has never been surpassed; it was an apprenticeship and is still practiced today in many professions.

Therefore, Jesus' disciples were not only to learn His new teaching, but they were to imitate His conduct. Like Him, they were to become meek and willing to serve others. They were to share their Master's troubles and witness all of His miracles. For His part, He was not to become just a master to them, but He was to look upon them as His own children. Since they were inexperienced in the truth which He was expounding, He often called them "little children." Jesus loved His disciples and was constantly concerned for their welfare and safety.

For a short while He had only four students. These men were two sets of brothers, fishermen whom He had known in the past. He did not call them by chance. He had examined their hearts and found that they were ready and willing to exchange their worldly occupations for something better, something spiritual which would make them live for generations to come and which would inscribe their names on the books of life.

These simple and illiterate fishermen had spent most of their time waiting patiently to catch a few fish. It required faith, patience, and perseverance, and they had prayed in their hearts before they cast their nets for help from God. But they were barely able to make a living; many times they had pulled out their nets and found them empty. Many times they had returned home embarrassed and empty handed. They had nothing in their purses with which to buy bread and the other necessities of life.

These, then, were the type of men whom Jesus wanted to train to become fishermen of men. Already trained to a great extent through experience, they could withstand the hardships of the world. They had been used to hunger and deprivation. Jesus discovered that it takes men like the rough and sturdy fishermen to change human hearts by becoming examples of the new way—citizens of the Kingdom of Heaven. If He could convert these illiterate and unpolished men, it would be easy to convert others. He was sure that they would accomplish something that the philosophers and other learned men had failed to accomplish because they relied on their wisdom and the strength of their arms for their livelihood, and thus the simple disciples understood the trials of their fellowmen better than those who had spent their lives studying without experiencing that which they had read.

These few poorly dressed young men, then, their large eyes wide open and eager to find something new, joined Jesus to become the first seeds of the new religion.

How many times passers-by saw Jesus and His disciples walking on the beach discussing plans for a better world order, a better society, a better way of life. And some of the passers-by wondered what these idlers were doing. Who would have believed that these few men were destined to change the world and alter the course of human history? And, as their eternal reward in the life to come, they would sit on the everlasting throne.

IO

THE
SERMON
ON THE
MOUNT

A NEW SPRING HAD COME, clothing the bleak countryside in green. Flowers filled the air with their sweet fragrance, an offering to God who had adorned them with His glory and majesty. How often had Jesus looked at the flowers during His lonely hours as a shepherd and wished that all peoples could live as the flowers—patiently and peacefully. Away from narrow, winding paths in the countryside, sowers scattered their seed into freshly plowed ground. They had done this every year, and nature had not failed them. Their forefathers had plowed these fields; their sons and grandsons would follow with the same faith and confidence, and the faith of these simple peasants was like that of little children who seldom doubt the words and promises of their parents.

The fame of the prophet from Nazareth spread rapidly

throughout Galilee and the adjacent lands. Wherever He went, large crowds followed Him, bringing the lame, the blind, the ill. Many carried baskets of food and gifts for the Healer, for even today pilgrims do not visit a holy man empty handed but always take a gift, usually food, to him. The people followed Him to the beach and even to the houses of men who had invited Him to dine. When He embarked for Tiberias, they followed Him along the water's edge and when the boat reached the shore, large crowds had already gathered. The roads to the town were choked with pilgrims, and Jesus looked upon them with compassion. He climbed a mountain near the town and sat upon a stone facing the gray, calm water of the lake of Galilee. His disciples sat at His feet and the crowds gathered around. Jesus was to explain the mysteries of nature and of man, to write a new chapter in the history of Judaism, inscribing a new law not on breakable stone tablets like the Mosaic Law, but on men's hearts to be handed down from one generation to the next.

And as the people waited impatiently, Jesus spoke:

Blessed are the humble, for theirs is the kingdom of heaven.

John had warned the people not to trust in their racial ancestry simply because they were descendants of Abraham. He had told them to bear good fruit like Abraham, for the ax is ready to cut down trees which are barren. By their good works only would they be known as the children of Abraham, not by ancestral pride. The most important thing in religion is the truth that lives forever: justice, mercy, love, forgiveness and the life hereafter. All people are the children of God, and God loves them all. Material possessions are ephemeral. They come like raindrops and disappear like vapor, or like the flower that blooms in the morning and is dried by evening.

Only the humble and pure in heart can become citizens in the Kingdom of Heaven. Only those willing to exchange all their temporal possessions for life eternal can enter the Kingdom.

Blessed are they who mourn, for they shall be comforted.

Blessed are they who mourn for the loss of something spiritual and enduring. God-fearing men do not grieve for material losses like Pharisees and Sadducees; they grieve when they think of the days gone by, when justice and truth meant more to the people and weighed heavier in the balance. These men mourn for the people who have traveled far from the religion of their forefathers and, because of their unfaithfulness to God, have delayed the fulfillment of the divine promises for a better future. These men will be compensated for their material losses by the good news of the Kingdom of Heaven, which is at hand.

Blessed are the meek, for they shall inherit the earth.

The meek are like trees that bend down when driving storms rage but which nevertheless continue to flourish. Those that do not bend are broken and beaten.

God blesses the meek by allowing them to inherit the lands of those who live by force and die fighting one another. It is difficult to bear hardship and humiliation, but it is better than resisting and being destroyed. Evil can be destroyed with love and gentleness even as fire is quenched by water.

The forefathers of the people, because of their meekness, were permitted to dwell wherever they wished. But when their descendants forgot meekness and gentleness, they fought one another as well as their enemies and were carried away into captivity. But God always spares a remnant that is made up of the meek, pure in heart and peacemakers and these, because of their suffering, patience and perseverance, will find their way to the Kingdom of God.

Blessed are they who hunger and thirst for justice, for they shall be well satisfied.

Justice is the foundation of all world religions and democratic institutions. Peace, progress, happiness, harmony, law and order—without justice, all are impossible. Justice is another name for truth; the universe is established on laws and true equations which bring the equilibrium that will endure forever. All nations that have flaunted justice have eventually been destroyed, for the wings of justice are patience and its weapon is time. Justice may come slowly, but it will always catch those who have violated it.

Blessed are the merciful, for they shall have mercy.

Jesus was aware of the universal law. He knew that those who were kind and charitable would receive kindness and charity, for those who give, to them shall it be given, and those who open their doors to strangers, doors will be open to them. The spirit which is the essence of life is indivisible. This is why when a man is drowning, others risk their lives, and sometimes lose them, to save him. There is a close relationship between all men, regardless of who they are, and sometimes this relationship causes men to lose all for the sake of helping a fellow man. Where would the world be without merciful men and women who constantly share with those who are in need? Man must be distinguished by acts of charity and mercy, not by mere words and observance, for a tree is known by its fruits and not by its leaves.

The whole of nature is founded on the principle of giving and receiving. This pattern was set by the wise Creator and when it is disturbed, all of life is disturbed.

Blessed are the pure in heart, for they shall see God.

The pure in heart are the pure in mind. They are those who have conquered the evil forces and have rid their hearts of evil thoughts that are contrary to the truth. They are the men and women who have come close to being perfect and who have transcended the material world, whose only aspiration is to work constructively in the interest of humanity.

The mind is the mirror of the soul. Even as a dirty mirror cannot reflect a clear image, so the mind, when it is filled with evil thoughts cannot reflect goodness. God, who is eternal purity, can only be seen through a pure heart free from all obstructions. All of men's actions, good and bad, are conceived in their minds. They must rid their minds of all evil in order to become a lamp for other men to light their paths.

After a brief pause to let the newcomers be seated, Jesus raised His arms as though to embrace the people and said,

Blessed are the peacemakers, for they shall be called sons of God.

Peace is the highest of all human desires, and peacemakers are those who have surrendered their hearts and souls to God and have made peace with themselves and with the world. They are the pious men who spend many hours settling quarrels and disputes with no compensation for their efforts. Not only do they have the same qualities as the meek and the humble, but they try to bring peace in order to avoid wars and famines. When a man says, "Peace be with you," which means, "I surrender to you," he first surrenders to God, the Father of all. And when he is greeted with the same words, peace and harmony reign. When the stranger and the host break bread and eat salt together, they are no longer strangers but brothers conceived of the same Father and born of the same mother.

The magic word "peace" destroys hatred and replaces it with love in the hearts of men. It is simple and practical, yet it is as difficult as "love your enemies and pray for those who hate you." It is not easy for a man to love his enemies and pray for them, for many believe that to love one's enemies means to humble oneself before them.

But peace is the shortest road to the Kingdom of Heaven.

Blessed are those who are persecuted for the sake of justice, for theirs is the kingdom of heaven.

Those who are persecuted are those who work and pray for the establishment of justice and the reign of righteousness, the reign of God instead of the reign of man.

Just as there are thousands of men hungry and thirsty for the reign of God and for peace and harmony, so there are millions who hunger and thirst for power and material possessions. These men would do anything to resist the message of the new Gospel and to preserve the world order as they know it. Men who have denied the immortality of the soul and believe death to be the end would certainly not sacrifice themselves, nor would they believe in laying up treasures in heaven in preparation for the eternal rewards in the life to come. As far as they are concerned, there is only one life—the life on this earth.

Justice cannot be established without sacrifice and suffering. Man has paid a heavy price for the comforts of life; he must pay a heavy price, too, for a government based on justice and truth. The heralders of the Gospel will become victims of thieves and bandits who wait for them, and they will stand before unjust judges and governors in order to condemn injustices.

All teachers of religion had promised abundant rewards and joys in the earthly life, but Jesus makes no such promises. Instead, He promises His followers a rough road, heavy crosses and possible death for His sake. But the men who are willing to accept the challenge and endure the suffering are those who will inherit the Kingdom of Heaven.

Blessed are you when men reproach you and persecute you and speak against you every kind of evil, falsely, for my sake. Then be glad and rejoice, for your reward is increased in heaven; for in this very manner they persecuted the prophets who were before you.

Purity is contrary to impurity, and falsehood is contrary to the truth. Therefore, when they meet, they clash. The preachers of the Gospel will be open to attacks from those who resist change. They will be persecuted, slandered, branded revolutionaries, and disturbers of the peace of the world because their way of life is contrary to that of other men.

When brass is burnished, it is placed in a heated furnace to burn the dross. Good character, like brass, can be neither smeared nor destroyed. In ancient days, the leaders had shamefully treated the prophets and the messengers of God who tried to lead them to God's way. So now will the world do the same to the preachers of the new Gospel. Only those who are willing to carry their crosses and drink from the bitter cup will be entitled to sit in the Kingdom. Man must love that which the world has hated and hate that which the world has loved. A new covenant and a new law must be written on the tablets of men's hearts, a covenant not written and sealed with the blood of animals, but with blood of man. Man must overcome temptations for something far richer and more satisfying.

Then Jesus summed up all that He had preached. The sun had gone down, and the day was drawing to a close.

> You are indeed the salt of the earth; but if the salt should lose its savor, with what could it be salted? It would not be worth anything but to be thrown outside and to be trodden down by men.

Salt is dug from the ground and must be carefully preserved in order not to lose its savor, for when salt loses it savor, there is nothing else to salt with and no way to bring its savor back.

The Jews were the people called by God, trained by His prophets and guided by His word in order to train others, but for many years they had lost their spiritual power and had become like the precious salt that has lost its savor. For centuries, because of their lack of faith, they had been trampled under the feet of the Gentiles. No longer did the Gentiles recognize the Jews as the people of God and come to seek healing and God's blessing from their hands, for they had not lived up to the promises made to their forefathers. Therefore, the Jews had to repent in order to find freedom, tranquillity and happiness.

You are indeed the light of the world; a city that is built upon a mountain cannot be hidden. Nor do they light a lamp and put it under a basket, but on a lamp stand, so that it gives light to all who are in the house.

The Jews were the only people blessed with the Light of God, the Torah, the Bible, God's commandments and His ordinances. But instead of upholding and revering the Law, they made a mockery of it. They had buried it under so many commentaries and other man-made devices that no one could see it. They had pretended concern about minor laws so they could break the more important ones; while condemning others, they illegally escaped condemnation themselves.

And Jesus ended His teaching by telling the people that all are children of the same Father—the Jewish God, the only God, the Father whose sun shines everyday upon Jews and Gentiles alike, upon good and bad, and whose stars shine upon all living beings no matter who they are.

When Jesus finished speaking on the Beatitudes, He took a deep breath and pointing at the people with His right hand, He said,

Do not suppose that I have come to weaken the law or the prophets; I have not come to weaken, but to fulfil. For truly I say to you, Until heaven and earth pass away, not

even a yoth or a dash shall pass away from the law until
all of it is fulfilled.

False rumors had been spread that Jesus' teaching was
aimed against the Law, the foundation of the Jewish religion, and the teachings of the Holy Prophets. People
became indignant if even a casual remark against the
Law and the prophets was dropped, and His enemies,
even some of His friends and followers, had wrongly in-
terpreted His attacks against the doctrine of the elders.
Men at the synagogues, who did not understand the new
Gospel, said that Jesus had come to destroy their religion,
and Jesus tried to explain to His audience what His purpose was: "I have not come to weaken, but to fulfil," to
teach them how to put the Law into practice.

As far as *weakening* was concerned, who could weaken
the words dictated by God to Moses? The only men who
had ever tried to violate the Law and change the words
of the prophets were the very men to whom the Law and
the prophets were entrusted—the scribes and the Pharisees. Through false interpretations and alterations and
loop holes in the text, they tried to make the Law and
the prophets read to their advantage. Twenty-six hundred years ago, the prophet Jeremiah condemned the
scribes because they had deliberately changed some of
the words of the Law in order to support their own interpretation: "How do you say, We are wise, and the law
of the Lord is with us? Lo, surely the lying pen of the
scribes has made it for falsehood." (Jeremiah 8:8) Whoever tries to weaken even one of the least commandments shall be regarded as one of the least in the Kingdom of Heaven, but anyone who observes and teaches
them shall be regarded as great. The Law is eternal; it
is the Word of God, food for the kingdom on earth as

well as for the Kingdom in Heaven. Nothing in it needs to be changed, nor can any other law supplant it.

So Jesus upbraided the hypocrites who pretended to uphold the Law and the prophets by condemning others on minor violations, thus shielding their own greater violations. He commanded His followers to uphold the Law and its commandments on mercy, charity, divorce, justice:

> For I say to you, that unless your righteousness exceeds that of the scribes and Pharisees, you shall not enter into the kingdom of heaven.

In other words, they must reject that which they had taught and teach that which they had rejected. At the banquets and feasts, they were to sit only in the lowest places, for all men are equal in the presence of God.

> You have heard that it was said to those who were before you, You shall not kill, and whoever kills is guilty before the court. But I say to you that whoever becomes angry with his brother for no reason is guilty before the court; and whoever should say to his brother *Raca* (which means I spit on you) is guilty before the congregation. . . .

According to Jesus' interpretation of the Law, the cause is far more important than the effect. A single offensive word like *Raca*, a defamatory phrase, is looked upon as murder, and some men would slay the offender, for spitting or an offensive remark is a debasement of a man's soul which is the image and likeness of God. In the East, nearly all quarrels that lead to murder are precipitated merely by a word. It is easier to conquer anger than to wait until murder has been committed. One can bring a fire under control when it first starts, but once it is blazing, it gets out of control. So Jesus wanted to bring under control the causes for murder, to stop trouble before it started. He taught that the most important way to prevent murder is to examine the causes leading to it. When a man is at peace with his brother and neighbor, there is no cause for abuse, so to subdue one's anger is far more important than offering a gift to God.

You have heard that it is said, You shall not commit adultery. But I say to you that whoever looks at a woman with lust, has already committed adultery with her in his heart.

Again, He goes back to the cause rather than the effect. He condemns a lustful look, for example, when a man sees a woman bathing and commits adultery with her in his mind by masturbating. That is, he tries to satisfy his desire by unnatural means. An evil habit, it still prevails in lands where men and women seldom see each other, where women cover not only their faces, but their entire bodies.

Centuries before, King David, walking on the roof of his palace, saw a beautiful woman bathing in her courtyard. Wishing her, he sent for her and committed adultery with her. He could have conquered his lust, but he did not want to. Instead, he had her husband, Uriah, a faithful general, put to death so he would not be considered the father of David's child.

But Jesus does not condemn man's natural desire for a woman when that desire is pure and for the purpose of marriage.

It has been said that whoever divorces his wife, must give her the divorce papers. But I say to you, that whoever divorces his wife, except for fornication, causes her to commit adultery; and whoever marries a woman who is separated but not divorced, commits adultery.

Here Jesus attacked the laxity of the Mosaic Law and the unjust treatment of women, who, in those days, were denied their rights. Considered inferior to men, they were thought of as chattels. Moses had decreed that when a man wished to divorce his wife, he had to give her the papers so that she could marry legally again. By the time of Jesus, the Jewish people had so far departed from the Law that they did not even take the trouble to obtain a divorce for they were afraid it would cost them money or a fee to the judge. Since there was no legal divorce, those who married again committed adultery since the women had no divorce papers and were still legally married to their first husbands. Jesus did not condemn the divorce itself; He condemned the injustices in the Law which made divorce easy for men but hard on women and their children.

Again you have heard that it was said to them who were before you, that you shall not lie in your oaths, but entrust your oaths to the Lord. But I say to you, never swear; neither by heaven, because it is God's throne; Nor by the earth, for it is a stool under his feet; nor by Jerusalem, for it is the city of a great king. Neither shall you swear by your own head, because you cannot create in it a single black or white hair. But let your words be yes, yes, and no, no; for anything which adds to these is a deception.

The people swore in the name of God and His temple because they believed in the sacred oaths and in a Higher Power, but they swore falsely. They used the name of

God to cover their dishonest actions, to further their own interests. Jesus reminded them that whatever they did to their fellow men, would in return be done to them. The whole of nature is built on the law of giving and receiving. The rain supplies the rivers with water, the water supplies the sea, and the sea meets the needs of the clouds which supply the brooks and the rivers. Any words in addition to a definite "yes" or "no" deceive.

> You have heard that it is said, An eye for an eye, and a tooth for a tooth. But I say to you that you should not resist evil; but whoever strikes you on your right cheek, turn to him the other also. And if anyone wishes to sue you at the court and take away your shirt, let him have your robe also. Whoever compels you to carry a burden for a mile, go with him two. Whoever asks from you, give him; and whoever wishes to borrow from you, do not refuse him.

In Jesus' day, bandits robbed men of their clothes and sold them in the marketplace. When the original owner found them on the back of a stranger, he would identify them as his garments and demand their return. But if the stranger refused, they could end up in court. Jesus said that if someone wishes to sue you for your shirt, give him your cloak, too, for He knew that if the stranger offered more than was demanded, the offer would be refused and a friendship would result.

Millions of Christians believe that this doctrine of not resisting evil is impractical, unacceptable and inconsistent with human dignity, but history has proven that those who have adhered to the principle of non-resistance have succeeded and their names are written in the pages of history.

This teaching of non-resistance is a repudiation of portions of the Mosaic Law. Jesus struck hard at the core of the Law by this teaching, but this code had not been given to man by God, but rather forced upon man by his own nature. The very nature of the Easterner is different from that of a Westerner. In the East, when a man strikes another on his cheek, the one who is struck turns his face and says, "You may strike on this side also." The man who struck the blow immediately feels shame and apologizes, for by the victim's turning his other cheek he becomes a mirror in which the attacker sees his real self.

Even though the doctrine of non-resistance goes against human nature, it is practicable not only in the East, but all over the world. Human nature and human aspiration is the same everywhere. In Aramaic, "turning the other cheek" means "stopping a trivial quarrel from becoming a fight." Jesus' admonition was practical. It did not mean cowardice, but meekness, gentleness and courage. Jesus knew it would be difficult to obey this command, for it went against that which the people had learned for centuries. But He also knew that some of His words would fall into the hearts of men and women who were tired of war and violence, and there bear fruit.

I I

FORGIVENESS
AND
HUMILITY

You have heard that it is said, Be kind to your friend, and hate your enemy; But I say to you, Love your enemies, bless anyone who curses you, do good to anyone who hates you, and pray for those who carry you away by force and persecute you.

IT IS EASY FOR A PERSON TO be kind to those whom he hates, to help them when they are in difficulties, but it is very difficult for him to *love* them. Jesus told His followers not only to be meek, but to carry the crosses of their enemies, to do for them what others would not.

The Mosaic Law recommended kindness too, for if a man helps to find the animals of his enemy, someday his enemy may help him. Indeed, kindness and mercy to others appears in the holy books of all religions be it Greek, Chinese or Jewish. But Jesus went one step further; He said, "Love your enemies" because love embraces all the good attributes in man. Love means a debt, a debt which every man owes to God and to his fellowman, a debt which a father owes his children, the children owe the parents. It is the only binding force that links all people of all races and cultures together. Love removes all barriers and unites people with a sacred bond. Kindness is temporal and is soon forgotten, but love is eternal.

To love one's enemies is harder than turning the other cheek, than going the extra mile, for man has been taught to pray for health, happiness and strength for himself but for death to his enemy. But when a man loves God with all his heart and with all his mind, he can overcome all obstacles. And in loving one another, all men become sons of our Father in heaven.

Jesus allowed no compromise. His words were clear and unequivocal. He left no doubt in the minds of His hearers by using qualifying phrases. His teaching was direct, and the people had but one alternative: To accept what He had told them or to reject it. No one can be loyal to God and at the same time compromise His truth.

The Golden Rule was then, and is now, the only true remedy for the human ills that Jesus had found. "Whatever you wish men to do for you, do likewise also for them." "If you love Me, you must obey My commandments," He told the people. "It is not he who says, 'My Lord, My Lord' who is My disciple, but the one who hears My words and does them." He repudiated lip service, long prayers, and repetitious and false adoration. He wanted action as the fruits of faith in Him.

He warned His disciples that no one can be His dis-

ciple unless he puts his relatives and all his human interests aside and puts the Kingdom of Heaven first.

He who comes to Me and does not put aside his father,
and his mother, and his brothers, and his sisters, and his
wife, and his children, and even his own life, he cannot
be a disciple unto Me.

Jesus and His teaching must be put in first place, for
God takes no second place. Millions have accepted Jesus'
name, but they have refused to obey His commandments,
even as thousands of those who heard Him on the mountain rejected Him and even challenged Him, asking,
"What miracles has He done, that we might believe in
Him?"

The Jewish people were not taught to hate their parents; they were taught to love them and honor them, but
not to honor them as God. How could one who admonished His followers to love their enemies and pray for
those who hate them ask them to hate their parents,
wives, brothers, sisters and children? The word "hate"
in other versions is a mistranslation.* A few decades after
His death and resurrection, thousands of Jesus' followers
forgave those who had persecuted them—blessed them
and prayed for those who were ready to execute them.

The living words that Jesus uttered on that beautiful
mountain in Galilee have served to transform many men
from beasts to human beings, from sinners to saints.

The second day on the mountain was nearly over. The
sun had traveled twice around the earth and in a few
more hours would slip behind the lofty hills of Galilee.
New crowds were pouring in from towns around the lake

* The Aramaic reads, "put aside," that is, put God and His truth
first.

and from the villages by the Jordan River. They still brought the sick, the blind, the lame, the insane with hopes of having them healed. Some traveled on donkeys; others walked; but all carried baskets of food. The mountain resembled a large camp filled with people hungry for the bread of life and thirst for the living water.

Jesus, having rested, began once again to expound the Scriptures, this time discussing alms-giving and prayer:

Be careful concerning your alms, not to do them in the presence of men, merely that they may see them; otherwise you have no reward with your Father in heaven. Therefore when you give alms, do not blow a trumpet before you, just as the hypocrites do in the synagogues and in the marketplaces, so that they may be glorified by men. Truly I say to you that they have already received their reward.

Pride is a heavy burden for those who carry it as well as for those who see it carried. Every burden has a destination, but pride rests continuously upon the shoulders of those who carry it. It has no destination. False glory is another weakness of man because it makes him constantly conscious of his position in society. These men sacrifice greater and far more important things in life for the sake of the lesser. The true followers of Jesus were to reject that which the world loved and love that which the world had rejected. He who exalts himself shall be humbled, and he who humbles himself shall be exalted.

In Biblical lands, when an honored guest sits on a low seat at a banquet, the host escorts him to a higher one. Likewise, when a less important guest occupies a higher seat, he is shown to a lower. This humiliates those who are asked to move to a lower seat and exalts those who are escorted to a higher place. (High and low seats in

Eastern homes are determined by their position in rela-
tion to the door. Those who are honored are seated on
quilts, cushions and pillows away from the door, but in
a conspicuous part of the room. The other guests with
hats on and their shoes removed, sit on the floor, for
there is no furniture.)

Jesus had seen men giving alms in public so they
might be seen and praised, so He told His followers to be
careful to give in private so they are not seen:

> But when you give alms, let not your left hand know
> what your right hand is doing. So that your alms may be
> done secretly, and your Father who sees in secret, shall
> himself reward you openly.

There is no greater reward than that which the Father
bestows upon those who succor His needy children, but
the rewards which mortal men bestow upon one another
are like perishable garlands that are worn for a few hours
and then are thrown away.

> And when you pray, do not be like the hypocrites, who
> like to pray, standing in the synagogues and at the street
> corners, so that they may be seen by men. Truly I say to
> you that they have already received their reward. But
> when you pray, enter into your inner chamber and lock
> your door, and pray to your Father who is in secret, and
> your Father who sees in secret shall himself reward you
> openly.

Pour out your heart before your unseen Father who is
in heaven and who is at the same time on earth. Time is
eliminated, and heaven and earth join hands in prayer.
For only in silence can you hear the inarticulate voice

of the Spirit, and only in the darkness can you see myriads of stars and feel the presence of God. God dwells in
the true temple, in your inner heart, and in silence and
meditation your soul will wander in the realms of the
Spirit.

And when you pray, you do not have to remind God
to do what He has not done, for God knows all your
needs and all that you have done or left undone. Do not
ask as though you are lacking, but rather give thanks as
though you have received.

And when you pray, do not repeat your words like the
pagans, for they think that because of much talking they
will be heard.

God knows your need and He is always ready to grant
sincere prayers. You have to be ready to receive divine
messages and admonitions. You have to be humble and
aware of God's presence, and you have to be ready to
know whether what you are praying for is good or not.
A man may pray for a large house and a big car, and God
may wish him to have a smaller house and a cheaper car.
Only through the help of God can we distinguish between
gifts good and bad.

Jesus admonished His followers not to pray publicly or
to stand in a public place to be seen by other men and
praised openly. On one occasion while He and His disciples were in the Temple, He noticed a Pharisee and a
tax collector standing opposite each other and praying.
The Pharisee praised himself and reminded God of the
wonderful things he had done and of his loyalty to his
religion. He pointed to the tax collector and thanked
God that he was not such a sinner. The tax collector, on

the other hand, prayed solemnly and sincerely, confessed his sins and humbly sought God's forgiveness.

Jesus turned to His disciples and told them that the prayers of the tax collector were acceptable to God, but not those of the Pharisee. He told them that if their prayers were not answered immediately not to be discouraged and stop praying, for they would be answered in time. He related to them the story of a poor widow whom a judge had refused to see because she was too poor to bribe him. But the widow would not give up, and she continued to call on the judge until finally he tired of her and saw her. If a wicked judge could do this, how, then, could our heavenly Father, the source of justice and mercy, refuse to answer the prayers of His children and meet their needs?

Then the disciples, who knew their Jewish prayers by heart, asked Him how they should pray. Should they continue to pray as they had in the past—through their spiritual fathers, Abraham, Isaac and Jacob, or should they pray differently?

Jesus answered:

When you pray, pray in this manner, in the new way which I have taught you. Pray directly to God, saying, "Our Father in heaven, hallowed be thy name. Thy kingdom come. Thy will be done, as in heaven so on earth. Give us bread for our needs from day to day. And forgive us our offences, as we have forgiven our offenders. And do not let us enter into temptation, but deliver us from evil. For thine is the kingdom and the power and the glory for ever and ever. Amen."

In this new prayer, men must forgive their enemies before seeking forgiveness for themselves, for how can they receive forgiveness when their own hearts are filled with hatred? How can they ask God to do something for them which they are unwilling to do for others? Forgiveness not only relieves one's mind from a heavy burden, but it makes room for God's blessing. Do not lay up treasures of gold or silver or other material things, but lay up treasures of good deeds, of kindness. Earthly treasures are temporal and may be stolen or lost, but treasures laid up in heaven are handed down from generation to generation, and the one who has laid them up lives in them.

The eye is the lamp of the body; if therefore your eye be bright, your whole body is also lighted. But if your eye is diseased, your whole body will be dark. If therefore the light that is in you is darkness, how much greater will be your darkness.

In other words, you cannot have your heart or mind occupied with earthly treasures and at the same time be mindful of your spiritual treasures. Your heart can take care of one, but not both at the same time. You should not worry, either, about your food or clothes. Watch the birds of the sky and the flowers of the earth and see how they are cared for by your heavenly Father. Are you not more important than the birds and the flowers? When you seek first the Kingdom of Heaven, all the material things will be given to you. So don't worry about tomorrow. The God who reigns today is the King tomorrow. When one pasture is exhausted, the shepherd finds another. God's resources and treasures are infinite. When one well runs dry, another is discovered.

Men were told to remove the beam from their own eyes before they told their neighbor of a splinter in his eye—not to look at the defects in others while forgetting their own. It is easier to see the faults of others because we try to find them, but we fail to see our own faults in the process. Jesus hated hypocrisy, for hypocrites shunned the company of the sinners, hated those who had fallen, and would not eat with foreigners. They washed their hands and their food for fear they had been touched by Gentiles or pagans. They washed the cup on the outside but left the inside dirty. They never tried to cleanse themselves of their own sins.

The Prophet from Nazareth had kept hundreds of people on the mountainside enthralled with His new teaching. They had forgotten about their daily chores as they sat listening to Him expounding the truths which He had brought from the Scriptures, truths which hitherto had not been understood, but which heralded fresh hopes for a brighter future. They had been listening to a teacher—a metaphysician who understood the ills of mankind, who was familiar with the underlying causes of their troubles and unhappiness. And He had found a simple and sure remedy:

Ask, and it shall be given to you; seek, and you shall find; knock and it shall be opened to you.

12

LOVE
AND
THE POWER
OF FAITH

⁂

IN HIS LONG DISCOURSE, JESUS touched upon the most important of all the commandments:

Whatever you wish men to do for you, do likewise also for them; for this is the law and the prophets.

If you wish men to love you, you must love them too. If you wish men to honor you, to lend you what you need, to help you, you must do likewise to them.

The people who listened to Jesus lived in a society in which each depended on his neighbor. They borrowed and lent not only money and jewels, but food, dishes, animals, clothes and the other necessities of life, knowing that someday they, too, might need help in return. This admonition applied to friends and enemies alike, for did not the Holy Scriptures say that if you should find your enemy hungry, you should give him food, and if he is thirsty, give him water to drink?

And if the people extend these courtesies to their neighbors and even to their enemies, then how much more should they do it for their own flesh and blood?

Or who is the man among you, who when his son asks him for bread, will hand him a stone? Or if he should ask him for fish, will he hand him a snake?

Syrian bread closely resembles a stone, and in the dark, a father would be careful not to mistake a stone for bread. Then, too, in sheep camps bread is stored in a pile of stones near the tent. And snakes sometimes slip into the tents themselves and thus get into the food supplies. In the dark, they can easily be mistaken for fish, so parents had to be very careful indeed when their children were hungry at night. How much more careful, then, is the heavenly Father, the source of love, the all-seeing and all-knowing. How much kinder is He than your earthly parents who feed, clothe and love you.

The people, in accordance with their Scriptures, were always mindful of helping one another, but they never knew that their true Father loved them more and would do more for them when they knocked at His door and asked Him for gifts. They had forgotten that they were made in the likeness of Him and therefore were His beloved children.

The greatest of all commandments is to love:

You must love the Lord your God with all your heart and with all your soul and with all your mind and with all your might; this is the first commandment.

All the difficulties in life are brought about by man himself because of wrong thinking and lack of understanding of the power of God. The commandment became necessary when men strayed from God's ways, and the prophets were sent to guide them back. When we love God with our whole self—our hearts, our minds and our strength—our problems will be solved and there will be no need for the Law or the prophets.

The whole system of ethics introduced by the Prophet from Nazareth is simple and practical. But being so simple, most people do not want to try it out but prefer to try things that are difficult or complicated. For example, we search for God and His truth in distant lands, and yet we fail to recognize that He is right in our midst, in our hearts. He is so close to us that we do not try to search for Him.

The door through which to enter into a world of harmony, peace and understanding is narrow. But the door that leads to destruction is wide, and many people travel through it. It seems easier to steal, lie and cheat than to be honest and God-fearing. It is easier to amass riches dishonestly but quickly than to amass them slowly and honestly. Indeed, the road to the Kingdom is narrow and the byways are filled with thorns, and few people are willing to travel them. Man has always rejected the truly easy way—the way which God had ordained for him. He has always listened to the false prophets and the advocates of destructive and untrue philosophies.

The people who had been listening to Jesus preach were hungry. They had shared their food with their neighbors and had nothing left for their long trips home. The disciples told Jesus of this and asked Him to dismiss them. But Jesus was not worried about the shortage of food, for He knew that God's supplies were inexhaustible and that the people who had been fed with the bread of life would be fed with physical bread as well. So when the disciples told Him there was no more food, He told them to look around and see if there was any bread. They did as He asked and found a boy who had five loaves of bread and two fishes. The boy willingly gave his food to the disciples, who took it to Jesus for His blessing, according to custom.

Jesus took the loaves and the fish and when He had given thanks, He distributed them among the disciples to give to the five thousand hungry people and not counting women and children. As those nearest the food started to eat, bread began to come miraculously from unexpected sources. Then more latecomers bearing gifts of food arrived and those gifts, too, were shared. The small amount of bread was spiritually multiplied through the power of God and came from sources which are hidden from human eyes. Easterners believe that when God blesses a loaf of bread, it multiplies. When they bake bread, they bless the dough and pray that God will include in it a share for the hungry visitor.

When all the people had eaten, Jesus ordered His disciples to gather the crumbs and fill twelve empty baskets that were lying on the ground. Bread is the most precious food in Biblical lands, and Jesus realized that many of the hungry would be happy to receive even a few crumbs.

Jesus' prayer, His divine presence and His inner knowledge of God's love were responsible for feeding the multitudes with so little. He knew that God, through His infinite love for His children, would reach the hearts of some of the rich men and women and cause them to bring large supplies of food with them. Then, too, thousands of people shared their supplies, and in the East, such an act of sharing is far greater than the sight of baskets of bread and fish falling from heaven. This is indeed a miracle. Whenever a great need is met, it is said, "It came from heaven." Thus, the people had sought spiritual truths, and their physical needs were met. It is the feeding of the hungry which counts as a miracle and not where the bread and baskets of fish came from.

Nevertheless, shortly after Jesus had miraculously multiplied the bread and fish to feed five thousand people, some of those who had witnessed the miracle met Him in Capernaum and asked Him, "What miracle do you perform that we may see and believe in you? What have you performed?" (John 6:30) for they were looking for something spectacular. Men sought Him out because He was a popular teacher of religion, and wherever He was entertained, the host fed the people who came with Him. But some of the guests came simply because they expected to get food, and this is why He said, "You seek Me because of the bread you eat." He knew they were not seeking the bread of life, nor were they impressed by the miracle they had seen on the mountain. They knew that no one went to a holy man without a gift of food, so they were not surprised. Moreover, the Hebrew prophets had also multiplied bread, healed people and raised the dead. The Messiah was expected to perform greater wonders and miracles. They wanted magic; they wanted to see a staff turned into a serpent, a stone changed into a loaf of bread, or the sun commanded to stop, but Jesus refused to perform magic. He knew that if He were to show them one sign, they would demand another, greater one. He had read in the Scriptures that despite the many miracles Moses had caused to happen before the people, they still did not believe in him or obey his ordinances. And the people themselves did not know what kind of miracle they expected. They did not know it, of course, but the only sign Jesus was going to show them was His resurrection from death and His triumph over the grave. There are no greater miracles than these. They would be the ultimate of all miracles.

As Jesus returned to Capernaum, large crowds followed Him, for the news of His great message and reassuring words had spread throughout the countryside. Suddenly a leper appeared and threw himself at Jesus' feet, saying with assurance, "My Lord, if you wish, you can cleanse me." He had so much faith in Jesus and was so anxious to be rid of his dreadful disease that Jesus compassionately reached out His hand and touching him, said, "I do wish this, be cleansed." And the leper was healed.

It was against Mosaic Law to touch a leper. The disease was so dreaded that the afflicted lived in seclusion until they were healed and a priest had pronounced them clean. But the leper who approached Jesus was so eager that he dared to mix with the crowd, and Jesus touched him to prove to him and to those who watched that He had power over the disease. His touch banished fear from the mind of the leper, and the leper was thus made whole again.

After he was healed, the leper was so excited that instead of going to a priest to be pronounced clean, he stood around talking to the other people until Jesus, mindful of the Mosaic ordinance, told him to find a priest. He wanted the man to comply with the Law and at the same time avoid trouble with the priests, who were also doctors.

As Jesus entered the town, a centurian, a captain in

the Roman army, came up to Him. A God-fearing man, he was familiar with the Jewish religion and the healing power of the Jewish God. He saluted Jesus, bowing low as was the custom, and begged Him to heal his son who was paralyzed and in great pain. Jesus consented and told him He would come to his house, but the centurian, touched by the positive answer of "I will come and heal him" rather than "I will come and I hope to heal him," became convinced that only a word from Jesus was necessary. He therefore humbly told Jesus that He need not trouble Himself, that he was not good enough for Jesus to enter under the shadow of his roof (an oriental way of showing humility), but that if He said just one word, the boy would be healed.

The centurian knew the meaning of a command, the power of the words that came from Caesar himself and that were obeyed by even the least important soldier in the field. He knew, too, that the healing power was not in the hand, the eye or the hair of healer, but in the words he spoke. And because he had such a tremendous faith, he believed that Jesus' words were enough to heal his son.

As Jesus listened to the centurian, He became greatly impressed and with great emotion, He said to the people, "Truly, I say to you that not even in all Israel have I found such faith as this." And then He added, "A great many will come from the east and from the west, and sit down with Abraham and Isaac and Jacob in the kingdom of heaven. But the sons of the kingdom will be put out into outer darkness; there shall be weeping and gnashing of teeth."

And when He had thus warned the people, He turned to the centurian and said, "Go, let it be done to you according to your belief." And the boy was healed.

The prophecy of Isaiah spoken centuries before was fulfilled:

> Sure he has borne our sorrows and carried our griefs; but we considered him stricken, smitten of God, and afflicted. But he was slain for our sins, he was afflicted for our iniquities; the chastisement of our peace was upon him, and with his wounds we are healed. (Isaiah 53:45)

Despite the crowds that followed Him and begged for His help, there were still many who opposed Him, who laughed at Him, even belittled His works. Because of these people, Jesus decided to leave Capernaum and go to a port just outside the town. There, a scribe approached Him and said, "O my teacher, I will follow you wherever you go," but Jesus rebuffed him, saying, "The foxes have holes, and the birds of the air a resting place, but the Son of man has nowhere even to lay his head," for He knew the scribe wanted only a share of the gifts the people brought Him and the wealth that came with them. But in His answer, Jesus told him that He had no place to rest, that His preaching was not a business, and He depended only on God.

Then one of His followers said to Him, "My Lord, permit me first to go and bury my father." In other words, my first duty is to my parents. Let me return home and take care of my father until he dies. (The Mosaic Law commanded every Jew to honor his father and his mother, and to take care of them in their old age. The parents are to be honored next to God.) Jesus understood what the man meant, but He replied, "Come after me, and let the dead [the village] bury their dead." In Aramaic the words "village" and "dead" are distinguished only by a dot over or under the word. I am inclined to believe that Jesus used the word "village" rather than "dead," which is a repulsive remark. Jesus could not have spoken rudely to the man. In Biblical lands when a man is in need, relatives and neighbors provide for him and when he dies, the town buries and mourns him.

Jesus wanted to emphasize that in the new Kingdom the Gospel must come first. He had already warned His disciples that those who loved their families more than Him were not worthy to be His disciples, but He also assured them that those who followed Him would receive one hundredfold for their earthly losses.

As the crowd grew at the port, Jesus and His disciples boarded a boat and started across the lake to the land of the Gadarenes. As they neared the center, a violent storm came up and the boat was tossed around by the waves. Even though the lake of Galilee is only about ninety square miles, storms on the water can be very severe. As the waves threatened to swamp the boat, the disciples became frightened and called on Jesus, who had been sleeping, to help them before they were drowned. He immediately reassured them by saying, "Why are you fearful, O you of little faith?" and then He rebuked the wind and the sea until there was calm again.

The disciples until now had been puzzled by the new teachings and doctrines which were contrary to what they had been brought up on, nor did they understand how a small band like themselves could change the world. They were frightened of the thorny road which had led many Jewish leaders before them to the cross. So when Jesus calmed the waters and the wind, He also calmed the hearts and minds of His disciples.

They continued on across the lake, and when they reached the land of the Gadarenes, they were greeted by two lunatics who had been living in empty sepulchers. Nevertheless, they had somehow heard of Jesus, and when they saw Him and His disciples, they immediately recognized them and cried out, "What business have we together, Jesus, son of God? Have you come here to torment us before the time? What have we got in common or have you come to torture us like everyone else?" But Jesus' kindness and compassion overcame them and shortly the two maniacs became calmer, and they realized He was one of the Jewish men of God whom the Syrians had always respected and gone to in need.

Near where they were standing was a large herd of swine, and the lunatics knew that the Jews never ate pork and hated swine, so they said to Jesus, "If you are going to heal us, permit us to enter into the swine," which means to attack the herd of swine. In other words, "If you heal us, we will become converts to Judaism and will destroy the swine that you hate." Jesus told them to do whatever they thought was right, so the two men chased the pigs over a cliff into the sea. The owners of the animals ran to the town to spread the news that the two insane men had been healed and when the townspeople came to the spot, they asked Jesus to leave the country, for they were afraid that He would convert so many to Judaism that they would stop eating pork and put the owners out of business. So Jesus and His followers returned to Capernaum.

Soon the house in which He was staying in the town was so full of people that there was no more room inside, and they stood outside. Among the people who came to see Him were four men who carried a paralytic. Realizing they could never get into the house through the doors, they carried the invalid to the roof and removing some of the grass and timber from the roof, lowered him to Jesus through the hole. When Jesus saw the paralyzed man lying before Him, He was touched by the faith of the four men and said to the paralytic, "Have courage, my son; your sins have been forgiven. Arise, take up your quilt and go to your home." But some of the Pharisees and scribes who were seated near Jesus considered the words blasphemy, for they did not realize that man himself is the author of sin and he can forgive it. Nor did they realize that Jesus was empowered by God to heal and to forgive sins. When they saw the man rise and walk, they gave glory to God, for they recognized the miracle.

As Jesus left Capernaum, He met a customs officer named Matthew, and He said to him, "Follow me," and Matthew followed Him. Customs officials and tax collectors were recruited by the Romans. They were Jews who, for the sake of making a living, were willing to levy unjust fines. Men who refused to pay or who had no money were publicly flogged until their wives or relatives were able somehow to raise the necessary money. Because of their duplicity, crookedness and cruelty they were regarded as traitors, men who had sold their souls for the sake of money. No good Jew would sit down at the same table with them. Yet while Jesus and His disciples were guests at Matthew's house, many tax collectors and other sinners arrived and shared the meal with them. Jesus taught that they would be forgiven since they did not know what they were doing, and they gathered around Him because He gave them hope of salvation and showed them the way to a new and better life.

When the scribes and the Pharisees saw these men who were known as sinners eating with Jesus, they complained to His disciples and said He should know better, but when Jesus heard them, He looked at them and said, "Those who are well need no doctor, but those who are seriously sick they need the doctor." Then He reminded them that the Scriptures said, "For I desired mercy and not sacrifice; and the knowledge of God more than burnt offerings." (Hosea 6:6) God is more interested in seeing men who have gone astray return to His way than in seeing material sacrifices. Then He added, "I came not to invite righteous men, but sinners."

Jesus never condemned tax collectors or other men who had gone astray, for their downfall was not their fault. They had been led astray by false leaders, and yet the Pharisees, Sadducees, and scribes hated tax collectors and customs officials because they thought the money collected would be given to the Temple treasuries to enrich the priests and the Levites.

From the beginning, Jesus had shown little interest in Jewish temple rituals and observances which He branded the doctrines of the elders. He had no faith in sacrifices and offerings because God had no need of them, and they were eaten by the priests and the Levites. His attitude worried the Pharisees, the Sadducees and the scribes, and even John's disciples finally came to Him and asked why they and the Pharisees had to fast while His disciples did not. He answered them by saying, "Is it possible for those at the wedding feast to fast as long as the bridegroom is with them? But the days are coming when the bridegroom will be taken from them, and then they will fast." The disciples understood, for had not their own master John called Jesus the bridegroom and he himself the best man? Therefore, as long as Jesus was with His disciples they did not have to fast any more than did the guests at a wedding feast as long as the groom was present.

Apparently, many of His friends wished to see Him come to an understanding with the religious authorities, to work with them rather than against them, but Jesus knew a new building cannot be built from old debris. It must be built completely with new materials. So He told them something that they knew well, for they had seen it done every day in their homes: No man puts a new patch on an old garment.

Neither do they pour new wine into worn-out skins so as to rend the skins and spill the wine, and the wine runs out and the skins are ruined; but they pour new wine into new skins, and both of them are well preserved.

Jesus' teaching was the "new wine" and the worn-out skins were decadent Judaism. The days since Moses had lived had changed. The old Jewish traditions were obsolete, too old and impractical to be of service, but Jesus' teaching was new, dynamic and clear like pure water coming from a rock. It could not be blended with the complicated and hair-splitting teaching of the Jews.

While Jesus was speaking, a leader from the synagogue arrived and told Him that his daughter had just died and he asked Jesus to come and put His hand upon her so she might live. He had so much faith in Jesus that he believed that if only He would touch the girl, she would live again.

On His way to the man's home, Jesus felt a touch on the hem of His cloak. A woman who had had a hemorrhage dared to mix in the crowd around Him in order to touch His cloak, for she knew she would have no chance to speak to Him. But Jesus felt the touch and turning to her, said, "Have courage, my daughter, your faith has healed you." And so it had.

When they arrived at the house, Jesus heard the laments of the professional singers who had been hired to mourn the dead girl. When He told them the child was not dead but only asleep, they laughed at Him, but when He said to the child, *"Talita, komi,"* which means, "Little girl, arise," she rose up. Jesus did not believe that death was final but rather a part of life, a sleep for rest, and it was because of this belief that He could raise the dead. Even before He had entered into the chamber where the child was lying, He had assured her parents that she was not dead, that her life had not ended, for life is eternal and indestructible.

As He was leaving the house, two blind men cried out to Him, "Have mercy on us, O son of David," for a good man is called the son of a good man who, because of his valiant deeds, has left a lasting impression. David had lived a thousand years before Jesus, but because of his loyalty to God and to his people, his name was constantly on the lips of the people who cried for freedom. Jesus accepted the high title humbly, but the Pharisees and scribes did not like it, for they did not believe that Jesus of Nazareth was either the promised Messiah or a descendant of David.

When the blind men followed Him, Jesus asked if they believed He could heal their eyes and when they answered, "Yes, our Lord," their eyes opened.

On that same day, Jesus healed a demented dumb man so he was able to speak again.

The people were amazed at these miracles, for such things had never before been seen in Israel. To be sure, the prophets had healed the sick and raised the dead, but not one of them had restored the sight to the blind or sanity to the insane. Jesus did not believe that God brought the illnesses upon the people as punishment for breaking His commandments. He knew that God is not the creator of evil, nor has He given power to anyone to punish. Rather, the wrong itself causes the afflictions and this is why Jesus was not afraid to confront any kind of illness.

The religious authorities could not deny the miracles that Jesus had performed before their very eyes. They saw that He never performed miracles just to prove that He was the Messiah or healed only those in whom He found true faith. Furthermore, He shunned those who followed Him just to see a miracle or to eat the abundant food that was offered to Him. His whole teaching was centered around one thing—faith in God, forgiveness, meekness and kindness. Nor did He believe in demonology which had been borrowed from the Babylonian and Persian religions. He ridiculed such beliefs and branded them alien to the Jewish belief of one God. He told the people that every kingdom divided against itself will fall, a house divided will fall, so if Satan would cast out Satan, he, too, would be divided and could not stand. He told them that all sins would be forgiven men, but the blasphemy against the Spirit would not. If they believed the healing was not done through God's power but rather through that of Satan, they would not be forgiven.

From the beginning, Jesus' work in Galilee had been successful, for He had met little or no opposition from the religious authorities. In Galilee there was an air of religious freedom, for the Galileans had come in contact with the Gentile world and were therefore less hostile. Indeed, the people were seeking more knowledge of God.

13

EXPANSION
OF
THE GOSPEL

HIS WORK OF TEACHING THE
Gospel in Galilee had been so successful that now Jesus
wanted to send some of His disciples to preach peace
and the Good News to the tribes that had been lost from
Israel. These tribes had been carried away into captivity
by the Assyrian kings and had settled in Syria, Asyria,
Iran, Babylon, Armenia, and other countries of the East.
Their capture had been foretold by Amos and other
prophets in the eighth century B.C. when he had warned
the Israelites that "The Lord God has sworn by his holi-
ness that, behold, the days are coming upon you when
they shall take you away with weapons and the last of
you shall be devoured." (Amos 4:2)

Josephus, the Jewish historian and a contemporary of
the apostles, wrote that the descendants of these captive

tribes in his day were still in the same lands in which
the Assyrian kings had settled them, and, indeed, some
of their descendants were brought to Palestine in 1948
and are settled in the state of Israel.

The original captive Israelites had for centuries been
separated from the Temple and the religious authorities
in Jerusalem. It had been prophesied centuries before
that Jesus the Messiah Christ would gather the scattered
people and bring them to the true religion of their forefathers, and they had been longing for the day of their
deliverance and restoration.

Although Luke states that Jesus sent seventy of His
followers, Matthew tells us that twelve were sent. He
warned His messengers to keep away from the Gentile
customs and told them not to enter a Samaritan city.
They were to adhere strictly to the Jewish code of morals
and to obey the ordinances and laws of the Jewish religion under which they had been raised because they
could not preach one thing and do another as the Pharisees and scribes did. Moreover, they were commissioned
to preach the Gospel of the Kingdom and to herald the
coming of the long-awaited reign of God. They were
not to accumulate gold and other treasures, but to be content with that which the people would offer them for their
services. Jesus admonished them carefully, for He knew
that valuables would only hamper their work and pos-
sibly endanger their lives. They were to take nothing with
them, but depend on the hospitality of those to whom
they would preach. They were to be wise like serpents,
but pure and harmless like doves. They were to know
where to go and where not to go, with whom to associate
and to whom to preach.

He encouraged the disciples by telling them that even
if they were persecuted and despised, they were not to

lose hope because the Holy Spirit would stand by them, guiding and strengthening them in every way. He warned them that their way would be hard, for they were no more important than their Master and they should not expect better treatment than He had received so many times before. They were never to compromise with the teachers of religion, but to acknowledge Jesus before the judges in courts and in the presence of governors. Never must they exchange His Gospel for false prophecies.

And so the disciples went forth upon their errand, and when they returned, they told Jesus of the warm reception they had received from the people. Assuredly, the new teaching would slowly but surely not only overthrow the existing false religions and ideologies, but it was destined as well to defeat the great powers of domination and oppression. Three centuries later, His prophecy was fulfilled. The truth of Jesus was causing war and strife between not only pagan and Christian, but between Christian and Christian, and it will continue to do so until His teaching is followed throughout the world.

When Jesus returned from Judea where He had instructed His disciples on their mission, He left Capernaum to continue traveling and preaching. Although His work had been gratifying to Him, nevertheless He realized there were still many who wanted only miracles to prove to them that He was the Messiah Christ. He knew, too, that many did not understand, that even His disciples did not understand His work completely, and there were many who flatly rejected Him. He still had much work to do.

It was the time of one of the Jewish Holy Days and as was His custom, Jesus went to Jerusalem. From all over Palestine and the neighboring countries, the Jews gathered for these feast days to pray in the Temple, to fulfill their vows and at the same time to see the Holy City and transact their business. Some came simply because of the abundant food, for thousands of sheep, goats and oxen were slaughtered.

When Jesus and His disciples arrived in the Holy City to meet the people and speak to them, they went to a baptismal pool, in Hebrew *Bethesda*, the house of mercy. There were five entrances to the pool and at these entrances were many sick people who believed that after an angel had stirred up the water, the one who went in first would be healed. Pilgrims and passers-by had pity on these sick and gave them money, food, and sometimes even clothes, so in effect some of them were beggars, who did not really want to be healed at all, but would prefer to trade in on their disability.

At one of the entrances to *Bethesda* lay a man on a quilt bed. He had been sick for thirty-eight years, but he had been brought to the pool and left there by people who had pitied him:

> Jesus saw this man lying down, and he knew that he had been waiting for a long time; so he said to him, Do you wish to be healed? The sick man answered, saying, Yes, my Lord; but I have no man, when the water is stirred up, to put me into the baptismal pool; but while I am coming another one goes in before me. Jesus said to him, Rise, take up your quilt and walk. And the man was healed immediately, and he got up and took his quilt and walked. (John 5:6–9)

But the Jews who saw this wonder reminded the man that it was the Sabbath and no man had the right to carry a quilt bed on the Sabbath, for the Sabbath had overshadowed all else in their religion. Strict observers would carry nothing on that day, not even a pitcher of water to quench a fire. Some would not help a sheep or a lamb in trouble and even went so far as to stand still and be killed rather than defend themselves on the Sabbath.

Later, when Jesus met the man in a crowd at the Temple, He said to him, "Behold, you are healed; do not sin again, for something worse might happen to you." And then the man knew that it was Jesus who had healed him, and he went and told the Jews. Because it was the Sabbath, though, the Jews resented Jesus and wanted to kill Him, for they did not know that the one who had told the sick man to get up and walk was greater even than the Holy Day. Then, too, Jesus and His disciples observed the Sabbath just as they observed and kept the other nine commandments. Those who were evil did not know that God had granted Jesus power to perform miracles, that the Messiah had authority even over the Sabbath. Everything that Jesus did was in accordance with God's law and will. Had He departed from God's way, God would not have given Him power to say to a sick man, "Rise up and walk," even on the Sabbath.

A short time later Jesus and the disciples returned to Galilee where the majority of the people were ready to listen and perhaps accept His teaching. Higher religious authorities had tried to ignore Him, had ridiculed His Messianic claims and had taken the whole affair very lightly, for they were reluctant to implicate themselves in any movement which would endanger their own precarious freedom and high positions. They said to one another, "Let Him preach and heal. Sooner or later the people will tire of Him because there will be no change in taxation and the other evils that the Romans have brought upon our people."

The Romans themselves did not worry about Him either. As far as they were concerned, there was only one kingdom in the world: their own. There was only one life: the life here on earth. They knew that all their subjects had their own political and religious beliefs and practices, but as long as they remained loyal to the Romans and paid their taxes, duties and tributes, the imperial government did not interfere with them.

In all His travels around Galilee and the surrounding countries, Jesus had been very careful not to speak against the Roman government or Herod Antiphas. Herod had already made it known that he would like to destroy Jesus, and having been warned, Jesus avoided him. Jesus never advocated political reform or revolt or any other action that might be construed as disagreement with the government. All of His teachings were directed against the Pharisees, Sadducees, scribes—the leaders of His own religion. He called them hypocrites, and these attacks pleased the Roman authorities because they divided the Jewish people.

Then Jesus became involved. While He was addressing a crowd, a shrewd scribe came forward and stood face to face with Him. In a courteous voice and with a false smile he said, "Rabbi, we know that you have come from God because of the great works you have been doing. We know that you are a great teacher, but Master, please tell us: Shall we pay head tax to Caesar or not? You know well that we are the free children of Abraham and citizens of the Davidic kingdom."

Jesus immediately realized that the sly scribe was trying to trap Him by forcing Him to say something that would offend either the Romans or the Jewish authorities. If He told the people that as descendants of Abraham and therefore citizens of the Kingdom of Heaven they should not pay taxes to a foreign ruler, then the Romans would arrest Him for being a revolutionary. On the other hand, if He told them to pay, then the Jewish leaders would rise against Him and accuse Him of treachery.

This question was one of the most dangerous that Jesus had ever faced. The tax question was a touchy matter. The Jews had objected to paying a head or poll tax, although they had no objection to other taxes. As God's people, they did not feel they could in conscience pay a head tax to a Roman emperor who was worshiped as the god of the Empire. Indeed, such an act would put them in the same class as animals upon whose heads taxes were levied.

Jesus reached out His hand and said, "Give me a coin." A Roman coin was given to Him. (It was easy to distinguish Roman money from the Temple money, for the shekel on the Temple coin had no image upon it. The coin that was given to Jesus had been minted in Rome and was not acceptable by the Temple treasury since it actually belonged to Caesar). Jesus held the coin up before the crowd and asked, "Whose image is this?" The answer came back, "Why, it is Caesar's." Then Jesus said, "Well, then, give what is Caesar's to Caesar and that which is God's to God."

And the people were amazed at His wisdom.

14

THE
DEBATES

IT WAS THE GREAT FEAST OF
the Tabernacles, which commemorated the days when the
Jewish forefathers lived in huts built from the branches
of trees and covered with grass. When they wandered
in the Sinai desert, they had lived in tents. All the people
looked forward to these feast days. They refreshed their
memories of bygone days and united them, enabling them
to forget that they were under the harsh yoke of the
Roman oppressors.

Jesus, too, wanted to go to Jerusalem for the Feast of
the Tabernacles. He loved to see the people happy in the
city which He Himself loved so much, but He hesitated.
On His previous visits, the leaders had threatened Him,
for He had made many enemies among them. He was not
afraid to die, but there was still work to be done, and

His time was not yet come, although He had already seen the cross in His imagination. That was why He warned those who would be His disciples that they must be willing to take up their crosses.

On one occasion, Jesus was preaching in a house in Capernaum when word was brought to Him that His mother, brothers and sisters were waiting to see Him. Jesus, instead of hurrying to them, said to the messenger, "Who is my mother and who are my brothers?" Then He pointed to the disciples and added, "Behold my mother and behold my brothers. For whoever does the will of God is my brother and my sister and my mother." (Mark 3:33–35)

A preacher of universal brotherhood, Jesus was not bound by His blood relations. Those who had left their own families and property to follow Him were His spiritual family, and He valued them more highly than He did His own family. Then, too, all but Mary thought He had gone insane and were ashamed of Him.

Even His brothers did not believe that their meek, humble, cheerful brother was the promised Messiah. All they could do was to apologize to the Jewish authorities for His actions and claim that He had lost His mind.

Thus, when the time came for Jesus to go to Jerusalem, His brothers taunted Him and sneered, "Depart from here and go to Judea, so that your disciples may see the works that you do. For there is no man who does anything in secret and yet wants it to become known. If you are doing these things, show yourself to the people." But Jesus replied, "My time has not yet come; but your time is always here. The world cannot hate you; but it hates me, because I testify against it, that its works are evil." (John 7:3–7)

Nevertheless, after His brothers and some of His followers went to Jerusalem, He followed them secretly. He was more careful than ever although word had spread that He would not be there. Thousands of people had gathered for the feast, and the narrow, crooked streets and the Temple grounds were thronged. Although His enemies searched, they did not find Him, for it was not easy to find a provincial among so many. The people were afraid, and even those who believed in Him and had witnessed some of His miracles did not dare to discuss Him openly, for they feared reprisals from the authorities.

When the feast was at its peak and the city was filled with pilgrims, Jesus went to the Temple grounds to teach as was His custom. The outer courts of the Gentile section of the Temple were filled with both Jews and Gentiles. Some of the merchants were selling animals for the offerings. Some were exchanging the Roman and Persian coins for the Temple skekels, the only legal tender for the Temple since foreign coins had images on them and were therefore considered improper as offerings to God. Some pilgrims were meeting with friends who had traveled far for the feast, and some were buying animals for the sacrifices.

Religion was discussed everywhere—on the streets, in the homes and in the marketplaces. It was the main topic of conversation, and teachers of religion would not miss such opportunities when large crowds were gathered to express and share their knowledge and throw light on such a vital subject. Prophets spoke in the Temple courtyard and expressed their opinions on foreign policy and religious and social matters. The princes, scribes and dignitaries spent considerable time watching the crowds and listening to the speakers—especially to Jesus of Nazareth, the Prophet from Galilee.

The people marveled at His teaching, for He spoke simply and in parables that were easily understood. He used logic to prove His points and quoted the Holy Scriptures to back His teachings. He knew the Bible by heart whereas those who challenged Him knew only the doctrines of the elders, the ordinances and other things that served only to complicate religion and confuse the people. Some of the Jews who knew nothing of Jesus' background asked one another, "How does this man know reading, when He has not received a formal education?" They did not know that He had been educated at the synagogue in Nazareth, had examined the Scriptures and found the truth. They only saw a man dressed in the simple, coarse Galilean garments made of wool or goat hair. He had no insignia, nor did He wear a coat with ground-length sleeves to indicate His high position as a teacher of religion. He was dressed like all other Galileans. In contrast, the Pharisees and scribes wore long garments with broad hems and long sleeves that touched the ground so that they could be easily recognized by the people.

As He taught and answered questions, Jesus heard the murmuring of the people who surrounded Him. Some were attacking Him while others were agreeing with Him. Suddenly, He turned to the people and said, "My teaching is not mine, but His who sent me." Then He added, "Those who believe in God and do His will, they will know that my teaching is from God. I have nothing of my own. I am not an advocate of a new teaching or a new philosophy. My teaching is based on the teachings of the prophets whom you revere, although your forefathers slew them centuries ago not because of the evil they did, but because the prophets acted as spokesmen for God."

He told them He had not broken the Sabbath by healing a sick man. He told them that even the Law of Moses permitted circumcision on the Sabbath and yet circumcision was not a portion of the Law which had been given to Moses, but an old ordinance that had come from the Fathers centuries before. The people listened carefully to Him, especially when He said their leaders wanted to kill Him not because they thought His works evil, but because of the acts of mercy He performed on the Sabbath.

"You are crazy," declared some of the men who heard Him. "Who wants to kill you?" They did not take seriously the rumors and threats that had been circulating. After all, if the Jewish leaders had wanted to kill Him, they could have done it secretly or by hiring someone to murder Him. John tells us that Jesus was speaking openly on the Temple grounds and yet no one interfered with Him. Some of the people, therefore, thought that the Jewish elders and religious authorities might have decided that He really was the Messiah Christ.

The men who debated with Jesus were startled at His teaching, for they found that some things that had been said about Him were not true. They found a strong, healthy, courageous, humble and sincere man addressing the people, quoting freely from the Law and the prophets, and admonishing them to turn from their evil ways. They did not hear a word against the government. The man they saw was wise like a serpent. He could quote any portion of the Scriptures to prove His point, yet He was harmless as a dove. His face radiated peace, yet His words were charged with power. His heart was full of love and compassion for mankind. Indeed, He was a man ready to give His life that others might live in peace.

All of this was true, but the people were still puzzled.

He had been raised in Galilee, so everyone considered Him a Galilean. He and His disciples spoke Aramaic, the dialect of Galilee. He dressed like a Galilean, but they had been taught that when the Christ came, no one would know where He came from.

Jesus said to them, "You know me, and you know whence I come; and yet I have not come of my own accord, but he who sent me is true, whom you do not know. But I know him; because I am from him, and he sent me." (John 7:28–29)

Thus, Jesus emerged triumphant from His debate, and the news of His success reached the ears of the Pharisees and the High Priests. They sent the Temple guards to arrest Him and bring Him before the council:

> Now on the greatest day, which is the last day of the feast, Jesus stood and cried out, saying, If any man is thirsty, let him come to me and drink. Whoever believes in me, just as the scriptures have said, the rivers of living water shall flow from within him. . . . Many of the people who heard his words were saying, This man truly is a prophet. Others were saying, He is the Christ; but others said, Is it possible that Christ should come from Galilee? Does not the scripture say that Christ will come from the seed of David and from Bethlehem, the town of David? (John 7:37–38; 40–42)

Both the Jewish leaders and their people had forgotten that the Messiah is greater than David, that the Messiah will come when all other human hopes for peace and freedom have failed. They had forgotten that some of their kings, the descendants of David, had paid tribute to the king of Assyria, to Pharaoh, to the king of Babylon. They had forgotten that some of their kings had been slain in battle while others had been carried away to Babylon.

They had been praying for a political messiah, a great human leader from the house of David. They could not see a spiritual Messiah, a leader greater than David, stronger than the kings of Babylon, Egypt and Assyria, and wiser than all philosophers, a new ruler who through love and meekness would establish a universal and lasting kingdom, a Mighty Counselor, an Everlasting Father. They did not yet know that the Messiah was to be a light to the Gentiles and a hope to the people who were walking in darkness. They had forgotten the words of Isaiah who centuries before had predicted:

The land of Zebulun and the land of Naphtali have rejoiced; the mighty dominion, the way by the sea, the country beyond the River Jordon, and Galilee of the Gentiles have rejoiced. The people who walked in darkness have seen a great light; those who dwelt in the land of the shadow of death, upon them has the light shined. (Isaiah 9:1-2)

There is always the human element. The people pray to God for help, but at the same time they rely on the the arm of man which has always failed. They make God's help conditional. Each race has thought it was superior, and many thousands of people have suffered because of it. This is why the world has been unable to achieve a lasting peace and why the Scriptures say, blessed are the humble and the meek. They are blessed because they seek peace and bless others. Like the flowers, they share of their fragrance. They give everything but seek nothing in return.

Thus, the people questioned Jesus' Messianic claims. Two years before, Nathaniel, who had since become a disciple, told Andrew that no good could come out of

Nazareth. Now, the men who had been sent to take Him to the Priests and the Pharisees could find nothing other than His Galilean background against Him. And Jesus did not deny it, nor was He ashamed that He was called a Nazarene, a citizen of the insignificant town in Galilee.

One day while the Pharisees and scribes were gathered together, Jesus asked them, "What do you say concerning the Christ? Whose son is he?" And they answered, "The son of David." Then Jesus quoted from a man whom they worshiped as a pious man, a great hero and the deliverer of Israel—David. "The Lord said to My Lord sit on my right hand until I set your enemies as a footstool under my feet." When the Pharisees and the scribes heard Him, they could say nothing, for they could not question the author of the Psalms of David.

And like them, the soldiers were amazed. They confessed that they had never before heard anyone like Him nor had they ever seen such a compassionate face. When the authorities asked them why they hadn't seized Him, they said they had found nothing wrong in His teaching. The authorities were angry and told the guards that they had been deceived just like the others: "Why have not any of the leaders of the Pharisees believed in Him? No one has believed in Him except this cursed people who do not know the law."

But one of the Pharisees, a man who had tried to visit Jesus during the night, tried to defend Him. This man, Nicodemus, admonished the council members not to convict a man before giving him a hearing, and they replied, "What! Are you also from Galilee? Search and see that no prophet will rise up from Galilee." (John 7:52) For the guardians and interpreters of the Law considered Galileans an alien people.

15

JEWISH
MORALITY

❧ ✦ ❧

THE MORAL CODE OF THE
Jews was very strict. A Jew would rather see one of his
sons dead than one of his daughters pregnant without
being married or caught in the act of adultery. Although
some Jewish men could commit adultery with Gentile
women, a Jewish woman had to be chaste. One of the
Mosaic ordinances states, "There shall be no harlot in
Israel," and because of this law, today there are fewer
delinquencies among the Jews and the Moslems. There
were no open houses of prostitution in Judea, although
some women were secretly harlots. Some of these women
had been raped and therefore could not find a husband;
some were girls who had broken the Mosaic Law. Sometimes harlots left the towns and were found wandering
along the country roads or sitting by them to entice men.

Indeed, it was by the road that Tamar, daughter-in-law of Judah, waited for him disguised as a harlot. Judah, who had no money, gave her a pledge, committed adultery with her, and she was later found to be with child.

The subtle Pharisees and the scribes for some time had been trying to find fault with Jesus' teachings so they could trap Him by accusing Him of blasphemy. Earlier, they had tried to trick Him into saying something against the head tax so they could accuse Him on political grounds, but they had been unsuccessful. Now they tried to make Him speak against the Mosaic Law so they could bring Him before the council, but Jesus was clever.

They brought before Him a woman: "Teacher, this woman was caught openly in the act of adultery. Now in the Law of Moses it is commanded that women such as these should be stoned; but what do you say?"

While they made their accusations against the frightened woman, Jesus had been leaning over and scratching in the ground or doodling. (The judges in that part of the world do this even today. They make lines on the ground with their forefinger, with a stone, or with a stick.) When the accusers were finished, Jesus straightened up and answered, "He who is among you without sin, let him first throw a stone at her." Then He resumed His scratchings in the dirt.

When the men heard His answer, they left one by one, for they had all visited the woman and were afraid Jesus could name the father of the child, and the culprit would be stoned along with the woman. When Jesus looked up once more, He was surprised to find that they had gone.

"Woman, where are they? Did no man condemn you?"

The woman replied, "No man, Lord."

Then Jesus said, "Neither do I condemn you; go away, and from henceforth, do not sin again."

This was not the answer the Pharisees and scribes had expected. They thought He would tell the woman she had broken no law by committing adultery or that He would tell the people she should be stoned. In either case, He would have implicated Himself and they could have brought their charges against Him.

The religious authorities were concerned solely with the Torah, the law that is the Light of God which shone from a spiritual world, and the temple rituals. They did not care about the truths found in the Mosaic Law, the books of the prophets and the ordinances. At that time, the Light of God was like a flickering lamp shining in a cold and dark world. The lives of the people revolved solely around the Torah and the Jewish leaders were so jealous of it that they permitted no criticism of it. These fanatic men thought that anything that differed from the Law of Moses was against the Law and any new interpretation of it that deviated from the doctrine of the elders was contrary to their precepts. Indeed, the Torah, the light so valued by the Jews, was only a spark of the Light of God which shone in Jesus Christ. The Law was given by Moses, but truth and grace came into the world through Jesus Christ: "For the very light which was in Him was the life of men."

Jesus spoke again to the people and said, "I am the light of the world; he who follows me shall not walk in darkness, but he shall find for himself the light of life." That is to say, whoever followed Jesus would find the true light that makes life worth while—the light which dispels darkness and causes even the Gentiles and pagans to see the Light of God.

Jesus performed many miracles, but the scribes and the

Pharisees denied their validity. They boasted that Abraham was their father, but they did not act like Abraham. They believed that God was their Father, but they resented Jesus when He told them, "Truly, I say to you, whosoever obeys my words shall never see death." They said to Him, "Now we are sure you are crazy. Why, even our father Abraham and the prophets have died. Whom do you make yourself to be?" And when He replied that Abraham rejoiced to see His day, they pointed out that He was not even fifty years old, for they did not know that the Messiah Christ was older than Abraham. The Jews picked up stones to throw at Him, but Jesus hid Himself in the throngs.

Trying to find a man in a crowd on a feast day in Jerusalem is like trying to find a needle in a haystack, so once again, Jesus escaped stoning. His time had not yet come. But when it did, He would walk openly and would die a death worse than stoning, the death on the cross, the most horrible, the most painful death.

As He moved to another part of the courtyard, Jesus saw a man who had been blind from birth, and in His compassion He felt He had to help him. But even before He made any move to speak to him or help him, His disciples asked Him, "Teacher, who did sin, this man or his parents, that he was born blind?" They had been taught that according to the Law of Moses, the parents eat sour grapes and the children's teeth are set on edge, that is, the sins of the parents are passed on to their children. In these lands, the children are compelled to pay the debts of their parents, for they are responsible for what their parents borrow. Therefore, the disciples thought that either the man himself or his parents had sinned, thereby causing him to be born blind. It is true that many evil deeds of the parents are passed on to the

children, but in many cases, like the sons of Eli, the High
Priest, and the prophet Samuel, the opposite is true. At
times, the children of pious parents turn out evil. So, too,
sometimes the children of evil parents turn out to be
good as did Josiah, the King of Judah.

Jesus pointed out to His disciples that there were other
causes of blindness: "Neither did he sin, nor his parents,
but that the works of God might be seen in him, I must
do the works of him who sent me, while it is day; the
night comes when no man can work," that is, when the
opportunity is at hand. Jesus wasted no time trying to
find the cause of the man's blindness but spitting on the
ground, He mixed some soil with His saliva and placed
it on the blinded eyes.

Later, when the people asked him how his eyes had
been healed, the man replied, "A man whose name is Jesus
made clay and placed it on my eyes, and he said to me,
Go and wash in the water of Shiloha; and I went and
washed, and I see," but when they asked him where this
Jesus was, he said he did not know.

Now Jesus had healed the man on the Sabbath and
even the small act of mixing His saliva with soil was considered work and therefore against the sabbath law. The
Pharisees said, "This man Jesus is not from God, because
he does not observe the sabbath," but others said, "How
can a man who is a sinner do these miracles?" So they
called the man before them and asked, "What do you
say concerning him who opened your eyes?" and he replied, "I say he is a prophet." But even this did not
satisfy the Pharisees and they called his parents.

"Is this your son, who you say was born blind? How
then does he now see?"

The parents answered, "We know that he is our son
and that he was born blind. But how he sees now or who

opened his eyes we do not know; he is of age, ask him, he will speak for himself."

So once again the Pharisees called the man before them and asked, "What did he do to you? How did he open your eyes?"

And the man answered them, "I have already told you, and you did not listen; why do you want to hear it again? What! do you also want to become his disciples?"

But the Pharisees still could not believe what the man said, for they could not understand how anyone could heal by breaking the Sabbath. They did not know that man is greater than the Sabbath, greater even than the Law. They did not know the truth which had been embedded in the Scriptures—to set men free from the doubts and false teaching. All their training, their knowledge, their reputations were in danger, for they told themselves that if the prophet from Galilee was right, then the whole system under which they lived and taught was doomed, and they were afraid.

Then Jesus raised His hands and spoke to the people:

I am the good shepherd; a good shepherd risks his life for the sake of his sheep. But the hired person who is not the shepherd and who is not the owner of the sheep, when he sees the wolf coming, leaves the sheep and runs away; and the wolf comes and seizes and scatters the sheep. The hired person runs away because he is hired and does not care for the sheep. I am the good shepherd, and I know my own, and my own know me. Just as my Father knows me, I also know my Father; and I lay down my life for the sake of the sheep. I have other sheep also, which are not of this fold; them too I must bring, and they will hear my voice; and all the sheep will become one flock and one shepherd.

(John 10:11–16)

Jesus was speaking of the Gentiles who were also seeking salvation and expecting deliverance from the foreign rulers.

But the parable of the sheep made no impression on some of the people, and they said to one another, "He is insane. Why should we waste our time listening to Him?" But others realized that His words were not those of an insane man. Besides, they reasoned, could an insane man have opened the eyes of the blind? Among those who were not impressed by His words were the Jewish leaders. They thought that He had blasphemed because He called God His Father, and they picked up stones to hurl at Him. Jesus reminded them that the Scriptures also call men gods and the sons of the Most High, but the Jewish leaders had forgotten the words of the Scriptures.

Sheep know their own shepherd and hear his voice. They trust him and will follow him to the pasture and water, and they know the difference between a good shepherd and a bad one. Jesus' words, "I am the good shepherd," were aimed at the Pharisees and scribes, the unfaithful shepherds of Israel who did not care for their own. But Jesus, being a good shepherd, cared for His people, fed them when they were hungry, healed them when they were sick, and was even willing, like the good shepherd, to die for the sake of those in His care. Then He told them, all those who have come before are thieves and bandits if the sheep did not hear their voice.

16

THE
RAISING
OF
LAZARUS

JESUS RETURNED TO THE JOR-
dan River not far from Jerusalem. It was here that His
cousin John had baptized the people and told them of
the coming of the Messiah. Now many came to Him and
told Him that while John had not performed miracles,
still they believed that what he had said about Jesus was
true, and they believed in Him. As we have said, this
was contrary to the religious authorities who, worried
about their organization and their Temple revenues, were
becoming more and more hostile toward Him. Twice
they had tried to seize Him, and twice He had escaped.

While Jesus and His disciples were preaching at the
Jordan, news reached them that Lazarus was seriously
ill. Lazarus and his two sisters, Martha and Mary, were
friends of Jesus', and He had often stayed at their home

in Beth Ania. Although at first He told the disciples that the sickness from which Lazarus suffered would not cause death, two days later while they were debating a question, Jesus suddenly said, "Our friend Lazarus is asleep, but I am going to awaken him." The disciples did not realize He spoke of Lazarus' death and said, "Lord, if he is sleeping, he will get well." (Jesus did not use the word *death* because to the Jews, death was an end of life while to Jesus it was a long sleep and not the end. When the Jews referred to the death of kings or holy men, they said, "He slept with his fathers," for to them the word *death* was frightening and repulsive.)

When Jesus told the disciples that He was going to Beth Ania, Thomas, one of the disciples, said to the others, "Let us also go and die with our Master," for there were rumors that Jesus would be arrested and put to death.

Beth Ania was about two miles from Jerusalem, and when they arrived, they found that Lazarus had been in his tomb for four days. When Martha heard that Jesus had come, she went out to meet Him. Bowing her head in grief and with tears in her eyes, she said, "My Lord, if you had been here, my brother would not have died. But even now I know that whatever you ask of God, He will give you," for she had so much faith that she felt that even now Jesus could raise her brother.

Jesus looked into her tear-streaked face and said to her reassuringly, "Your brother will rise up," but Martha misunderstood and thought that He was speaking of the day of resurrection when all the dead will rise. When Jesus saw that she did not understand, He added, "I am the resurrection and the life; he who believes in me, even though he die, he shall live. And whoever is alive and believes in me shall never die. Do you believe this?" And Martha replied, "Yes, my Lord; I do believe that you are the Christ, the Son of God, who is to come to the world."

Then she went to get her sister, Mary, who threw herself at His feet and said to Him, "My Lord, if you had been here, my brother would not have died." Her words, the same as those spoken by Martha, disturbed Jesus, and He wept, not for Lazarus, but for the people's disbelief in Him. They had heard that He had raised others, that He had healed the blind, yet even though they believed He was the Messiah, they doubted that He could raise Lazarus. These people, even though they were trained in the Jewish religion and had seen miracles, still did not understand the mercy and power of God.

After a few minutes, He raised His head and asked them where Lazarus was laid. One of the mourners pointed to a cave in which was the tomb and said, "Master, there is the tomb." Jesus told them to take away the stone from the entrance of the cave, but Martha protested, saying, "My Lord, already his body stinks, for he has been dead four days," for she was afraid the body would be decomposed and even though she believed in Jesus' power, she was reluctant to have the tomb opened and the body of her brother exposed.

Then Jesus, as though scolding her for her disbelief, said angrily, "Did I not say to you that if you believe, you will see the glory of God?" Martha lowered her eyes in embarrassment and made no further protest as the stone was removed. Then Jesus lifted His eyes to heaven and prayed to God, the author of life and death: "O Father, I thank thee for thou hast heard me, and I know that thou always hearest me; but I say these things just because of these people who stand around, so that they may believe that thou hast sent me." And then He stretched forth His hand toward the tomb and cried, "Lazarus, come out." And the dead man came out, his hands and feet lightly bound with burial clothes. (The Jews never disturb the body of the dead. They dress the corpse in white cotton garments, and the hands and feet are loosely wrapped in the same material.)

Death was defeated by life, and Lazarus appeared limping. Jesus told the people to remove the burial garments, and for a while Lazarus, who did not realize that he had come forth from another world, mixed with his friends.

As a result of this miracle, which was so evident that none could deny it, many Jews who had witnessed it believed in Jesus.

A dead man had been brought back to life only a few miles from Jerusalem, and the Pharisees, the scribes and the High Priests began to worry even more about the Prophet from Galilee. The council, fearing the people might officially proclaim Him the Messiah and thus start a rebellion, met and decided He had to be destroyed. They realized that although they could challenge His Messianic claims and prove to the people that the meek man whom they had heard preaching was no match for the Romans, how could they challenge His healing power? It would be difficult to explain to the people that Jesus was evil when God had granted Him such power that He could raise a man who had been dead for four days.

Had they realized that the man they hated and feared was really the Messiah, they would have carried Him in triumph to the Temple, but they did not know. Jesus' teaching was so new, so contrary to all they had learned that they could not believe. Even though His own disciples lived with Him, ate with Him, and sat at His feet listening to Him, they could not fully understand His teaching. How, then, could He blame the religious authorities who believed only in the doctrines of force for force, life for life, and evil for evil?

Even Peter, one of Jesus' stanchest and most faithful disciples, relied on force when he saw that his Master was in danger at Gethsemane. He drew a knife and cut off the ear of one of the servants of the High Priests', but Jesus rebuked him: "Put your sword away, for those who take up swords perish by the sword." And when the sons of Zebedee asked Him to bring fire down upon a village which had refused to give them hospitality, Jesus had to remind them, "Love your enemies and pray for those who hate you; and render no evil for evil, but good for evil."

He was careful to make it clear in His teaching that forgiveness must be reciprocal, that he who is forgiven must in turn also forgive. The parable of the prodigal son is a true example of forgiveness. The loving father had shown him the meaning of forgiveness when the son returned home after having spent his money foolishly and having been disloyal to his father. The son, who earned forgiveness the hard way and therefore understood it fully, would not hold anything against those who had offended him. But some people plead for forgiveness when they themselves would not forgive; some expect mercy and compassion from others when they have no mercy or compassion in their own hearts. These are the people who do not understand what it means to forgive.

To give another illustration of forgiveness, Jesus related the parable of a king who called one of his officials before him to give an account of the money he had lent the man. In Biblical lands, all the ministers, governors, heads of the army and the palace ministers speak of themselves as servants when they are summoned by the king. They do this as a token of respect to their ruler, although many are princes, rich men and dignitaries with businesses of their own, for they are all in service to the realm. Sometimes they borrow money from, or lend it to, one another or even the king.

In Jesus' parable, the king found that one of his ministers owed him ten thousand talents, a large amount in those days. The man had been negligent in paying back the loan, and the king, in order to have the obligation paid, decided to punish him by confiscating all his property and having his family sold to raise the necessary funds. The minister, however, threw himself at the feet of the king, kissing his feet and grasping the hem of the king's robe. He begged for mercy and promised that he would pay the debt if the king would only have patience and compassion upon him and his family. The king was greatly moved by the supplications of the minister and forgave him by canceling the entire debt.

A few days later, this same minister found that one of the least of the king's servants was unable to repay some money he had borrowed from the minister. The minister demanded the money and threatened to confiscate all his property and sell his family to pay the debt. The servant threw himself on the ground, grasping the feet of the creditor, and begged him for mercy. He promised to repay the loan if the minister would only have patience with him, but the minister's heart was as cold as ice, and he would not grant him more time. Already had he forgotten his own dramatic and clever appeal before the king that had resulted in the cancellation of his debt. Instead of following the king's example, he threw the servant into prison and confiscated all his property.

The good king symbolizes God, who is merciful, compassionate and always ready to forgive His children when they turn to Him in true need. The borrowers are the people who appeal for mercy for themselves but then forget what God has done for them and refuse to help others in need. If a servant and his master would think of each other's problems and try to help one another, most of the difficult problems in life would be overcome.

This forgiveness of sins was one of the greatest stumbling blocks between the teaching of the Pharisees and that of Jesus. The Pharisees and scribes were disturbed when Jesus healed on the Sabbath and when He told the sick their sins were forgiven because they believed that only God could forgive sins. They were astonished that sins could be forgiven without the sacrifices and gifts prescribed in the Law of Moses. Then, too, the priests, the Levites and all the workers in the temples lived by means of these sacrifices, which were the main source of income for the houses of worship.

The parables that Jesus related gave His disciples and His listeners a new, clearer concept of God as a loving and forgiving father, constantly watching and caring for His people. This was the direct opposite of the old concept of a tyrannical God whose forgiveness could be obtained only by vows, fasting, prayers, sacrifices and other gift offerings, and with all these, only with the help of the High Priests in the temple.

Centuries before Jesus, Joshua, the son of Nun, ordered Akan and his family to be burned because Akan had stolen some offerings intended for God. Akan had confessed and begged Joshua for mercy, but there was little mercy and forgiveness in the old law.

Jesus authorized His disciples neither to forgive nor to forget the sins of those who were not worthy of forgiveness, but to forgive those who were worthy. The power extended to heaven as well as on earth, for in the new Kingdom of Heaven, the new earth and heaven were to join hands and become one. No such authority had ever been granted to any of the prophets and men of God before this time. None but the High Priest could forgive sins, and religious responsibilities were so heavy that the people were always afraid they had broken a particular religious law by, for example, walking a few steps more on the Sabbath or eating without washing their hands. This is why so many flocked to Jesus, and this is why the sinners, the wicked, the tax collectors, and those who had fallen and were hopeless took refuge under His shadow and found comfort and relief for their weary souls, heavy burdens and harsh yokes.

In Jesus' teaching of forgiveness, a sinner could be forgiven not only seven times, but seventy times seven, that is, as many times as he had sinned and repented. This was the first time such hope had been offered to sinners. The hopeless found hope, and the sinners became saints who, generations later, were to be emulated by the people and revered as men of God.

Those who follow Jesus can ask anything in His name and they have the assurance that it will be granted to them. If only two men are worthy, the request will be granted, for to be worthy means to be sincere, faithful and truthful:

> Again I say to you that if two of you are worthy on earth, anything that they would ask will be done for them by my Father in heaven. For wherever two or three are gathered in my name, I am there among them. (Matthew 18:19–20)

Two thousand years before, Abraham petitioned God to spare Sodom and Gomorrah (Aramaic: *Amorah*), pleading that there might be some righteous men there. God was willing to grant the request and spare the two cities if only Abraham could show Him ten righteous men, but to Abraham's great disappointment, not even two could be found. Nevertheless, this shows that God is mindful of the remnant and respects it and has mercy on it. He spared Lot and Lot's family when He destroyed Sodom and Gomorrah. He would do no less for the followers of Jesus Christ. Even sinners forgive one another and help each other. Even creditors forgive their debtors when they find they are poverty-stricken and unable to pay their debts. How much more, then, will our Heavenly Father, the fountain of mercy and loving kindness, whose rain falls upon the pastures of good men and bad men alike, grant the requests of His righteous men.

17

THE RICH MAN

JESUS LEFT GALILEE AND RE-
turned to Judea near the crossing of the Jordan River.
As always, a great many people followed Him, and He
healed many sick men and women. Soon the Pharisees
and His other enemies came to Him and tried to tempt
Him by trapping Him into contradicting the Mosaic Law.
They asked Him if it was lawful for a man to divorce his
wife for any reason, whether moral, social or political.
Jesus, however, reminded them of the Scriptures:

Have you not read, that He who made them from the
beginning made them male and female? Because of this, a
man shall leave his father and his mother, and shall be
joined to his wife, and the two shall be one flesh. Hence-

forth they are not two, but one body; therefore what God has joined together, let not man separate.

But the Pharisees persisted, for they wanted to force Jesus into saying something that could be considered an offense against the Law—and blasphemy was punishable by stoning. They quoted the Mosaic Law and reminded Jesus that Moses had commanded that a man can give a woman a letter of separation and then divorce her. But Jesus knew what they were up to, and now He came with a blast against Moses himself: "Moses knew the hardness of your hearts and gave you permission to divorce your wives, but from the beginning it was not so." ("Moses" here refers to the books of Moses which were often altered by the scribes to satisfy the people.)

Then Jesus expounded on the Law and the way it should be applied. "But I say to you, Whoever leaves his wife without a charge of adultery and marries another commits adultery; and he who marries a woman thus separated commits adultery."

Jesus had touched on divorce when He had delivered the Sermon on the Mount, but now even His own disciples were bewildered. They had been born and raised in Judaism and now they could not understand why there should be such difficulty in divorcing a woman. For years they had seen men deserting their wives, sometimes just by giving a small gift to a scribe and obtaining a divorce paper. Some men divorced their wives for no reason at all. After all, in those days women had no status or rights. Considered chattels, they were often mere servants. According to Jesus, though, men and women were equal children of God, created male and female by Him, neither one inferior to the other.

The disciples were dismayed to hear their Master up-

holding the rights of women so strongly, so Jesus told
them that what He had said regarding divorce did not
apply to all men, nor did it apply to all women:

> For there are eunuchs who were born this way from their
> mother's womb; and there are eunuchs who were made
> eunuchs by men; and there are eunuchs who made them-
> selves eunuchs for the sake of the kingdom of heaven.

Because the Jewish moral code was extremely strict and
delinquencies were punishable by death, most men knew
nothing about women until they were married, for they
were never permitted to associate with the opposite sex
before marriage. Therefore, in cases when men were
found to be eunuchs, or impotent, the marriage was dis-
solved or nullified. This was also the case with women
who for one reason or another were not found to be
physically normal after marriage. Divorce in such cases
was granted. This law is still upheld today by the Church
of the East. (The author was appointed twice to sit in
judgment to determine the validity of marriages.)

In Syria, Palestine and Arabia, one of the fondest desires of parents is to have their children—always boys,
for girls are never exposed to strangers regardless of their
age—blessed by the holy men or priests. Some parents
will walk long distances just so their sons can stand before the men of God and have His name and His blessings
invoked. Usually, this practice of presenting the boys to
be blessed is discouraged by those around the holy men
who fear the guest is tired and does not want to be disturbed, although usually the holy men gladly welcome
the children to come before them to receive the blessing,
and some of them take the boys on their laps and talk
kindly to them.

Thus it was that when the parents heard that Jesus was in their town, they took their little boys to Him that He might lay His hand upon them and bless them. The children would remember the blessing all the rest of their lives and the words of grace would sink into their hearts as spring rain sinks into dry ground. The picture of the holy man before whom they stood would never be forgotten. Jesus Himself had been blessed at the Temple in Jerusalem when He was forty days old. He was blessed again when He was given the Bar Mitzvah at twelve, and many other times He had been blessed by rabbis. Now He in turn was blessing others that they might continue in the true doctrine.

Now when the children were brought to Jesus, His disciples rebuked the parents and tried to chase them away. But Jesus stopped them, saying, "Allow the little boys to come to me and do not stop them, for the kingdom of heaven is for such as these." And He laid His hand on them, blessed them, and continued on His way.

Once when His disciples were arguing among themselves as to who would take the place of their Master should He be arrested and put to death, Jesus called a little boy and made him stand in their midst. Then He pointed His finger at the child and told the disciples to be humble like the child, to be unconcerned about greatness, but to melt like salt so they might savor the world around them. He urged them not to be like the Gentiles whose leaders were lords over them, but to be meek and humble like little children.

Jesus loved all children and they responded to this love by loving Him. Whenever they gathered around Him, He would hold their little hands and speak to them in their own pure and innocent, simple vocabulary which endeared Him to them. He told them little stories and anecdotes, and they loved to listen to Him.

Jesus was not married, for He had dedicated His life to serving the world and mankind. He had no children of His own, yet all children were His.

Metaphorically, *children* also means those men and women who are born again, those who change their way of life and take on the image of their Creator.

The teaching of Jesus differed from that of the rabbis and elders. Jesus wanted men to humble themselves, to become harmless and innocent like children, free from malice, prejudice and worldy ambitions. For the little children, like the flowers and the birds, have no worry for tomorrow, no fear of dangers, no thoughts of evil. They know their parents watch over them and care for them. Jewish elders, on the other hand, taught the children to emulate the elders themselves, to acquire their wisdom and aspire to that which they had achieved. They taught that wisdom belonged only to the men with gray hair and knowledge only to the men of experience. They did not know that man's knowledge is often polluted, whereas a little child is a perfect being and the image of God, free from all human folly. The greatest objective of all religions is to cause man to be born again, to change to be his real self, simple, honest and sincere.

While Jesus and His disciples were on their way to Jerusalem, they stopped by the road to rest and to eat. As usual, they were soon surrounded and while Jesus was addressing the crowd that pressed close to Him, a man came up to Him and said, "O, good teacher, what is the best that I should do to have life eternal?" Since every great rabbi recommended what he considered the most important way into the Kingdom of Heaven, he wished to hear what Jesus would say.

But at first Jesus did not answer the question. Instead, He asked, "Why do you call me good teacher? No one is good. God is the only good teacher, the only one who can answer every secret and knows every thought in the human heart." (*Good* here means experience; it does not refer to character.) Jesus, of course, was good, but He was humble in refusing to accept the title. Then He continued and answered the question: "If you want to enter the life, then obey the commandments of God," that is to say, if you want to enter into the life eternal, live up to the teaching of the commandments, for they are the core of all religion and the foundation of justice.

The man had expected Jesus to have a new answer, a new doctrine, but Jesus knew what he wanted, so He answered him accordingly, pointing out that reverence to God and the keeping of the commandments were the most important aspects of the Jewish religion. And when the man asked more questions, Jesus answered him by quoting the commandments. Apparently, the man had been a strict observer of the ordinances of the elders all his life, for he said to Jesus, "But I've done all this since youth," to which Jesus replied, "Then sell everything and give it to the poor."

The man paled, his shoulders sagged, and he turned his eyes from Jesus. All of his material possessions appeared before his eyes, and he could see them being sold and given away to the poor. He remembered everything that had helped him to amass his great wealth, when he had sold his very soul to make a profit, when he had sworn falsely in the Temple, when he had refused to help his needy friends and neighbors. The words of Jesus pierced his heart. Never before had he heard a religious man talk like that. He had never met a teacher who loved the poor as Jesus did. Perhaps his teachers had told him to tithe more, to give more to the priests and to give more to the Lord, but never to the poor. He did not understand Jesus' words.

Those words, "Go and sell your possessions and give them to the poor and you will have a treasure in heaven; then follow me," are probably misunderstood more than any others that Jesus spoke. Many people who took the meaning literally sold everything they had and gave it to the poor. But that was not what Jesus meant at all. His remarks were aimed at one man, a rich man who was searching for the truth that would lead him into eternal life, a man who was searching for the shortest way to peace and eternity. Apparently, the man was impressed by the teaching of Jesus and wanted to be one of His disciples and travel with Him. Therefore, it was perfectly natural for Jesus to tell him to divest himself of his sheep, cattle, property, slaves and other material things which he valued more than the new Gospel. But the rich man was horrified at Jesus' words, and he chose his worldly possessions rather than the Kingdom of Heaven and eternal life. He believed that his possessions were more valuable than something that was promised but was not certain.

When Jesus saw his sad expression, He turned to His disciples and said:

Truly I say to you, It is difficult for a rich man to enter into the kingdom of heaven. Again, I say to you, It is easier for a rope to go through the eye of a needle, than for a rich man to enter into the kingdom of God. (Matthew 19:23-24)

Jesus used a common idiom which was familiar to, and understood by, the people. They all knew what a large wooden needle and a cord or a rope were. The needle to

which Jesus referred was not the tiny steel needle we
know today, but the large wooden needle made from oak.
These needles were in common use in the East until fairly
recently and in fact are still used by nomads today for
sewing sacks, tents and rugs. Some women could pass a
thick cord through the eye of one of these needles and
while passing it through, some part of the woolen rope
would pry from it. In other words, it is difficult to pass
a rope through the eye of a wooden needle, but it is not
impossible. Had He used the term *camel,* He would have
said, "It is *impossible* for a man to enter into the kingdom
of heaven," rather than *difficult.*

Nevertheless, the disciples were shocked when they
heard their Master telling the rich man to sell everything or give it away. They did not understand that Jesus
did not condemn the wealth itself, but the love of wealth
and the trust that men put in it.

Jesus told them that while it is impossible for man to
give up everything by himself, with God's help anything
is possible. Elisha gave up his possessions when Elijah
asked him to follow him. When men learn to love God
with all their hearts and with all their minds, their false
love of wealth will disappear and they will have an everlasting treasure in heaven. God can help men to have
abundant wealth, but He will grant them power to possess it—not to worship it as a god.

18

TO ENTER
THE KINGDOM
OF HEAVEN

ON ONE OCCASION, A SCRIBE, who wished to test Jesus' teaching to see whether it differed from that of the Jewish authorities, asked Him, "Teacher, what shall I do to inherit eternal life?" Apparently, Jesus understood the reason behind the question, for He answered, "What is written in the law? How do you read it?" The scribe replied, "You must love the Lord your God with all your heart, and with all your strength, and with all your mind, and your neighbor as yourself," and Jesus said to him, "You said the truth. Do this, and you shall live."

But the scribe was not finished yet, and to prove his piety, he asked, "And who is my neighbor?" Now, he knew very well that all Jews were considered his neighbors, and he also knew that all men are indebted to each other regardless of religion, race or color and that the Law had even recommended mercy to the Gentiles and strangers. But he did not realize that people other than the Jews were also his neighbors.

In the days when the Mosaic Law was written, the Jewish concept of God was different. God was the God of Israel and the laws were given to Moses for the benefit of the Israelites only. The Gentiles and the pagans had their own laws and their own gods. At that time, too, there were many teachers of Judaism, and each individual teacher advocated those methods through which he believed salvation and eternal life could be gained. The pagans, too, had their own doctrines. The Zoroastrians believed in keeping the sacred fire burning in the temple, for they believed the sun was the god of the universe and fire is a spark of the sun. Other pagans believed in the worship of the sun itself and in the other celestial bodies, for in them they saw beauty, power and eternity.

So the scribe wanted to know who his neighbor was, that is, to which class of people the Law alluded. He did not know that in God's eyes there is no class, no color, no Gentile, no Jew, for all are His children and He cares for them alike. In order to make the scribe understand this truth, Jesus related for him the parable of the Good Samaritan:

There was once a man who went down from Jerusalem to Jericho on a road which winds through mountains and hills and valleys—a narrow way which resembled the valley of the shadow of death and on which bandits lay in wait for travelers. As the man entered the deep valley that leads to the plains of Jericho, the bandits attacked him. After they had robbed him, they beat him severely and left him for dead on the road.

It so happened that a priest came along the road, and

he saw the wounded man lying near death, but when he saw the blood on the road and on the man's clothes, he went his way as though he had not seen him. The Mosaic Law forbids the Jews to touch either human blood or dead bodies, and to the priest, the keeping of the Law was far more important than helping a fellow human being.

A little later, a Levite, traveling along the road, saw the victim, too, lying helpless, but like the priest, he, too, passed by. To this religious man, like the priest, the mere observance of the Law was far more important than mercy and compassion, although he had read in the Scriptures that this was against the will of God. He sacrificed the greatest of all laws for the sake of keeping an ordinance that was not even a part of the Law.

Then a Samaritan happened along. When he saw the injured man, he halted his donkey, dismounted and took oil and a small skin of wine to the victim. He treated the wounds with the oil and wine and then putting the man on the donkey, took him to an inn nearby. There, the Samaritan continued to care for the stranger all night and in the morning he gave two dinars to the innkeeper with instructions to care for the patient.

After Jesus had finished telling the story, the scribe acknowledged that the one who had had compassion on the injured man was truly his neighbor.

When a fellow human being needs help, race, religion and color are forgotten, for it is the spirit that responds, and all spirits are one—the Spirit of God. How many thousands of men and women have risked their lives to rescue a drowning person without knowing anything about the victim? How many thousands of men have died that others may live? When one loves God with his whole heart, he loves all humanity. When one loves his neighbor, he loves his real self.

Just as there is a single source of life, so there is a single Kingdom prepared by God for all the peoples of this world. No one can enter into this Kingdom without the qualifications and the calling by the King. Just knowing the commandments by heart and observing the holy days and the traditions of the elders do not entitle one to enter into the eternal life. There is something more and greater—the good works which put faith in action, "For faith without works is dead."

Jesus related another parable to illustrate to the Jews that willingness to obey God's commands and to work are the most important ways to enter the Kingdom of Heaven. He compared the Kingdom of Heaven to a householder who, early one morning, went out to hire workers for his vineyard. He bargained with the laborers, agreeing finally to pay them a penny a day, and he sent them to his vineyard. A little later he saw other workers standing idle in the marketplace, and he said to them, "You also go to the vineyard, and I will give you what is right." And they, too, went. Late in the afternoon, he went out again and found still more laborers standing idle and when he asked them why, they replied that no one had hired them. And the householder said, "You also go to the vineyard, and you will receive what is right."

When evening came, the owner of the vineyard said to his steward, "Call the laborers, and pay them their wages, and begin with the ones who started work last." Those who had been hired at the eleventh hour received a penny, but when the first ones arrived, they expected to be paid more, for they had worked longer, but they, too, received a penny. When they received it, they shook their heads in surprise and said, "These last ones have worked only one hour, and you have made them equal with us who have borne the burden of the day and its heat." But the hirer said, "My friends, I am not doing you an injustice; did you not bargain with me for a penny? Take what is yours and go away. I wish to give to this last one the same as to you."

The owner of the vineyard paid the laborers he had hired last the same wages as those hired first because they had been waiting to work, and it was not their fault that no one had hired them sooner.

The first laborers who were hired were the Jews who worked in the vineyard of God and who had suffered much for the sake of their religion. They had been working a long time before the Gentiles and pagans were called by God and hired to work in His vineyard too. When God called Abraham and asked him to leave his native land and go to Palestine, there were other righteous men in other parts of the world. But God first chose one pious man and his family. God never works with committees; He always calls one man.

The Gentiles always sought the true God and were ready for God's calling. Many had sought healing from the hands of the Hebrew prophets. They knew that the Jewish God was the most powerful God, but His vineyard, His religion, was too small. The Hebrew workers were enough to take care of it, but as the vineyard enlarged and spread out, God needed more workers for it. The Gentiles had been waiting patiently, and when God said to them, "Why do you stand idle?" they replied that no one had hired them. They and the pagans were hired late and had not suffered like the Jews from the heat of the day (persecution).

The good householder, the loving God, paid them all the same wages because their wages were their only livelihood. God rewarded the Jews and Gentiles alike because they were all His children, and if they could not work, they would go hungry.

The Pharisees and the scribes did not like Jesus' references to the Gentiles, but Jesus knew that the day was coming when the prophecy of Isaiah would be fulfilled, when the Gentiles would return to the fold, and when Jesus the Messiah would be a light to them and a glory to Israel.

The gates of God's great vineyard, His Universal Kingdom, were open to people of all races, colors and classes, and in His house were many rooms for all His people. The Jews and the Gentiles had never believed they could live together in peace and harmony. For centuries, they had been hating and fighting one another and they wondered how, since they could not live together on earth, they could live together in heaven. They did not realize that the teachings of Jesus were to make them a new and holy people, that racial boundaries erected by men would be removed.

The parable of the vineyard also answered the question of neoplatonism which had sprung from a doctrine advanced by the great Greek philosopher Socrates. Socrates advocated state ownership and control of wealth and that all people should have an equal share and equal opportunity. This was one of the beginnings of what we today call *Communism*. It was a splendid doctrine, but the world was obviously not ready for it. People could not see the value of such human fraternity. The householder in the parable who paid the laborers equally even though some of them had worked in his vineyard longer hours than others settled this question of ownership once and for all. Jesus stated that the employer had the right to do whatever he pleased with his money, and no one had the right to complain or interfere. The householder, God, had the right to invite the Gentiles and pagans into His Kingdom and to reward them as He pleased and the Jews had no right to complain. He had the right to place the poor and the meek higher and the great and the proud lower in His Kingdom.

In this parable, too, Jesus upheld honest and true capitalism gained through hard labor, which is the only workable system of remuneration. All Jewish patriarchs were wealthy men whom God had blessed abundantly with material possessions for themselves and for their tribes. In Syria, Arabia and other Eastern lands, where generosity is admired and emulated when one man was blessed, others were also blessed. Unfortunately, now, many of these ancient customs have almost disappeared, for foreign influences have taught the people fear of tomorrow and have changed their willingness to share into greed and selfishness.

19

DAYS
DARKEN

❧❦

THE THIRD AND LAST YEAR OF
Jesus' ministry was the hardest, the most tiring, the most
discouraging year for His disciples and followers. There
was gloom and dissatisfaction in the ranks of His followers and there was strong opposition from His enemies.
The people themselves were dissatisfied with the slow
progress of the new Gospel.

The miracles which Jesus had performed, instead of
softening the hearts of the Pharisees and scribes and
changing their attitude toward Him, had made them even
more hostile and suspicious. His preaching and the ex-
positions of the Kingdom of Heaven, the Messianic Kingdom, had failed to impress them. They still did not believe that Jesus was the coming Deliverer whom the
prophets had predicted—the Messiah.

Those who opposed Him misunderstood His religious conduct. They looked upon Him as a renegade who was weakening the Law and the prophets instead of strengthening them, and they regarded Him as a friend of sinners and outcasts. Two years before, the religious authorities had sent men to see Him and to examine His teaching and then to report to the high authorities in Jerusalem. These examiners had found Him eating without washing His hands, healing men on the Sabbath, and not washing the foods His disciples brought from the marketplace. He had even asked a Samaritan woman, a member of a strange religion who had a bad reputation to give Him a drink of water.

For centuries the Jews had been washing the cup from the outside and leaving the inside dirty. They had been so strict in their observance of the Sabbath that they would not perform any act of mercy on that day, even helping a man who had fallen.

Jesus in His debates with them had successfully answered all of their arguments and accusations. He had told them that even David and his men had eaten the holy bread when they were hungry, that the Law was not broken, for life is greater than any law. He had also explained to them that the One who had made the outside of the cup had also made the inside and that it is better to wash the inside, for it is dirtier than the outside. That which enters into a man does not defile him, but that which goes out of a man needs to be cleansed, that is, malice, covetness and evil thoughts. They had heard Him praise the Gentiles who had received healing at the hands of their prophets, but He had belittled the suffering Israelites who were not healed because of their lack of faith in their prophets. They were enraged when Jesus commended Naaman for his faith in Elisha or the pious Syrian woman who had fed the prophet during the famine. Last but not least, they had seen with their own eyes a man who was born blind, healed, and a man who had been buried in his tomb for four days commanded to come forth—and he had obeyed.

Jesus' actions had confused the leaders of the Jewish religion as well as some of His own followers, and there were many deserters from His ranks, for they did not know what to make of Him. Finally, when their patience was exhausted, they decided to get rid of Him. They told Him bluntly that if He *was* the Messiah to show them a sign, to do something which they would ask Him to do, and do it right in their presence. Probably, they would have asked Him to turn stones into bread or to leap from the pinnacle of a temple or to cause the sun to revolve backward or some other spectacular act, for the Pharisees and scribes were not interested in miracles and signs to help human suffering. What they wanted to see was something contrary to the laws of the universe or impossible for man because they had been taught that the Messiah would be able to perform such feats. But Jesus refused to tempt God by working against His unchangeable laws.

Thus, the last year in His ministry was a year of bitterness, of trials, of doubts, of anxiety and of disappointment. Sometimes Jesus traveled secretly and avoided speaking openly because of the threats from the Jewish authorities. In order to escape arrest, for His time of death on the cross had not come, He spent considerable time in the little town of Peria by the Jordan River. His disciples were still dependent on Him, for it was difficult for them to understand His new Gospel.

Jesus had changed. He was no longer the meek preacher of two years before who would not hurt even the feelings of His enemies. Now He became belligerent and used a totally different language, sometimes abusive and harsh. He denounced the Pharisees, the Sadducees, the scribes, and even the higher authorities, calling them hypocrites, embezzlers, blind teachers leading blind men, men who could not even see the truth or understand the Scriptures themselves. At times He was so bitter that He condemned their actions in a manner which, had His own disciples used it just a year before, He would have criticized. The humble Prophet had turned into a fearless and militant teacher.

Furthermore, hitherto He had never spoken of His suffering on the cross or of His death. His disciples, like all other Jews, expected the Messiah to live and rule forever. Anything about His death on the cross would have weakened His ranks and caused even more of His followers to leave Him.

But Jesus knew the end of His great drama was drawing near. He could see the crown of thorns ahead of Him. His disciples had heard rumors relative to His arrest and condemnation; they had seen Him flee in order to avoid arrest; they had seen Him moving secretly at the feasts, trying to avoid His enemies. Some of them had admonished Him not to go to Jerusalem, and some had vowed to die with Him. Yet they did not understand why He had to die, nor had they understood the Scriptures relative to the rejection and death of the Messiah.

Even though the Pharisees believed in the resurrection of bodies, they knew little about immortality of the soul and the life hereafter. They did not know that this life is the beginning of a larger and more beautiful life, and they were unaware that he who values this life and is concerned about it will lose it, but he who loses it for the sake of the eternal life will live forever. Indeed, it was

hard for the Jews and the Gentiles and even the pagans
to see a victory after death, to see success, honor, glory,
and eternal rewards after the grave. As far as most of the
people were concerned, death was a finality—an end. The
defeated went down into the grave with shame, and the
victor entered the cities triumphantly.

Jesus' teaching was too far ahead of His time. All of the
great men who had been defeated or slain had gone
into oblivion; all the great emperors who had ruled the
world were gone, and some of them had been forgotten.

In the eyes of the people, death and the grave were
unconquerable. To die the shameful death on the cross
and yet to triumph and create a new Kingdom—a new
order based on peace and justice for which humanity had
been praying for centuries—was unthinkable and seemingly impossible. No one had been successful before. Not
even the prophets with their deep insight and mystical
minds had dreamed of such a reign and such a change in
the world.

Things do not happen until they happen. Miracles do
not take place until they are performed. Jesus was sure
about His success after the grave and the establishment
of a Universal Kingdom after His death. He was as sure
of the success of His Gospel as He was that the sun would
be shining in the sky the next day. But how could He dis-
close this profound secret to His simple and unlearned
disciples? How could He convince the Jews of it? No miracle in the world would convince the people that a
prophet, even the Messiah, could save the world through
His defeat, disgrace and death on the cross.

The only recourse left to Jesus was to make His disciples, His followers and the people understand something about the Kingdom of Heaven by speaking in
parables; to illustrate His teaching so that they might

understand what He was endeavoring to accomplish. Eight centuries before, Isaiah had written that the people have eyes, but they cannot see, and ears, but they cannot hear. The people to whom Jesus was preaching were the descendants of the people who had rejected Isaiah and the other prophets, but because they lived in a more evil world, they were even more stubborn than their fore-bearers. Simple peasants who are born and raised in small towns or in tents, who constantly live with their sheep and cattle, are slow to understand and grasp metaphysical truths. However, riddles illustrated by parables derived from the things with which they were familiar help them to understand.

So, Jesus spoke in parables to explain the mysteries of the Kingdom and its coming. The people thought that it would come suddenly, and this misunderstanding had to be clarified by the new Gospel and the inner meaning of the Kingdom of Heaven. The people had to be made to understand that such a spiritual Kingdom could not come without a long period of tranformation, without a change in their hearts. One may compel or bribe a man to depart from his religion and worship an alien god, but he cannot change his heart.

The citizens of the Kingdom of Heaven were to be gentle and kind toward their fellow men. They were to love their enemies, to be pious, patient and generous. They were to be just and therefore different from others. In other words, they were to shun that which the world loved, and seek that which the world rejected. Indeed, such a change was difficult—but it was possible.

Jesus, with all His persuasive power, had not succeeded in convincing the people of the characteristics of the spiritual Kingdom. Therefore, He decided to go north into Syria with His disciples and there openly reveal His rejection and death to them. For more than two years He had spoken obliquely about His rejection by the religious authorities and His death on the cross. He had imparted it in parables and in figurative speech, but His disciples had not understood what He was talking about. Just as they did not understand that the term "leaven" meant "teaching" and not "bread," so they could not understand the simple parable of the seed even after Jesus had explained it to them. Even though these young men had sat near the greatest master the world had ever known and had occupied places of importance close to Him, they were like children who do not understand maxims, metaphors and subtle speech. They understand only the plain, pure and sincere language that they have learned from the lips of their mothers.

Apparently, Jesus had left Capernaum for good. He had found that the Gentiles and the Jews who were far from the large Jewish centers and who had not been indoctrinated by the teachings and traditions of the elders were more open and ready to receive Him and His teaching. Some of these non-Jewish people were so eager to see Him and to hear Him speak that they were satisfied just to touch the hem of His robe.

The faith of a sick Syrian woman was so great that she believed that if she could only touch His mantle, she would be healed. And another sought Jesus to heal her daughter. Jesus told her that it was not right to give the children's bread to dogs—it is not right to give the truth and the ministry of healing to the Gentiles—but the woman was not offended and replied only that even dogs eat the crumbs that fall from the table of their master. The Syrians for centuries had seen glimpses of light from the Jewish religion and even their princes and kings had sought healing from the hands of the Hebrew prophets.

After all, the Syrians and Jews were kindred people and they spoke the same language.

Jesus and His disciples arrived in the country of Caesarea of Philippi, the region where Philip, the brother of Herod Antipas, had formerly reigned, an area of desert between Syria and Jordan. Jesus wanted to speak more openly to His disciples, for He wanted to know what the people and His own disciples thought of Him. Easterners are very sensitive and do not wish to hurt their friends and neighbors. Thus, they would tell others what they thought of a person rather than tell the person himself. The disciples were far more informed about the public opinion concerning their Master than He was Himself. They had heard people praise Him, and they had heard people laugh at Him and mock Him. They had listened to the learned rabbis and the elders who had criticized Him and who did not know what to make of Him. They had seen some of His followers leave Him because they were doubtful, but they had also listened to those who believed in Him, praised His miracles and looked upon Him as a great teacher and healer of bodies and souls. Ever since John the Baptist had acclaimed Him by the River Jordan as the Blessed Messiah, the people had held various opinions of Him, and even King Herod himself, who was haunted by the spirit of John the Baptist, was afraid that Jesus might be John risen from the dead.

All of these things the disciples told Jesus, and when they had finished speaking, Jesus turned to them and said, "What do men say concerning me, that I am merely a son of man?" (meaning a simple, ordinary man). And they answered Him, "There are some who say you are John the Baptist, others, Elijah, and still others, Jeremiah or one of the prophets."

When Jesus heard their answer, he smiled, and asked

them, "Whom do you say that I am?" for although they
had told Him what others said about Him, they had
not said what they themselves thought of Him. The disciples hesitated and stared at each other, for they did
not know what to say and each expected the other to give
his answer first. Then *Shimon Kepa*, Simon Peter, looked
straight into His Master's face and thinking that Jesus
questioned the disciples' faith in Him, answered simply
but firmly, "You are the Messiah, the Christ, the Son of
the Living God."

Peter was not a learned man that he should give such
an answer, nor was he an eloquent speaker to say so much
in so few words. His answer was like that of a child, plain,
terse, yet meaningful. "You are the Christ, the Son of the
Living God." The Holy Spirit had put the words in his
mouth. One might expect such an unequivocal answer
from a scribe who had made a thorough study of the
Scriptures, a rabbi or an elder of the synagogue, but not
from a simple, slow-thinking, slow-reasoning illiterate fisherman, whose name bore witness to his slow thinking
and reasoning.

It was not by accident that he had been given the nick-
name *Kepa* (stone or stone-headed). His name was Shimon, which means "hearing," but he was called Peter
because he was unpolished. In the East, the large and
roughhewn stones are placed as cornerstones. It was divinely planned that Peter should receive this name, for he
was to become the foundation stone for the new religion
and the leader of Jesus' followers.

Several of Jesus' disciples were educated. Matthew had
been the chief customs officer and could read and write;
Judah of Iscariot and Bartholomew were both brilliant
men and must have had some education, yet they did
not speak for they did not know what to say.

Jesus was not surprised that from all of His disciples only Peter gave such a bold and true answer, so He said to him:

> Blessed are you, Simon son of Jonah, for flesh and blood did not reveal it to you, but my Father in heaven. I tell you also that you are *kepa*, stone, and upon this stone I will build my church; and the doors of Sheol shall not shut upon it. I will give you the keys of the kingdom of heaven; and whatever you bind on earth shall be bound in heaven, and whatever you loose on earth shall be loosed in heaven. (Matthew 16:17–19)

In that hour Peter was born again. Now he was born of the Spirit and could see that which the learned men and the rabbis could not see. Now He could recognize the Great Teacher, at whose feet he had been sitting, as the Savior of Israel and of the world. He could discern that which the other disciples could not.

Therefore, Jesus gave him the keys to the Kingdom, keys to open the door for all who were waiting and willing to enter, whether Jew or Gentile. These are the keys of authority, the keys to determine what is right and what is wrong; what is good and what is bad, the keys to open the mysteries of religion and to explain that which for centuries had been hidden from all eyes. These keys could free those whose souls had been imprisoned by teachers, would open the doors of the spiritual world.

Peter's faith in Jesus had been wavering. It was not that he did not believe in Him, but because he was uneducated, he could not reason things out. Now the words that Jesus spoke and the keys of authority that He had given him strengthened his faith. His simple and child-like life made his love toward Jesus greater and stronger

than all the other disciples'. Jesus, however, knew both
Peter's strength and his weakness, and he knew that later
Peter would stumble and fall. He also knew that only
those who fall appreciate rising, and only those who have
gone astray long to return home.

Now the twilight of His mission on earth was gradually
turning to darkness. The opposition to His Messianic
claims was growing everywhere, and Jesus knew that
His popularity was declining even as the danger against
His life was increasing. The time had come when He must
open His heart to His disciples. He must speak to them
openly about His death, His rejection, and His crowning
on the cross. So He spoke to them plainly, without parables, telling them that soon He would go to Jerusalem
where He would suffer a great deal at the hands of the
elders, that He would be killed but that on the third day
He would rise up again. He wanted His followers to know
that His triumph would be completely different from that
of earthly kings. The people would build no triumphal
arch for His entry into Jerusalem. No delegation of priests
and elders would welcome Him, no bread and salt, no
white horse, but an ass, the symbol of humility.

This was indeed a dark picture, contrary to what the
disciples had expected, and it was beyond their understanding. They were stunned and dismayed and stared
at each other speechless. They had, of course, heard the
rumors about their Master's fate, but they had not taken
them seriously. Now Jesus Himself was telling them, con-
firming those rumors. For more than two years He had
tried to prepare them for this solemn hour, but their hearts
were dull and their eyes were dim. They felt that their
work had ended, and there was no hope left in them.

Then Peter, the simplest disciple of them all, felt that
he had to encourage his Master. He went to Him and

gently took His arm not as a disciple, but as a friend, and they walked a little distance away. Then Peter rebuked Jesus and said, "Far be it from you, my Lord, that these things should happen to you!" Peter was so sure of his Master that he could not conceive of such a tragedy befalling Him. He expected Jesus to thank him for his comforting words, but Jesus came back with a sharp and unexpected retort that He had never used before: "Get behind me, Satan. You are a stumbling block to me, for you are not thinking of the things of God but of men!"

Peter did not know that the Messiah had to suffer in order to enter into His glory and triumph over death. His concern was for Jesus' earthly life and the interests of the disciples. He did not have the perspective to see the long-range, divine plan of God to save the world. As far as Peter was concerned, Messiah was to reign over the Davidic kingdom which He was soon to restore. So after Jesus had spoken so sharply, Peter returned peevishly to the others. He could not know that some of them would be living when Christianity became a great religion while those who gave up everything for the sake of His Gospel would live in the Gospel itself.

20

THE
TRANSFIGURATION

JESUS TOOK THREE OF HIS DIS-
ciples, Peter, James and James's brother John, to Mount
Hermon, the tallest mountain in Palestine and Syria. This
mountain is so high that its peaks are covered with snow
even in the hot summer months. This journey symbolized
the summit in Jesus' mission which had started at another
mountain, the Mount of Temptation below sea level. It
had been on that mountain that Jesus had decided to
embark on His great though hazardous mission to reform
Judaism, to share the Light of God with the Gentile
world and to create a universal state based on law, justice and righteousness. And it had been here at the low
point of His ministry that Satan had tempted Him, offering great earthly rewards in order to persuade Him not
to embark on such a mission.

Now Jesus and three of His closest disciples were ascending the highest mountain in the Biblical lands, from whence He would embark on another, even greater mission—to reveal His true self to His disciples and to triumph over the evil forces and death. *Hermon* means "dark," and the mountain was so-named because it was as yet in darkness. It was through this darkness that the disciples would see the divinity of Jesus and know that the Man at whose feet they had been studying was the Blessed Messiah. Only through thick darkness are the far-distant stars in the sky revealed and the glory of God made manifest to the human eye.

On the majestic peaks of Mount Hermon the wheels of time stopped so that past, present and future met. Here on these heights were the two great Hebrew prophets, Moses and Elijah, to meet with Jesus, pay homage to Him and confirm the faith of His disciples in Him. The people expected that some of the great prophets would prepare the way for the coming of the Christ: Moses had promised that a great prophet, greater than himself, would come; Elijah had ascended in a glorious chariot of fire and he, too, was expected to return to teach the people change of heart.

As they climbed the mountain, the disciples thought of the sad news their Master had told them and of their forthcoming dangerous journey to Jerusalem. Peter still pondered the harsh words he had received from Jesus. Their faith was beginning to waver again. Perhaps they were following another false prophet, they thought. After all, Moses and Elijah had not appeared, and even the disciples could not see how the Messiah could come before the way was prepared for Him.

When they reached the summit of the mountain, they saw the other majestic peaks about them covered with dazzling snow and, where the snow had melted, late-blooming flowers. Their human imagination was captured with the beauty, and they felt they were in a new world, a world free from fear and anxiety. These three fishermen who had in the past patiently spent most of their time searching for fish were now on top of the world, and they had never seen such a beautiful and virgin scene in all their lives. Indeed, they may never have seen snow before.

Suddenly, before their eyes Jesus was transfigured. His face shone like the sun, His eyes were like sapphires, and His raiment became white as the snow. These three disciples who for more than two years had walked with a Man, a Prophet, a Miracle Worker had never seen His Divinity, the Spirit of the Lord with which He was anointed. And as their imaginations were carried into timeless space, there appeared to them in a trance Moses and Elijah talking with Jesus. Then Peter said to Jesus, "It is better to remain and if you wish, we will make three shelters here, one for you, one for Moses and one for Elijah," and as he spoke a bright cloud appeared over them, and a voice came out of the cloud saying, "This is my beloved Son. I am pleased with him." The voice confirmed that Jesus was the Messiah and that God was pleased with His teaching and His willingness to challenge the forces of evil, and through His death to triumph over death.

But the disciples were so frightened that they threw themselves on the ground and covered their heads. The glorious transfiguration was too much for them to see or understand. They had read about Moses and Elijah, had wished that they could see their faces, and now, lo and behold, they saw the great prophets seated beside their Master. Soon Jesus came to them, telling them not to be frightened, and when they opened their eyes, they saw that He was alone. The vision that had transported their minds into another world had vanished. Moses and Elijah, having done their part, disappeared.

The voice from the cloud had been the same voice that had spoken to Him by the banks of the Jordan River and for a while, the disciples' faith was once more strengthened. The fear of death disappeared, for they had seen what no other human eye had seen. What other proof did they need?

As they descended from the mountain, Jesus told them not to reveal the vision until He had risen from the dead, for the people would not understand and would ask why the prophets appeared only to the three disciples. They would not understand that in a vision one has to transcend this physical world, that Moses and Elijah could appear to all who believed, but not to the religious authorities who taught their own laws and ordinances.

Jesus was stern in His warning to His disciples, for He knew that they were not yet prepared to see a spiritual triumph through His death on the cross. They were still unaware that Jesus would shortly be taken away from them, and they would be left, bereaved.

21

WHO IS
THE GREATEST?

THE GREAT JEWISH FEAST OF
Passover, the day of rejoicing, was nearing. Dark clouds
were gathering on the blue Palestinian sky as rumors of
Jesus' arrest, judgment and death spread quickly. The
High Priests, the Pharisees, the Sadducees and the scribes
had taken council and had decided to get rid of Jesus
or else face a disastrous revolt against the imperial Roman
army that ruled Judea with an iron hand. They were
concerned for their special liberties, granted to them by
the Roman authorities, and then, too, there had been false
christs before who had led the people into butchery instead of freedom and happiness. The Jewish leaders did
not wish to see this happen again.

At the beginning of Jesus' ministry, high religious leaders looked upon Him merely as a poor and dissatisfied

Galilean peasant who preached to His poverty-stricken people. They saw no danger in this preaching and since some thought Him insane, they left Him alone. But now the once-obscure rabbi, the teacher from Nazareth, had thousands of followers not only in Galilee, but also in Judea and Syria and even in Jerusalem, the center of the Jewish religion. He had eleven young and healthy Galileans and one Jew (Judah) traveling with Him. Instead of the revolutionary movement that He had started dying out as they had expected, they saw it gain momentum until now it was flourishing and spreading like fire in dry stubble. At last, they felt the movement had to be stopped even at the cost of the life of its leader.

For a long time Jesus had tried to prepare His disciples for the crucial events which were to take place in Jerusalem—His rejection by the religious authorities, His trial, His death on the cross. But His words had made no impression on them. He had told them about His death in Caesarea of Philippi, but they had taken Him so lightly that Peter had taken Him aside and told Him never to speak in such a manner again. He had again spoken of His death when He said, "When I am lifted up from the earth, I will draw every man to me." ("Lifted up" means to be crucified, and we are told He said this to show what kind of death He was to die.) Now on the road to Jerusalem, He took His disciples aside once more to tell them that His hour was at hand, that death was only a few days away:

Behold, we are going up to Jerusalem, and the Son of man will be delivered to the high priest, and the scribes, and they will condemn Him to death, and they will deliver Him to the Gentiles, and they will mock Him, and scourge Him and crucify Him; and on the third day He will rise up.

The Christ who had raised the dead and restored the sight of the blind knew that His time to die was near. Hitherto, He had always said His time had not come. When the fruit on a tree is ripe, it falls off. The wheels of time cannot be turned backward, nor can they be speeded forward. When time comes, it comes and no force in the world can stop it. Jesus' time had come, but He was going to rise again. Even as He was so sure about His death, so was He sure of His glorious resurrection and triumph over death and evil forces.

Now nothing could deter Him from His tragic journey to the historic city which had slain so many prophets and ambassadors of God. Nothing could make Him escape from His enemies as He had done on previous occasions. Now His mind was made up. The hour had come, and He was going like a lamb to the slaughter. Every prophecy about Him was to be fulfilled.

And still His disciples did not believe. On the contrary, they expected a wonderful reception from the Holy City and the sudden restoration of the Davidic kingdom. They had heard Him promise great rewards to those who would leave their families and possessions to follow Him, and they expected to receive these rewards on earth. They had no understanding of the spiritual world to come, for they had not yet succeeded in transcending the material world.

No sooner had Jesus stopped speaking than the wife of Zebedee came up to Him with her two sons, James and John, to request a favor. When Jesus asked her what she wanted, she said to Him, "Command that these two sons of mine may sit, one at your right and one at your left, in your kingdom." By this, she meant would Jesus make them high ministers of state in the new Kingdom. The disciples had already begun debating among them-

selves as to who was the greatest and who should succeed
Jesus in case He was put to death, and Zebedee's wife
naturally wanted her sons to get the best. Like the other
people, this simple and illiterate peasant woman did not
understand any kingdom other than the earthly ones, and
she was sure the Messiah would live forever. Jesus, realizing that they did not understand, turned to the mother
and her sons and said, "You do not know what you are
asking. Can you drink the cup that I am ready to drink, or
be baptized with the baptism with which I am to be
baptized?" And when they said they could, He continued,
"Indeed my cup you shall drink, and the baptism with
which I am to be baptized, you too shall be baptized
with; but to sit at my right hand and at my left, that is
not mine to give, but it is for those for whom it is prepared by my Father."

When the other disciples heard this conversation, they
were angry with the brothers. They had thought that
James and John had gone to Jesus to comfort Him in His
dark hour, and they were shocked when they found that
instead of comforting, they were asking for high positions in His kingdom. John and James had no idea that
in the Messianic Kingdom the first were to be the last—
the most honorable, the most humble—so Jesus called to
them and said:

You know that the princes of the Gentiles are also their
lords; and their officials rule over them. Let not this be so
among you; but whoever wishes to be great among you, let
him be a minister to you; And whoever wishes to be first
among you, let him be a servant to you; Just as the Son
of man did not come to be ministered to, but to minister and
to give His life as a salvation for the sake of many. (Matthew
20:25–28)

As they drew nearer to Jerusalem, they stopped in Capernaum, and while they were there, a man brought his epileptic son to Jesus to be healed. He told Jesus that he had taken the boy to the disciples, but they had not healed him. Jesus said to him, "If you can believe, everything is possible to him who believes," and the boy's father cried out, "I do believe, help my little faith." The father had faith in Jesus as a healer, but the disciples had no faith that *they* could heal. A spark of fire contains all the power that is in fire and just this spark could burn all the forests in the world. So, too, the father's faith, small though it was, was sufficient to spark the healing of his son.

One day, Peter entered the house where Jesus was staying. He looked worried, and Jesus realized it was time for the collection of the poll (head) tax—a silver coin—that the Romans had levied upon each male. The Jews, understandably, resented having to pay this tax. They paid heavy tithes to the Temple, they maintained the expensive Herodian government, but above all, they hated paying a head tax to the government that had enslaved them. Jesus knew that He, like all the other men, had to pay the tax. One could see the tax collectors going from house to house collecting the taxes in whatever commodity the people were able to pay. In the Near East, taxes, up until World War I, were paid in kind, that is, in sheep, goats, cheese, butter, wheat, fish, or whatever the people could spare. Money was scarce and most of what there was belonged to the rich and the other privileged classes who stored it in the ground.

And as Simon Peter stood bewildered, Jesus looked at him and said, "What do you think, Simon? From whom do the kings of the earth collect custom duties and head tax, from their sons or from strangers?" Simon answered,

"From strangers," and Jesus replied, "Then the sons are free. But so as not to offend them, go to the sea, and throw out a hook, and the first fish which comes up, open its mouth and you will find a coin; take it and give it for me and for you." (In these lands, people refer to an article by quoting its value in coins, for example, "I see only two coins in the jar of cheese; ten coins in the ox; three coins in the lamb," which means the jar of cheese is worth two coins, and so on.) Now some people may wonder how the fish would come to the hook while a coin was in its mouth. Of course, Jesus, through His divine power, could have done anything that seems impossible to us, but Jesus never resorted to magic. The answer is simple: Through Jesus' divine power, a large fish was caught and was sold for enough coins to pay the taxes for two men. Peter did not see why his Master, the King of kings and Lord of lords should pay taxes. He did not understand that even his own Lord had to pay taxes like any other man so as not to offend the tax collectors and thereby perhaps incite a revolt among the people against the government. Jesus was willing to conform and pay taxes rather than resist and offend those in power. As long as He was in this world, He was subject to its laws and had to comply with them.

The people in Galilee openly discussed the rumors of Jesus' arrest and death, and the disciples wanted to be prepared in case the rumors were true. They wanted to know who would be the greatest in the Kingdom of Heaven. Jesus had not explained to them the characteristics of the Kingdom, that all men and women would live together like brothers and sisters, that all people would be treated equally. But they were to be shown later when their Master knelt down and washed and dried their feet.

Now they came and asked Jesus, "Who is the greatest

in the kingdom of heaven?" They expected Him to start
with Himself and then name each disciple according to
his ability, knowledge and rank so that after His death
they would be able to carry on the work which He had
started. It was natural for them to want to know who was
to succeed Him. When David was approaching his last
days, he named Solomon, his younger son, as his heir and
had him enthroned while David was still living. Jesus read
their inner thoughts, and His answer was a great surprise to them. Instead of naming one of them as His
successor, He looked around. From a group of little boys
who had come to watch Him as most boys in the East do
when a prominent man is entertained, He called one
over and made him stand in the midst of the disciples.
Then He answered the question:

> Truly I say to you, Unless you change and become like
> little children, you shall not enter into the kingdom of
> heaven. Whoever therefore will humble himself like this
> little child, shall be great in the kingdom of heaven. And he
> who will welcome one like this little child, in my name,
> welcomes me. And whoever misleads one of these little ones
> who believe in me, it would be better for him that an ass's
> millstone were hanged on his neck and he were sunk in the
> depths of the sea. (Matthew 18:3–6)

This was an admonishment to the disciples who had
been thinking in terms of the earthly kingdom and aspir-
ing to high positions for themselves. They were to strip
themselves of all material things of this world and re-
nounce all that this world offers and accept that which
the world rejects. In short, they were to become like
children—humble, pure in heart and unconcerned about
earthly aspiration. They were to be pruned like trees in

order to produce good fruits. Jesus loved children and wished that all men were innocent like them. In them, Jesus saw a perfect human society and a new concept for a perfect government based on freedom, justice, equality and truth.

Christ had come to raise all who had fallen, to redeem all who had been sinful, to release the prisoners and to declare all men equal before God His Father.

The God of Jesus was different from the God of the Old Testament whose presence shook the mountains, the God of anger who was thirsty for the blood of sacrifice, and who sought vengence even to the third and fourth generations. The God of Jesus was a forgiving and compassionate Father who seeks the lost and forgives the sinners. In order to make the people understand the true characteristics of this new God, Jesus related several parables.

In order to clarify further His concept of God as loving father, Jesus related the parable of the prodigal son, an ungrateful boy who had gone astray and who later returned to his father:

There was a well-to-do man who had two sons, probably the only children he had, and he loved them both, for he was their father and they were his flesh and blood. The older son was his father's heir who someday would take his place and carry on his business. The younger son was a little more favored simply because he was still looked upon as a child.

In Biblical lands, oftentimes the father is a little more lenient toward his firstborn, but the mother always takes the side of the younger because he is forever a child to her and therefore, inexperienced. Rebekah loved Jacob more than his brother Esau, yet both were born just a few minutes apart. Brothers in the East are rivals who often do not like each other and are jealous of one another, as we see from the Scriptures. The first two brothers, Cain and Abel, could not get along together and eventually Cain slew Abel. Esau and Jacob hated one another.

In the story of the prodigal son, the younger boy grew up under the discipline of his father and his older brother, whom he hated because he knew that someday his brother would take his father's place and might disinherit him. He would rather take orders from the servants than from his own brother. Apparently, the younger boy was extravagant, as most young men are. He entertained his friends, attended wedding feasts, participated in games and gave money to the poor, but his brother was frugal, sedate, calm and shrewd in all his dealings. He had been told from childhood that someday he would inherit the property and that he would surpass his father's wealth. Because of the difference between them, they invariably quarreled, much to their father's distress, for he could not take sides. His advice was in vain. The younger brother gradually made up his mind to leave home while his father was still alive so he could take his share of the inheritance with him. He was sure his father would give him his share, but he distrusted his brother.

One morning when a servant came to awaken him to give him instructions for the day from his brother, the youth told the servant to tell his father that he was ill. The father had risen early and had gone into the field with the hired reapers, but when he heard that his younger son was not well, he hastily returned home. When he entered the chamber of his younger son, to his surprise he found him dressed in one of his best garments, his belongings packed into a large saddlebag. When he asked the boy where he was going, the boy answered, "Father, I hate to tell you because you know well how I love you, but I am leaving. I can no longer stand the taunts and insults of my brother." Then he fell at his father's feet and with tears in his eyes, he begged, "My father, please permit me to go. Please give me whatever you will and let me go. I must go away from my brother and then I will find peace and happiness."

His father sorrowfully agreed and taking him to a nearby field, uncovered two earthen pots that had been buried there. One was filled with silver and the other with gold, and he gave both to his son.

A servant had already saddled a horse, and the young man kissed his father once more, mounted and rode off. His sad father stood watching until horse and rider disappeared behind the hills.

When the son reached the highway, he found a small caravan on its way to Syria, and he joined it until they came to a large city. There he spent a few days with a merchant whom he had met on the trip and then he decided to rent a large house. He hired servants and began to live the life of a prince. He spent his evenings at the public houses and enjoyed fine wines, and he watched scantily clad girls dancing to the music of tabrets, for this was something he had never seen or heard of in his little village.

Then he started entertaining lavishly, and his fame spread among the merrymakers, harlots, dancers and others who lived carefree lives instead of working. But one day he found that the bag of silver was empty, and his gold was slowly diminishing. Still he kept on entertaining until finally all his money was gone, and he had sold all his furniture and clothing, and the house was bare. Now all his friends, the men and women who had graced his generous table, disappeared, too, and only beggars came to his door. Finally, he was forced to leave town and sought refuge among the peasants where he could find food and shelter, for these people were simple like his own people, and they lived off the land. He secured a job as a swineherder, the lowest position in the land, for the Jews not only did not eat pork, but they would not even look at pigs. But since life is dearer than sacred customs, he accepted the lowly job in order to live. Now with his job he had a place to lay his head at night and two or three loaves of Syrian bread each day. But during a severe famine, his ration was cut to only a small loaf of bread daily, and he became thinner and thinner until his fat was gone, and his skin shriveled. He was so hungry that he started to eat carob beans, which are fed to pigs, and the roots of vegetables, as people do when they are hungry.

One day he began to think about his father, the man who had loved him. He thought to himself, "How many hired workers are now in my father's house who have plenty of bread, and I am here perishing with hunger! I will rise and go to my father and say to him, My father, I have sinned before heaven and before you; And I am no longer worthy to be called your son; just make me like one of your hired workers." (Luke 15:17–19) So finally, he returned to his father's house.

The brokenhearted father in the meantime had constantly asked about his son from merchants who were returning from foreign lands and from strangers who passed by his house, but he had always received disappointing answers, for none knew where the boy was. One day, to his great surprise, his wayward son appeared on the road. When he saw him, the old man forgot his age and began to run as he had in his youth, and when he reached his son, he took him in his arms and kissed him. Then his son looked humbly at the ground and said, "My father, I have sinned before heaven and before you, and I am no longer worthy to be called your son." But his father, instead of scolding him, ordered the servants to bring the best robe, and he placed a ring on his hand and shoes on his feet. Then he had a fatted ox slaughtered and invited all his friends to celebrate the return of his son.

When the older son returned from an errand, he saw the house lit up, and as he drew nearer, he heard music and singing and saw dancing. When he alighted from his horse, he asked a servant what was happening, and the servant answered, "Your brother has come; and your father has killed the fat ox because he received him safe and well." The older brother became very angry and refused to go into the house, so his father came out to plead with him. The son said, "Behold, how many years I have served you, and I never disobeyed your commandment; and yet you never gave me even a kid that I might make merry with my friends. But for this son of yours, after he had wasted your wealth with harlots and has come back, you have killed the fat ox." His father looked at him a moment and then answered, "My son, you are always with me, and everything which is mine is yours. It was right for us to make merry and rejoice; for this your brother was dead and has come to life; and was lost and is found." (Luke 15:28–32)

If a human father would do so much for his son who had offended him and gone astray, how much more our heavenly father, the source of infinite love and mercy, would do for His wayward children. Such will be the joy in heaven when a sinner returns.

Then, in order to make His point on God's love for His children even stronger, Jesus cited another parable, this time about something with which all the people were familiar. All Jewish people were pastoral and knew something about the shepherd and his flock or about the sheep which were entrusted to him.

Now it happened that a shepherd discovered that one of the sheep in his flock was missing. The shepherds know their sheep just as a father knows his children. When this particular shepherd called the sheep by their names, he found one was missing. So he left the ninety and nine other sheep and went back to the places where they had fed searching for the stray. When he found her, he put her upon his shoulders and brought her back. The shepherd was happier over finding this one sheep than he was over the ones he had left behind, for he loved all of them and would have been unhappy if one had been lost.

Men who have one hundred sheep are looked upon as wealthy. The number one hundred is well known. To people who have to count on their fingers, it is a large number, and to some it sounds like infinity. Many work hard in order to increase the number of their sheep to one hundred—the highest and most desired number as far as they are concerned.

Just as the shepherd was happy that he had found the one sheep that had gone astray, so God our Heavenly Father rejoices when a sinner is converted or when one of His children who has gone astray returns. A father has more compassion upon the children who are weak and who fall or go astray, for he can be nothing less than a loving father who loves all of his children.

Then Jesus recited another parable, this one about a woman who, while entertaining a group of women in her home, broke her necklace. The precious coins that comprised the necklace fell to the ground, but all save one were recovered. The woman searched for it diligently, but she could not find it. The lost coin was one her husband had given her when they had been married, and because it was so dear to her, she continued searching for it. Finally, she found it, and in her delight, she ran outside crying, "Rejoice with me, for I have found my coin which was lost." (Luke 15:9)

Now, if a woman would search so long for a little silver coin, if a shepherd searches long and hard for a lost sheep, how much more would God search for His children when they are lost and how much more does He rejoice when they are found and restored? The good always belong to God, but His great concern is for those who are lost, those who have gone astray from the true path of life.

22

JERUSALEM

ON THIS LAST JOURNEY TO
Jerusalem, Christ stopped at Jericho. As He neared the
town, Matthew, a customs officer who was later known as
Zacheus, went out to meet Him. Zacheus had known Jesus
at Capernaum where he had been a customs officer before
going to Jericho. Because he was short and the crowd
was large, he climbed a mulberry tree so as to see the
great teacher. When Jesus saw him up in the mulberry
tree, He called to him, "Come down. I will be your guest
today." So Zacheus climbed down out of the tree and
gave a banquet for Jesus. The banquet was a great success, for a great many noblemen, Pharisees and scribes attended, but it angered the religious authorities to see a
man who proclaimed Himself the Messiah accepting the
hospitality of a man whose character was questionable,
a hated customs officer and tax collector who had be-

come a Roman stooge. No pious Jew would ever associate himself with a renegade like Zacheus, much less eat with him.

After the feast, as Jesus was leaving the town, two blind men heard His name, and they cried out, "Our Lord, have mercy upon us, Son of David," for this was their last opportunity to be near the great healer of whom they had heard so much. Jesus stopped, touched their eyes, and their sight was restored.

As Jesus and His disciples neared Jerusalem, instead of entering the Holy City, they went to a town named Beth-Pagey, which was not far from Beth Ania on the eastern side of the Mount of Olives. Since it was a feast day, Jesus did not wish to enter Jerusalem without making some advance preparations. The city was choked with pilgrims not only from Palestine, but from all over the Roman Empire. Even though the Jews, like the Arabs, are known for their hospitality, on a feast day no one would invite thirteen men to eat and lodge, since there would not be enough room for all of them. Jesus was determined to spend the last week of His life with His dear disciples and to eat His last Passover with them.

After they had rested for a while, Jesus commanded two of the disciples to bring a she donkey and her colt to Him that He might ride the colt into the city not as a conqueror, but as a humble and meek man:

And he said to them, Go to that village which is in front of you, and straightway you will find an ass which is tied up, and a colt with her; untie them and bring them to me. (Matthew 21:2)

Until a few decades ago in these ancient lands, one could see donkeys for hire or loan tied up at the doors of houses. Jesus was well known in the villages around Jerusalem, and He knew that no one would refuse to lend Him a donkey or even a horse. The disciples would need only say, "It is for our Lord," and the reply would be, "Take it and keep it as long as you wish," for Easterners never refuse the request of a holy man.

Zechariah long ago had prophesied that the Messiah would enter the historic city riding a lowly animal, the ass:

> Rejoice greatly, O daughter of Zion! Shout, O daughter of Jerusalem! Behold, your King comes to you; he is righteous and a Savior, lowly and riding upon an ass, upon a colt the foal of an ass. (Zechariah 9:9)

How many times Jesus had read these words. How many times had He pictured Himself entering Jerusalem on an ass and surrounded by His disciples and a few of His followers. Again and again, had He seen His rejection by the religious authorities and the political leaders, His condemnation by the priests, and His crucifixion by the Romans. Zechariah had also seen the rejection of the Christ and like Isaiah, he had portrayed His humiliation. He knew the priests, the Temple authorities and the scribes would resist any changes or reforms just as their forefathers had rejected the admonitions of the Holy Prophets. The Messiah Christ was to inaugurate a new Kingdom of meekness and justice, and he knew Jesus was to suffer for the sake of His seemingly revolutionary teaching.

The disciples, although they still expected a reception quite the opposite of what it was to be, did as Jesus commanded and brought Him the she ass and her colt. The she ass was necessary, for Jesus was to ride the unbroken colt, and a colt will not move unless its mother goes ahead of it. (Jesus rode upon the colt only. He did not ride upon both animals as the Western versions of the Bible state.) An ass is the most despised animal in the East. It is a beast of burden and although it is stupid, sometimes it is smarter than its rider. When the prophet Baalam was going on a mission to curse Israel, his donkey halted when she saw an angel in front of her, and the donkey warned the prophet of his wrong-doing.

The colt the disciples brought Jesus did not buck and kick when Jesus mounted it, for He had ridden donkeys in His boyhood. In the East, poor people own only asses and use them for transportation, while those who are wealthy own both horses and donkeys. Riding an ass is symbolic of poverty, meekness and even disgrace. When a man is found guilty of blasphemy of some other heinous crime, the authorities place him upon an ass and parade him in the street as punishment. Men who were honored, on the other hand, rode horses.

Jesus, however, rode the ass to impress on His disciples that He was not a political messiah. Then, too, He wanted to be an example of meekness so that henceforth none who followed Him would try to rule over the others. He also wanted them to know that He would be rejected, for they still expected a warm reception which they were not to receive. By entering the city so humbly, His enemies would not be able to humiliate Him, and He could show that He was not an earthly king.

When all the preparations were made and the ass and the colt were ready, some of His disciples and followers were stunned. Their dreams of a triumphant entry and welcome were shattered forever. Judah, particularly, was disappointed. He had never expected His Lord, the Messiah, to ride upon the stupid and despised beast of burden. He, more than the others, had expected elaborate preparations in Jerusalem and a delegation from the High Priests and scribes sent to Beth Ania to see the entry. Judah, like other disciples, had followed Jesus for the sake of glory and material possessions. He had seen great opportunities for himself by following the Prophet as He traveled around the countryside teaching and healing and performing miracles. He had seen the people bring gifts of food and money to Jesus and had seen Jesus with His divine power meet the needs of His disciples and feed thousands of hungry people. Apparently, Judah was a shrewd businessman and merchant who was constantly mindful of his profits and losses. His one purpose in following Jesus was to make more money and to achieve a higher station in life for himself. Because of his shrewdness, he had been made the treasurer for the group, the keeper of the purse, the receiver of all contributions, the buyer of food and other necessities.

But now suddenly the whole thing seemed ridiculous. He was smart enough to realize that no one would come out to greet a man riding on an ass and realizing that nothing lay ahead but disaster, he was sorely depressed. He thought he had been deceived and had lost out.

When the procession reached the summit of the Mount of Olives, it halted and all gazed at the Holy City with its beautiful Temple, and as they were halted, they were met by a large group of Jesus' followers who were already in Jerusalem but who had not expected Him to attend the feast.

Jesus' entry into Jerusalem has been one of the most misunderstood episodes of His ministry. In spite of His own words that He would be rejected by the priests, scribes and the elders, judged by the council, condemned and delivered to the Romans for crucifixion, scholars still believe He entered the city in triumph.

The small procession of Galileans began to descend the narrow road that winds along the edge of the old Jewish cemetery on the outskirts of the city. The people were singing hosannahs, the holy songs which were to be sung before the Messiah, and throwing branches from trees before Him as He rode along on His donkey. As they passed by the cemetery, some Pharisees met them and told Jesus to stop the songs, but Jesus pointed toward the tombs at the side of the road and replied, "I say to you that if these should keep silent, the stones would cry out," in other words, the dead in the sepulchers had hoped to see the day when the Messiah would enter the city, and if He stopped the living from singing, the dead would take up the songs.

But the singing was soon drowned out by the noise of the pilgrims, merchants and merrymakers who had come to Jerusalem for Passover and by the lowing of the oxen and bleating of the sheep that had been brought to be sold for sacrifices.

When they entered the city, Jesus and His disciples went straight to the Gentiles' Court of the Temple, the place where He always spoke to the crowds, the place where He had made both friends and enemies and where He had debated with the scribes, elders and other learned men on His previous visits. The Temple precinct was a small city unto itself. It contained the Holy of Holies, which no one could enter except the High Priest, and he only to absolve the people of their sins once a year. There were also rooms for the priests and the Levites, storerooms for the offerings and the properties of the Temple as well as the part where the Jews worshiped and into which Gentiles could not enter. The outer portion of the Temple complex was called the Gentiles' Court. Some of the space was occupied by shops which were rented to the merchants and money changers and in these places business transactions were carried on much as they were in the public markets. At the markets, however, customers could go into different shops to obtain the best bargains, but at the Temple shops, they had no choice and were often taken advantage of by dishonest merchants. These Temple shops were necessary, for the Jews who came long distances to the Temple could not bring offerings and sacrifices with them, and their foreign coins were not acceptable to the Temple authorities, for they had images on them and violated the second commandment. The Temple shekel was the only legal tender, and all foreign money had to be exchanged for these shekels. The great Temple, therefore, which had been built about nine hundred years before by the great and wise King Solomon as a house of prayer, was thus turned into a mart—a den of thieves—for dishonest business.

The treasury in the Temple was the cause of the invasions by kings of Egypt, Assyria and Babylon, for the wealth had become a byword. It was because of this wealth that the ten tribes of Israel left King Rehoboam, the son of King Solomon. Jeroboam, a servant of Solomon, saw that all the wealth from the North was pouring into Jerusalem, so he built another temple at Bethel and told the members of the Ten Tribes to worship there instead.

The Temple at Jerusalem, because of the iniquities which were practiced in it, was finally destroyed by Nebuchadnezzar, the king of Babylon, and all the treasures were carried off to that country. The Temple in the time of Jesus was the third and had been enlarged and beautified by Herod in order to win the favor of the Jews. For centuries it had been the only business in Judea, for the land was poor and nothing could be grown for export. The Temple revenues were the only wealth in the lands and supported thousands of priests and Levites and their families. We are told that when Pompey entered the Holy of Holies, instead of seeing the Jewish deity, he saw piles of golden talents. Indeed, the Temple was the life of the city, and without it, Jerusalem would have died.

Now when Jesus entered the Temple and went to the Gentiles' Court, He saw the dishonest business dealings that were being carried on. Before, He had held His peace, only taking the opportunity to preach to the merchants and moneychangers in the hope that they would heed His admonitions and change. But He no longer had any patience with the crooked merchants. He had to condemn the evil practices not only by words, but with action. He had to rebuke those who had turned the holy house of God into a den of thieves and drive them out, even at the cost of His own life, and He knew this was His last chance.

As He entered the court, He saw thousands of animals waiting to be sacrificed for the sins of men—that which no animal blood can cleanse. And He saw the religious authorities and others walking proudly around in their ornate robes and watching the merchants bargaining and swearing falsely in the name of God. Sometimes they disagreed with customers and cursed one another, but when they made a good profit, they blessed the customer, for all the merchants who had shops in the Temple had to make good or fail. They had paid high prices to the priests and they had to make high profits in order to offer gifts to the elders and scribes.

Jesus made a whip from the grass that was strewn about the courtyard and with it, He tried to expel all those who were conducting business in the Temple. He was so enraged He overturned the trays of the moneychangers, saying to them as He did so, "It is written, My house is the house of prayer; but you have made it a cave of bandits." The people were bewildered by His actions, and some of the Pharisees and merchants were bitter, but they said nothing. They were afraid the people in the provinces who had accepted the Prophet from Nazareth as the Messiah were at the feast and would fight to defend Him. Furthermore, Jesus had many strong followers among the pilgrims and Jews in Jerusalem and the religious authorities were afraid of a rebellion, for the people were tired of the corruption in their land. Then, too, Jesus was surrounded by twelve stalwart and fearless young Galileans, a people noted for bravery in war. The priests and scribes had waited a long time to arrest Him, and they felt they could wait a day or two more. Meanwhile, Jesus had returned to His healing and preaching in the Gentiles' Court as though nothing had happened.

At sunset, He and the disciples left the Temple and walked to Beth Ania, where they spent the night.

Apparently, they left the town the next morning without eating breakfast, for when they were within sight of the Temple at Jerusalem, Jesus saw a fig tree by the road and went to it in the hope of finding some fruit to eat. In the East, all fruit trees at the roadside belong to travelers and the poor, but most of their fruit is picked early in the season by little boys. This is evidently what had happened by the time Jesus and His disciples reached the tree, for there was nothing left on it but leaves. Mark tells us ". . . for it was not yet time for figs," but these words must have been written by a later scribe who thought he had found the answer as to why there was no fruit on the fig tree. If this had been the case, though, Jesus would not have expected to find figs.

When He found nothing but leaves on the tree, Jesus lost His temper as a man and said to the tree, "From now and forever let no man eat of your fruit," and the tree shortly after withered and died.

The cursing of the tree and its death taught the disciples a great lesson, for when they remarked about it, Jesus said to them:

> Truly I say to you, If you have faith and do not doubt, you will perform a deed not only like this of the fig tree, but should you say even to this mountain [pointing to the Mount of Olives], Be removed and fall into the sea, it shall be done. And everything that you will ask in prayer believing, you shall receive. (Matthew 21:21–22) [The term "mountain" is used metaphorically meaning a very difficult problem.]

What better purpose could a fig tree have served?

One does not need to have faith like a mountain, but only a little faith like a mustard seed, the smallest seed in the world. A spark of fire can burn a whole world. The disciples saw faith demonstrated not only in words, but in deed. Hitherto they had been dependent on their Master and had never tried to learn to preach, to heal the sick or to teach. As long as He was with them, they felt there was no need for them to do what He was doing, nor did they have the slightest idea that He was going to leave them shortly. It never occurred to them that this was the last week that they would be with Him, to walk with Him and to eat with Him.

The fig tree died in order to become a reminder to them of the faith and power of their Lord and Teacher. Another tree was to become lifeless temporarily, the earthly body of their Master. Jesus was ready to die to demonstrate that life is eternal, that the spiritual man is indestructible. He was ready to die and rise up again in order to strengthen the faith of His disciples and followers in the new and everlasting Kingdom which was ahead of them. He was ready to die that humanity might find eternal life.

While Jesus was preaching at the Temple, some priests, Pharisees, scribes and elders came to Him and asked, "By what authority do you do these things? and who gave you this authority?" As far as they were concerned, such authority came from Moses and from the priests, the descendants of Aaron, who were anointed and given power to preach, heal and expound the Holy Scriptures. No other person had this authority. These leaders had heard what had happened in the Gentiles' Court of the Temple the day before, and they had received complaints from the merchants who bought and sold legally in the Temple and who had never been disturbed before. They asked Him where He got His authority in the hope that they could trap Him and thus have Him arrested and arraigned before the Sanhedrin, the highest Jewish tribunal which had been spared by the Romans. Jesus knew what they were after and instead of answering their questions, he replied by asking *them* one that He knew they could not answer without getting into trouble. "I will also ask you a question, and if you answer me, I will then tell you by what authority I do these things. Whence is the baptism of John? Is it from heaven, or from men?"

The leaders debated among themselves, for they did not know how to answer the question. If they said from heaven, Jesus would ask them why they did not believe in him, and if they said from men, they would be afraid of the people, for all regarded John as a prophet. Since, no matter what answer they gave it would get them in trouble, they were caught in their own trap. Jesus had effectively silenced them before the crowd who had been listening to the debate, and the people must have been amused to see the bewilderment on the faces of their leaders. Finally, they came up with an answer. "We do not know," and Jesus replied with a grin, "Neither will I tell you by what authority I do these things."

Had Jesus told them that His authority was given by God, they would not have believed Him and would say that He had blasphemed. Then He related a short parable:

> A man had two sons, and he came to the first one and said to him, My son, go and work today in the vineyard. He answered, saying, I do not want to, but later he regretted and went. And he came to the other one and spoke to him likewise. And he answered, saying, Here am I, my lord, and yet he did not go. (Matthew 21:28–30)

When He was finished, He asked the men, "Which of these two did the will of his father?" and the answer came back, "The first one." Then Jesus said, "Truly I say to you that even the tax collectors and harlots will precede you into the kingdom of God."

This was one of the sharpest denunciations of the Jewish leaders Jesus ever made in the presence of the high-ranking Priests and Temple authorities. The first son symbolizes the Gentile world who, when they were asked if they would work in the vineyard, said they would not. Nevertheless, when the time came to work, they were on hand. The other son is symbolic of the Jews who were always ready and willing to work in the vineyard of God, but when the time came for their help they found excuses and refused to work. The Jewish leaders confessed that the first son had done the will of his father, the owner of the vineyard. They knew that the parable was aimed directly against them, for they had turned deaf ears to all the good works that Jesus had done. His denunciations were milder than those of the Hebrew prophets who had preceded Him, but what had enraged the leaders was His implication that the Gentiles would be heirs in the vineyard of God. They also wanted to discredit Him on the grounds that He was a Galilean and therefore could not be the promised Messiah. Furthermore, eleven of His disciples were also Galileans, as were most of those who had greeted Him as He entered Jerusalem. The Jews who had prayed for the coming of the Messiah and had agreed to work in the new vineyard of God refused to go out to greet Him, nor had anyone offered Him food and shelter.

On the day of His birth, Jesus slept in a cave. Now, during the last few days of His life, He was to sleep in a dirty and desolate place wrapped in a soiled mantle against the chill of the April night.

Then Jesus told another parable:

There was a man who was a householder, and he planted a vineyard and fenced it, and he dug in it a winepress and built a tower, and then he leased it to laborers and went away on a journey. And when the fruit season was at hand, he sent his servants to the laborers, that they might send him some of the fruits of his vineyard. And the laborers seized his servants, and some were beaten and some were stoned and some were killed. Again he sent other ser-

vants, many more than the first; and they did likewise
to them. At last he sent his son to them, saying, They might
feel ashamed before my son. But when the laborers saw the
son, they said among themselves, This is the heir; come, let
us kill him and retain his inheritance. So they seized him,
and took him out of the vineyard and killed him. When
therefore the owner of the vineyard comes, what will he
do to those laborers? (Matthew 21:33-40)

The leaders answered, "He will destroy them savagely,
and lease his vineyard to other laborers, who will give
him fruits in their seasons."

This parable was aimed directly at those leaders who
had rejected the prophets and messengers of God and
who had killed some of them. The vineyard was Judaism,
the true religion that God had planted in Palestine. The
householder was God; the laborers to whom the vineyard was leased were the priests, the Pharisees, the Sadducees, and the scribes. The servants whom the householder sent first were the early prophets, and the second
group of servants were later prophets who had met the
fate of their predecessors. The son of the householder
was Jesus Himself, the Messiah, the beloved Son of God.
The wicked laborers were ready to seize Him and deliver
Him for punishment to the Romans.

The parable placed the Jewish leaders on the spot.
They were not only guilty of seizing the vineyard, but
also of slaying God's prophets—Isaiah had been sawn
asunder by order of the wicked King Manasseh; Jeremiah
had been stoned in Egypt; Ezekiel had been slain in
Chaldea. All of God's ambassadors who had been sent
to lead the people to God's way had been murdered not
by the people, but by their leaders who had conspired
against God. Now the time had come when God, the

owner of the vineyard, was to reckon with the wicked laborers, destroy them and lease His vineyard to strange laborers, the Gentiles. The first were to be last, and the last were to be first.

The priests and elders who patiently listened to the parable knew it was aimed at their evil conduct, and Jesus did not want to leave any doubt in their minds that they were soon to be destroyed.

Then He told another parable:

> The kingdom of heaven is like a king who gave a marriage feast for his son. And he sent his servants to call those who were invited to the marriage feast, but they would not come. Again he sent other servants and said, Tell those who are invited, Behold my supper is ready, and my oxen and fatlings are killed, and everything is prepared; come to the marriage feast. But they sneered at it, and went away, one to his field, another to his business; And the rest seized his servants and mocked them and killed them. When the king heard it he was angry; and he sent out his armies and destroyed those murderers and burned their city. Then he said to his servants, Now the marriage feast is ready, and those who were invited were unworthy. Go, therefore, to the main roads, and whomever you may find, invite them to the marriage feast. So the servants went out to the roads and gathered together every one they could find, bad and good; and the banqueting house was filled with guests. (Matthew 22:1–10)

The king was God, and the marriage feast was symbolic of the inauguration of a new religion. The son was the Messiah, Jesus of Nazareth, and the servants were the prophets. The guests who were invited first and who refused to attend were the leaders of the Jewish religion.

When they refused, the King sent His other servants, the apostles, to invite anyone they could find—the poor, the rich, the good and the bad. These new guests were the Gentiles, pagans and members of other religions and cults who had been waiting for their call. Now they were in the Kingdom.

A few days hence the High Priests and other leaders were to relinquish their seats to the simple Galileans who were ready to go out and invite more guests until the house of their Lord was full, until the true religion of Judaism was shared all over the world. A new religion based on the teachings of the Hebrew prophets was on its way, founded on meekness, forgiveness and loving kindness instead of on force and the sword.

In a few days a new Covenant was to be written and sealed not with the blood of deaf and dumb animals, but with the precious blood of the most innocent Man who had ever trod the soil of this earth, who, by His meekness and the shedding of His blood on the cross, was to make all men of all races and colors worthy to enter the new Kingdom that was prepared for them.

23

RESURRECTION,
REFORM
AND
HYPOCRITES

AFTER THE PRIESTS AND THE
learned scribes had left disappointed because they could
not trap Jesus, the Sadducees, the righteous ones, came
to Him. They did not believe in the resurrection of the
body, Judgment Day or the life hereafter. They were
satisfied with only one life. Most were well to do and
many were employed by the government. The Pharisees,
the chosen ones, were nationalists. They worked hard
to restore the defunct kingdom of David and were zealous
in their keeping of the Mosaic Law and its observances.
Unlike the Sadducees, they believed in the resurrection
and in the Judgment Day when everyone, regardless of
their position in life, would answer for their deeds on
earth.

The Sadducees had come to ask Jesus a question about

the resurrection and the life hereafter. They were eager
to learn about them from a man who had raised the dead
and who was not himself afraid to die. Apparently, they
were not sure about their own beliefs, for, after all, the
prophet Daniel had given them, as Jews, the hope of
resurrection and the life hereafter. Nevertheless, this new
doctrine was in its beginning stages. There had been little
or nothing about it prior to the Babylonian captivity. The
Old Testament tells us that both the good and wicked
went to Sheol, a place underground for the departed
souls, but the early Israelites knew nothing about Hell.
And before Daniel, the Hebrew prophets had told the
people that they would punish themselves with their
own evil acts and reward themselves with their own good.
Man, being in the image of God, can create whatever he
wishes. Nowhere do the Scriptures attribute the author-
ship of evil to God.

Now the Sadducees could witness a great prophet,
greater than Daniel, greater even than Moses, Elijah and
Isaiah, a prophet who had been hailed by all the great
prophets as the Messiah—Jesus of Nazareth, who had
raised the dead and opened the eyes of the blind, a
prophet who had foretold His own death and resurrection. Surely this Man could give them an answer about
the resurrection.

So they came up to Him and said politely:

Teacher, Moses has told us, If a man dies without sons,
let his brother take his wife and raise up an offspring for
his brother. Now there were with us seven brothers; the
first married and died, and because he had no sons, he left
his wife to his brother. Likewise the second, also the third,
up to the seventh. And after them all, the woman also died.

Therefore at the resurrection, to which of these seven will she be a wife? for they all married her. (Matthew 22:24–29)

Jesus, after meditating for a few moments, looked at them and replied:

You err, because you do not understand the scriptures nor the power of God. For at the resurrection of the dead, men neither marry women, nor are women given to men in marriage, but they are like the angels of God in heaven. But concerning the resurrection of the dead, have you not read what was told you by God, saying, I am the God of Abraham, the God of Isaac, the God of Jacob? And yet God is not the God of the dead, but of the living. (Matthew 22: 29–32)

Sixteen hundred years before, the Hebrews, Egyptians and Babylonians had different concepts of life and death. The Babylonians and Egyptians were so sure of the resurrection of the body that they buried furniture, food and other worldly goods with the dead. In some cases, even the wives and servants of a ruler were buried with him to serve him when he rose up in the grave. The Hebrews, being a pastoral people had little or no knowledge of the resurrection of bodies, but they nevertheless believed that the souls of their forefathers lived. All of these ancient people believed the body would rise up. They did not understand that the human body is a temporal garment but that the spiritual man, being the image of God, is indestructible. Then, too, the Hebrews thought that the dead lived through their posterity and that if a man died with no heir, that was the end of the man unless his brother took his widow and raised a male child as an heir of the deceased.

The Sadducees did not know that God was the God of the living and not the God of the dead. They were not aware that there is only one Life and one Spirit, and that man is eternal because God his Father is eternal. Many of the prophets had died without an issue, yet all of them are still living. At the resurrection there will be no marriage and no physical world. The men and women will be like angels, stripped of their physical desires, for the resurrection is a rebirth, the rebirth of the spiritual man living in a spiritual world.

The Sadducees were amazed at Jesus' answer. The interpreters of the Law had erred, for they had taken everything literally. When the Pharisees and scribes saw that Jesus had silenced the Sadducees, they gathered around Him as though pleased that He had defended the doctrine of the resurrection so successfully, and one said to Him in a friendly manner, "Rabbi, which is the greatest commandment in the law?" and Jesus replied:

Love the Lord your God with all your heart and with all your soul and with all your might and with all your mind. This is the greatest and first commandment. And the second is like to it, Love your neighbor as yourself. On these two commandments hang the law and the prophets.

The Jews knew that their religion had to be reformed and that they had to return to the way of God in order to be freed from their Roman masters. The Holy Scriptures bore witness to the early reforms that had been carried out by the Holy Prophets whose forefathers had slain them. Now the people venerated them. Despite the opposition from their leaders, the Jewish people had been flocking to Jesus and accepting Him as a great reformer. They could not understand the opposition from the

scribes, nor could they understand the opposition from
the Pharisees, who, like the scribes, wore long embroidered robes with fringes as an insignia of their high office
and who rejoiced when the people bowed to them and
called them rabbis, doctors of the law and instructors in
religion.

By means of their literal, and false, interpretations of
the Law and the prophets, the scribes had succeeded in
holding high positions in Jewish society and were respected not only by their own people, but by the Romans
as well. Many men could read in those days, but writing
was rare. A scribe was therefore looked upon much as we
look upon scientists today. The scribes understood everything literally and would argue for hours on end over a
dot or a letter, but they had completely forgotten the
objective of the Law. They did not understand that it
had been given by their God as a guide to serve as a
lamp at their feet and as a light to their path so they
might not stumble and err.

Since the return of the Jews from Babylon more than
four centuries before, the scribes and Pharisees spent all
their time in contradictory explanations of what God
had revealed to Moses and to the prophets. God had admonished Moses to write clearly and simply so that all
could understand, but the Law, thanks to the Pharisees
and scribes, had become difficult to understand even by
themselves, yet they could not bring themselves to dis-
card the wrong commentaries and law, thereby refuting
some of the distinguished rabbinical authorities, in order
to go back to the original truth that had been so simple
and clear. To do this, they would have had to confess
their error and that of their predecessors, and this they
were unwilling to do. Furthermore, some of the passages
in the Law and the prophets were forged or modified

to suit the purposes of the interpreters. The words in Semitic languages could easily be altered by removing the positions of tiny dots, and the Babylonian captivity had dealt a severe blow to the Scriptures because the people had lost their original tongue.

These religious leaders, and not the people, were an obstacle in the way of Jesus' acceptance as the Messiah. They saw that even though He was a learned man, He was poor, so they rejected Him and tried to prove from the Scriptures that the Christ would be a mighty warrior who, with the breath of His mouth, would destroy His enemies. The scribes again and again read to the people those passages that state that when the Messiah comes, the people will change completely and an everlasting peace will be established. What could ignorant people say against these passages? They had been written by some of their greatest prophets. They did not read the other passages which predicted the death and rejection of the Messiah.

The same question has been raised again and again in our own day. Some Christians still think that Christ has not come simply because His followers have forged more deadly instruments of war than ever before and because powerful nations still exploit and oppress smaller and weaker ones. The Pharisees and learned scribes who sat on the chair of Moses interpreting the Scriptures and teaching the people had a strong point for rejecting the meek and humble prophet from Nazareth. Millions of men and women today refuse to believe in Him for the same reason. The angels sang the song of peace, but where is the peace?

Had not the great prophet Isaiah seen Christ's rejection more than eight centuries before? He knew it would be difficult to change the hearts of the people and teach them to sacrifice the lesser for the greater, the temporal for the eternal, and the material for the spiritual. As Jesus told the learned rabbi Nicodemus, men have to be reborn in order to see the new world of Spirit and Truth. The prophet knew that those who believed in force and violence and who derived the comforts of life from existing corrupt orders would resist any change and would fight and die for the only world they knew—the world of the here and now. Isaiah had seen, too, the death of the Messiah, but the Pharisees, scribes and other Jewish leaders did not understand the change in his prophecy from a political messiah to a suffering servant— a man who could not even break a bruised reed. They did not know that as Isaiah grew spirtually, he saw a new image of the Messiah.

The Jewish leaders tried to understand the strange Prophet from Nazareth, but they failed to see His qualifications as a political deliverer of Israel from her oppressors, so they rejected Him. No longer could they stand still and watch Him challenging their authority and interpreting the Scriptures in His own way, thus contradicting their revered authorities. They said to one another, "If His teaching is true, then centuries of studies and efforts by the rabbinical schools have been wasted and the Temple will be deserted and the sacrifices will cease." In the eyes of these men, honors, reputations and positions weighed more in the balance than the truth.

Through the centuries many Christians have condemned the Pharisees, the Sadducees, the scribes and the elders who were the pillars of the Jewish religion, and yet they themselves have hated, rejected, imprisoned and persecuted men who expounded certain truths which were alien to the doctrines of their respective denominations. They have treated them even more shamefully and cruelly than the leaders of the Jewish religion treated Jesus. For it is difficult to change the old way of life that has been tried and proved for something new and uncertain, no matter how good or practical it is.

On the other hand, some religious leaders through the centuries have been themselves like the Pharisees and scribes—more mindful of their own high positions, honors and glory than of the truth they should represent. Many centuries have elapsed since the scribes and the Pharisees rejected Jesus of Nazareth, yet only a few of His followers have been willing to take up their crosses, risk their honor and possessions for the sake of the truth that Jesus entrusted to them. Only a few have searched for the narrow and thorny road and have tried to walk on it.

I believe that in this century only one man, Pope John XXIII, has tried to walk the narrow and thorny road on which Jesus traveled nearly two thousand years ago. He would have risked everything—even his own life—for the sake of the teaching of his Lord Jesus Christ. And yet, Pope John's honors and glory were greater than the honors and glory of all the Christian kings and presidents of his day. Thank God, there have been many other sincere Christian men and women who have died for the sake of the truth. They, like Pope John, have served as guideposts for others to follow in their footsteps. The time has come for the followers of Jesus to look with the eyes of their Master at the Jewish leaders of the past, for if they had been in their place, they would have done the same and probably worse. The Jewish leaders of Jesus' day should be forgiven, for they did not know what they were doing. Jesus invoked His Father to forgive the Gentiles who crucified Him, for they did not know what they were doing. The light of the Gospel had not shone upon the world, and the words of Jesus on the cross were aimed not only at those who crucified Him, but at all those who opposed Him and wanted to do away with Him, for they thought they were serving a great cause.

The Jewish elders and religious leaders were guilty simply because they did not carefully examine the Scriptures. They remained loyal to the doctrines and teachings of men rather than the true teaching of the prophets who had sacrificed their lives for the sake of truth. These leaders advocated good things, but they themselves would not do them. They lay heavy burdens upon the people who trusted them and believed in them, but they did not try to help them carry these burdens.

These men were to answer to God for all the things they had done that they knew were evil. The days were coming when they would be summoned before the bar of justice to be requited for all their evil deeds. Jesus condemned them not for that which they did unknowingly, but for the wrongs of which they were aware. He admonished the people to obey the scribes and do the things which they were commanded to do, but not to act as they acted. In other words, what the scribes said was good, but what they did, was not. The words and the actions of these religious men were too far apart.

Hitherto, Jesus had denounced the scribes and Pharisees lightly as a teacher might denounce his students for their failure to learn their lessons. But now He began His tirade against them in hard words which were befitting to criminals and men who had gone astray from God and sold their souls. He was going to expose the self-appointed guardians of the Jewish religion, reveal their true selves and their deception of the people, for they were like tarnished sepulchers—pretty on the outside but dirty on the inside.

Woe to you, scribes and Pharisees, hypocrites! for you embezzle the property of widows, with the pretense that you make long prayers; because of this you shall receive a greater judgment. (Matthew 23:13)

The scribes and Pharisees prayed long and vehement prayers in the synagogues and on the street corners where they could be easily seen and heard by the simple, faithful people to prove that they were pious so that widows would appoint them guardians of their estates. These hypocrites acted like spiders who weave a fine web—a haven for the insects—so they might trap and devour them. They used their religion to defraud people instead of helping them. Their condemnation, therefore, would be greater because they were using their religion for the sake of worldly gain.

Woe to you, scribes and Pharisees, hypocrites! for you have shut off the kingdom of heaven against men; for you do not enter into it yourselves, and do not permit those who would enter. (Matthew 23:14)

The scribes and Pharisees, through their false interpretations of the Scriptures, had given the people a wrong concept of the Law and the prophets, thereby causing the faithful to go astray. They portrayed God as a tyrant, always angry with His people, a God to be appeased by means of gifts and sacrifices. They tried to hide the truth from the pious people, that the Kingdom of Heaven was at hand and the faithful could enter it immediately. They did not have to wait for its future coming. It does not come by observation or in a package; it starts in the heart. Instead of reading and teaching from the books of the prophets, which were the only key to open the doors of the Kingdom of Heaven, they read their own obscure and confusing commentaries, and laid more burdens upon the people.

> Woe to you, scribes and Pharisees, hypocrites! for you traverse sea and land to make one proselyte; and when he becomes one, you make him the son of hell twice more than yourselves. (Matthew 23:15)

This attack was one of the strongest charges Jesus had hurled against the Jewish priests, for they had tried to convert people of other races and religions not to the true religion of their forefathers, but to doctrines which they themselves had devised.

> Woe to you, blind guides; for you say, Whoever swears by the temple, it is nothing; but whoever swears by the gold which is in the temple, he is guilty! (Matthew 23:16)

Since the day Aaron made the golden calf and told the Israelites, "Here is your God," gold had become the soul of the material world, more precious and holy than the Temple and God's oracles. Some of the priests and prophets sold their souls for it, for they did not know that the Temple itself was greater and holier than gold. They did not know that the altar, through the Spirit of God, sanctified the offerings which were placed upon it. The scribes and Pharisees were far more concerned about the gifts than they were about the hard stones from which the altar was made and for what it stood.

> Woe to you, scribes and Pharisees, hypocrites! for you take tithes of mint, dill and cummin, and you have over-looked the more important matters of the law, such as jus-

tice, mercy, and trustworthiness. These were necessary for you to have done, and these very things (justice, mercy and trustworthiness) by no means to have left undone. (Matthew 23:23)

The scribes and Pharisees were constantly mindful of the Temple revenues, tithes, will and votive offerings. They even took tithes from men who had raised mint, dill and cummin in their small gardens, but they forgot justice. They had forgotten that the whole objective of religion was to execute justice and to help the poor and the needy. In their cold and hostile world, justice and mercy were far more important than the collection of tithes which they had no right to collect and of which God had no need. Justice and mercy should never have been forgotten, for when justice is trampled on, the whole system of government, society and religion collapses.

Woe to you, scribes and Pharisees, hypocrites! you clean the outside of the cup and of the plate, but inside they are full of extortion and iniquity. Blind Pharisees! clean first the inside of the cup and of the plate, so that their outside may also be clean. (Matthew 23:25–26)

The doctrines of men had supplanted the Word of God. It was easy for the scribes and Pharisees to appear in public places in their long religious garments, their heads anointed with oil, their hands and faces washed clean. They were like a cup that is clean on the outside, but dirty on the inside.

Woe to you, scribes and Pharisees, hypocrites! for you are like tombs painted white, which look beautiful from

the outside, but inside are full of dead bones and all kinds
of corruption. (Matthew 23:27)

Since the day Moses ordained his brother Aaron to the
priesthood, clothed him in an embroidered white linen
robe, and placed a miter on his head, many religious
men have laid more emphasis on the external than on the
internal. They have tried to impress worshipers by the
outer ritual rather than by inward truth and genuine
piety. This had not been true in the beginning when
religion was an inner, spiritual expression springing forth
from the hearts of men and devoid of all man-made
paraphernalia. In the old days, religious men were
known by their piety and good deeds just as a good tree
is known by its good fruits as well as by its beautiful
leaves and boughs. The pious faces and eyes revealed the
hidden goodness in the bottom of their hearts, and their
words and deeds spoke loudly for their good characters.
But by the time of Jesus, all this had changed, and truth
and sincerity had given way to hypocrisy. The religion
of the heart had become love of money, honors and high
positions. The religious leaders who were carried away
with worldliness could see the blunders that their forefathers had committed by murdering the prophets who
had been sent to bring them to God's way. Now they
built tombs over the prophets' graves and whitewashed
them to symbolize the innocence of the victims. Thus,
the conspicuous white tombs stood as witness to the evil
deeds of their forefathers. They said to themselves, "If
we had been in the place of our fathers, we would not
have done it," and yet during that very Passover week
they were conspiring to deliver an even greater prophet
to the Romans for punishment, oblivious to the fact that

they would have to pay for the blood that had been spilled in the past.

Jesus warned them that all the innocent blood that had been shed was to be avenged, but the leaders would not repent. Jerusalem had been deaf to the ambassadors of God in the past and her streets and palaces had been drenched with blood. Now the city was doomed just as it had been doomed when the Chaldean army had captured it and burned its Temple. The same disaster which had befallen her in the past was to come upon her again, and just as the prophet Jeremiah had lamented her fall six hundred years before, so Jesus was mourning her impending fall now.

24

THE
MOUNT
OF OLIVES

✥❧ ❧✥

AS JESUS AND HIS DISCIPLES
were leaving the Temple on their way to the Mount of
Olives, the disciples started discussing the large stones in
the Temple that had been hewn in Lebanon of Corinthian
marble and the other magnificent artwork with which
Solomon and Herod had made the house of God.

It was one of the greatest wonders in the world, and
people came from distant lands to see it, bringing with
them rich gifts and offerings. King Herod the Great had
spent most of the revenues from his kingdom on it,
and it had taken forty years to rebuild after its destruction.

When the disciples had finished talking, Jesus said to
them, "Behold, do you not see all of these? Truly I say to
you, Not a stone shall be left here upon another stone,

which will not be torn down." (Matthew 24:2) His prophecy was fulfilled in A.D. 70 when General Titus captured the city, demolished the Temple and slaughtered thousands of Jews. The building was the last to fall, for it was used as a fortress by the valiant Jewish defenders who gave their lives rather than see the Gentile armies enter it. In A.D. 117, Emperor Hadrian uprooted both city and Temple, and the large and once-sacred stones were taken back to their place of origin, Baalbeck, a small town in Lebanon, which, since it was in the path of many conquerors, itself was destroyed. Not one word of Jesus' prophecy failed to come true. Jerusalem paid a heavy price for her evil doings and her obstinance.

While Jesus and the disciples were on the Mount of Olives, the disciples asked Him when these events would take place. Jesus did not tell them, but He warned them to be careful that no man should deceive them. Then He added, "When you see the sign of uncleanness and desolation, as spoken by the prophet Daniel, accumulating in the holy place, Then let those who are in Judea flee to the mountain." (Matthew 24:15–16)

In other words, when the Temple sanctuary is defiled by foreign invaders, that is the sign, and the Judeans should flee for their lives to the mountain. The disaster was to be so great and so sudden that those who were sleeping on the housetops would have no time to come down and rescue clothes or valuables and those in the fields would not have time to return home. There was to be great suffering—a great massacre of the Jews.

Then Jesus warned them of false christs who would come to deceive the faithful, for during disasters and afterward, people can easily be deceived by false prophets and false teachers. They follow any secular or religious leader at such times:

> Then if any man should say to you, Behold, here is the Christ, or there; do not believe it. For there will rise false Christs and lying prophets, and they will show signs and great wonders, so as to mislead, if possible, even the chosen ones. (Matthew 24:23-24)

The sun will be darkened, the moon will give no light, and stars will fall from the sky, which is to say, the universe will mourn and share in this great calamity.

Jesus revealed His second coming to His disciples, that it will be like lightning which comes from the east and is seen even in the west. The Spiritual Christ will be seen by people of all races and all colors, and He will appear to them whether they believe in Him or not. The signs of the times will indicate His coming. Then Jesus said,

> Truly I say to you that this race will not pass away until all these things happen. Even heaven and earth will pass away, but my words shall not pass away. (Matthew 24:34-35)

The Jewish race was to remain to the end of time as a witness to God's truth and His revelations to the prophets, for these truths were to be embedded in the Christ's teachings. A new and spiritual temple, not built by human hands, was to rise up.

The precise times of the coming of the Kingdom of Heaven and the second coming of Christ are known only to God the Father, and even Jesus Himself was kept in ignorance. The prophets had seen this Kingdom in their dreams and in their meditations, but because the concept of a new and perfect order must grow slowly in the hearts of men, every man should be constantly ready and alert so that when it comes, he may enter into it.

To illustrate this, Jesus related another of His many interesting and enlightening parables, this one of the ten virgins:

News of a wedding feast spread through the town, and as soon as the ten virgins heard, they opened their wooden chests and took out their wedding garments and jewelry. When they had dressed in their finery, each one took a lamp and went out, according to custom, to greet the bride and bridegroom. Five of the virgins knew from past experience that the wedding couple seldom arrived at the wedding house on time, and sometimes they were as much as five or six hours late. (In the East, time is irrelevant; to be three or four hours late means nothing.) The wise virgins also knew that on the nuptial day, both bride and bridegroom are bathed, and as water is scarce, it can take a long time to procure it. These five took extra oil so that if the couple were delayed, they would have sufficient oil and their lamps would burn for the procession and the feast afterward. But the other five virgins were foolish and took no extra oil with them, for they did not think the procession would be late. Then all ten joined the other people waiting in the street.

But it happened that the bridegroom was delayed, and since the virgins were tired, they went to sleep. Suddenly at midnight a herald cried out that the groom was coming, and a few minutes later the sound of the tambourines, drums and singers could be heard and the nuptial procession came into sight on its way to the wedding house.

All the virgins woke up and lit their lamps, but the foolish ones who had not brought extra oil, said to the wise virgins, "Give us some of your oil, for our lamps are going out." But the wise ones answered, "Why, our oil would not be enough for us and for you. Go to those who sell oil and buy some for yourselves." So the five went to try to buy some oil. The shopkeepers, however, were also watching the wedding, and all the shops were closed up. The wise virgins, in the meantime, had joined the procession and were welcomed at the wedding house since their lamps were burning and they had plenty of oil to help light the festivities all night. The foolish girls, however, missed the procession, and they did not want to miss the wedding feast as well, for they had looked forward to it for a long time. This was a day when they hoped to find prospective husbands, a day when they could dance and be merry. They therefore went to the house, but to their disappointment, they found the door locked. They looked through holes in the door and saw the people dancing and rejoicing and when the door-keeper did not open the door at their request, they pleaded, "Our Lord, our Lord, please open to us." But he answered, "Truly I say to you, I do not know you," for the house was crowded, and those who had failed in their early preparations were not welcome inside.

Jesus' disciples listened carefully to this familiar parable, and they realized that no one but God Himself knows when the Kingdom will come. It also served as a reminder to those who followed the disciples that they should always be prepared for His return and for the inauguration of the Heavenly Kingdom.

The Lord Jesus had shown His disciples and followers the richest field in the world—a field filled with the treasures that had been buried by their forefathers. Now, however, this treasure had been found again, but the disciples had to continue to work in order to own the field and the treasures which had lain hidden for so many years. Judaism was this field, and what God had given to the Jews He had not given to the people of other races and religions. His revelations to them were priceless, and the Lamp of God—the Holy Bible—that gave them light was one of these treasures. Jesus had warned His disciples of the disaster that was to befall Jerusalem, but He also wanted to tell them of the people's disloyalty to their God, so once again, He used a parable.

In the Bible lands, rich landlords entrust large sums of money to their servants so the servants can buy dairy products, cattle and sheep, and sell them at a profit. Generally, they buy when commodities are cheap and then hold them until the price rises before reselling them at a profit for themselves and for their master.

A rich landlord, before he left on a trip, called three of his servants to him and gave them some money. To one, he gave five talents; to another, two talents; and to the third, one talent. They were to trade with this money and make a profit.

The one who received five talents bought and sold and traded and thus gained five more talents. Likewise, the second gained two more talents by buying and selling; but the third servant who had received only one talent was afraid to trade, so he buried it in the ground. When the master returned, he called the servants to him for an accounting. The first said, "My Lord, you gave me five talents; behold, I have added five others to them," and his master said, "Well done, good and reliable servant. You have been faithful over a little, I will appoint you over much; enter into your master's joy."

Then the one who had received two talents came and said, "My Lord, you gave me two talents, behold I have added two others to them." The master said, "Well done, good and reliable servant, you have been faithful over a little, I will appoint you over much; enter into your master's joy."

Then the one who had received one talent came and stood hopefully before him. "My Lord, I knew that you are a hard man, and you reap where you do not sow and gather where you do not scatter. So I was afraid, and I went and hid your talent in the ground; here is the very one you gave me." His master answered, "O wicked and lazy servant, you knew me that I reap where I did not sow and gather where I did not scatter. You should then have put my money in the exchange, and when I returned I would have demanded my own with interest." And he took away the talent and gave it to the servant who had ten:

> For to him who has, it shall be given, and it shall increase to him; but he who has not, even that which he has shall be taken away from him. And the idle servant they threw into the outer darkness; there will be weeping and gnashing of teeth (regrets). (Matthew 25:29–30)

This parable was aimed at those rebellious and slothful religious leaders who had forgotten their calling and buried their talents in the ground because they were jealous of their religion and fearful of God. Now their talent was to be taken away and given to the Gentiles who were to use it and multiply it a hundredfold. It was a warning to the disciples who in a few days were to become the possessors of the richest treasure in the world, a teaching which all peoples of the world would accept and which would heal the wounds of nations.

The followers of Jesus were to work hard in order to make more converts, and they were admonished not to bury His precious teaching in the dark edifices as the

Jewish religious leaders had done, but to preach it openly so that all would hear it. The simple but sincere Galileans were to receive the gift of the Holy Spirit and the power to preach the word and heal the sick, and the more they used it, the more it would increase, and the better they would understand it. The word of God is like a seed. When it is sown, it multiplies, but if it is not sown, it remains a single seed.

When the Son of man comes in his glory, and all his holy angels with him, then he will sit upon the throne of his glory. And all nations will gather before him; and he will separate them one from another, just as a shepherd separates the sheep from the goats. (Matthew 25:31)

On Judgment Day, when the King of kings and the Lord of lords sits upon the throne, the great Scroll of Life will be opened and the works of man, both good and evil, will be revealed. Then Jesus (the Shepherd) will set the good people (the sheep) at His right hand and the evil people (the goats) at His left. And to those at His right, He will say:

Come, you blessed of my Father, inherit the kingdom which has been prepared for you from the foundation of the world. For I was hungry, and you gave me food; I was thirsty, and you gave me drink; I was a stranger and you took me in; I was naked, and you clothed me; I was sick, and you visited me; I was in prison, and you came to me. Then the righteous will say to him, Our Lord, when did we see you hungry, and feed you? or thirsty and give you drink? And when did we see you a stranger, and took you in? Or that you were naked and clothed you? And when did we see you sick or in prison and came to you? The King then will answer, saying to them, Truly I tell you, Inasmuch as you have done it to one of the least of these my brethren, you did it to me. Then He will also say to those at his left, Go away from me, you cursed, to the everlasting fire which is prepared for the adversary and his angels. For I was hungry and you did not give me food; I was thirsty and you did not give me drink; I was a stranger and you did not take me in; I was naked and you did not clothe me; I was sick and in prison and you did not visit me. Then they also will answer and say, Our Lord, when did we see you hungry or thirsty or a stranger or naked or sick or in prison, and did not minister to you? Then he will answer and say to them, Truly I say to you, Inasmuch as you did not do it to one of these least ones, you also did not do it to me. And these shall go into everlasting torment, and the righteous into eternal life. (Matthew 25:34-46)

Jesus was mindful of the welfare of His disciples and of His followers, and He wanted to assure them that He was not going to leave them alone but would be with them forever. His Spirit, the Christ in Him, was to guide them, strengthen them during their trials. They were the disciples of a Teacher who soon was to triumph over the material world, death and the grave, and unite life on this earth with the Life hereafter.

Jesus was going away to prepare a place for them. He was going to die in order to demonstrate that there is no death in the realm of the Spirit and to prove that Heaven begins here on earth, and the Kingdom of God was at hand. Henceforth, the gates of heaven were to be open not only for the Jews, but also for all other peoples, not only for the good, but for the repentant sinner, thereby giving the wicked hope which they never had before. All

the disciples had to do was to have faith in Him and
His future triumph:

> Let not your heart be troubled; believe in God, and be-
> lieve in me also. In my Father's house are many rooms; if
> it were not so, I would have told you. I go to prepare a
> place for you. And if I go and prepare a place for you, I will
> come again and take you to me, so that where I am you may
> be also. You know where I am going and you know the
> way. (John 14:1–4)

But His disciples did not know where He was going,
nor did they know the way. In Aramaic, the term "going"
means "dying," and "way" means "religion." That is the
way which Christ had revealed to them—the true religion of love and meekness, the way of harmony, peace
and understanding, the way which leads directly to
heaven. The disciples could not understand the terms
their Master was using. To them, death was the end, for
no one had ever risen from the dead to reveal its mystery.
But Christ had assured them of His resurrection and life
hereafter:

> I am the way and the truth and the life; no man comes to
> my Father except by me (which means, by my way or
> religion). If you had known me, you would have known
> my Father also; from henceforth you know Him and you
> have seen Him. (John 14:6–7)

Then Philip, one of the disciples, asked Jesus to show
him the Father, the mysterious and mighty God of Israel
—the God whose face even Moses had been unable to
see—for Philip, like many others, did not know that God
was Spirit, Life and Truth, and that whosoever had seen

Jesus had seen God. When Jesus heard this request, He replied,

> All this time I have been with you, and yet you do not know me, Philip? He who sees me has seen the Father; and how do you say, Show us the Father? Do you not believe that I am with my Father and my Father is with me? The words that I speak, I do not speak of myself; but my Father who abides with me does these works. Believe that I am with my Father and my Father is with me; and if not, believe because of the works. (John 14:9–11)

No one without God's help could have done the things that Jesus did, and these things bore witness to His Messiahship and to His being in one accord with God. In other words, Jesus was the express image and likeness of God revealed in human form. Therefore, he who sees Jesus sees God. Jesus had found the true way, "way" means religion, which leads men into peace and harmony, a way that no one had found before—the way of meekness and humility.

25

THE
HOLY
SPIRIT

❧❧ ❧❧

JESUS HAD TOLD THE WOMAN
in Samaria that God is the Spirit, the only Spirit and
Truth, and can be worshiped everywhere. The same Spirit
that spoke through the Holy Prophets was to speak
through His disciples and their followers. The Aramaic
term "Spirit" means "all embracing," that is, there is no
space in the universe where there is no Spirit.

During the time of Jesus, the Jews had lost the teaching
of their prophets and knew little of the power of the
Spirit of God. Human teachers had shorn Him of His
omnipresence, and He had become the God of a certain
area just as had the gods of the pagans. Worshipers,
therefore, had to walk long distances to pray and com-
mune with Him in the specified area. The Holy Prophets
had been slain centuries before, but their words were

heard daily in the synagogues, on the street corners and along the roadways. The Spirit was still living and operative, and that same Spirit that had guided the prophets was now to guide and help the apostles and those who followed them.

The time had come when the disciples themselves were to take over the work of their Master and to put into practice all they had learned at His feet. The Holy Spirit would nourish it and cause it to grow and spread. Not until Elijah had been taken away and his spirit had descended on his disciple Elisha did Elisha start to preach and heal. So, too, as God had been with Jesus, He would be with the disciples to see that they were cared for, protected and guided in all they did.

Not long before Jesus had told His disciples, "Now is the judgment of this world; now the leaders of this world will be cast out. And I, when I am lifted up from the earth will draw every man to me." A just man was soon to be delivered into the hands of the wicked and unjust, to be raised to the cross and crucified in order to become an everlasting example of meekness and forgiveness and to confirm with His own blood what He had taught His followers. When Jesus was lifted to the cross, He would draw humanity to Himself, and all those who had been tired of war and hatred and who were carrying heavy burdens would turn to His religion.

Peace on earth has been the core of the teaching of all prophets and religious founders. Philosophers and kings have sought it; priests and the pious have prayed for it; yet the world has sought it in the wrong places. Men have searched for it in books, on the tops of high mountains, in foreign lands, and in alliances and treaties, but they have failed to search for it in the depths of their own hearts, for they have not realized that they have to be peaceful within themselves before they can find it outside.

Jesus was to leave His disciples in a turbulent and wicked world, but He was not to forsake them. His Spirit would remain with them until the end of time. He was to enshrine in their hearts a new peace, a peace that would be like armor about them, a peace that would cause both conqueror and vanquished to embrace one another. This peace would be the inner peace of the soul, the peace of God which passes all human understanding. Jesus had no fear of death on the cross, for His heart was with His disciples who were soon to be bereaved. His request to see the deadly cup removed was for their sake, but to drink from it and thus become an example of humility to the world was more important than to remain with those who had followed Him.

All that Jesus wanted from His disciples during the darkest hour of His life was that they remain united, loyal to Him, and continue to preach His Gospel. In the past, many great teachers had died and their disciples had abandoned their teachings, so Jesus prayed that His disciples would remain with Him and draw strength from Him just as the branches of a vine remain with the root in order to receive nourishment.

"Vine" is symbolic of a race of people, and Israel was portrayed as a vine which God had planted in Palestine and the branches of which reached Egypt, Babylon and other distant lands. The whole objective of Judaism was to keep these branches pruned, strong and healthy, and to nourish the vine itself with pure streams of water so it would produce and spread all over the world. God had told Abraham that with his seed, all the nations of the earth would be blessed.

Now Jesus was the true vine, the reborn Judaism, the true teaching for which the prophets had died, and God was the husbandman. Every branch (man) of the vine that did not produce good fruit would be cut off and those that bore fruit, Jesus would prune so more fruit would be produced. The disciples and their followers were already pruned, that is to say, they had been educated by Jesus and nourished by His Spirit.

I am the vine, you are the branches. He who remains with me, and I with him, will bear abundant fruit; for without me you can do nothing. Unless a man remains with me, he will be cast outside like a branch which is withered, which they pick up and throw into the fire to be burned. If you remain with me, and my words remain with you, whatever you ask shall be done for you. . . . This is my commandment: That you love one another just as I have loved you. There is no greater love than this, that a man lay down his life for the sake of his friends. You are my friends if you do everything that I command you. Henceforth I will not call you servants, because a servant does not know what his master does; but I have always called you my friends, because everything that I heard from my Father I have made known to you. I command these things to you so that you may love one another. (John 15:5-7; 12-15, 17)

Love is the only answer to all of the world's problems, for it can accomplish that which force and hatred have failed to do. From time immemorial, the world has been dominated by force and only those in power rule. The humble have been trampled on. A thousand years before Jesus, the Israelites asked King Rehoboam, the son of Solomon, to lower their taxes, but he was advised to demand more, so the suffering people finally revolted against him. Under the Roman's iron yoke, however, revolt was impossible, for the Roman legionnaires had crushed every attempt, sometimes before it even started.

Even though Jesus knew His hour had come, He did not flee. He had decided to do the will of His Father and to drink the bitter cup (death) that was prepared for Him:

> Hereafter I will not talk much with you; for the prince of this world comes; and yet he has nothing against me. But that the world may know that I love my Father, and as my Father has commanded me, so I do. (John 14:30–31)

The world had hated Jesus and rejected the Truth He had preached. Now it was ready to crucify Him, and it would do the same to His disciples, for a disciple is not more important than his master nor a servant than his lord. Jesus wanted to remind His disciples of the difficulties that lay ahead of them, so they would remember what He had told them:

> I have spoken these things to you so that you may not stumble. For they will put you out of their synagogues; and the hour will come that whoever kills you will think that he has offered an offering to God. And these things they will do because they have not known my Father, nor me. I have spoken these things to you that when their time does come, you may remember them, and that I told you. And these things I did not tell you before because I was with you. (John 16:1–4)

Now the disciples at last understood that when He said, "I am going away," He referred to His departure from this life, not, as they had previously thought, that He was going on a journey as He had done in the past.

> But I tell you the truth, It is better for you that I should go away; for if I do not go away, the Comforter will not

come to you; but if I should go, I will send him to you. (John 16:7)

The Holy Spirit would vindicate Jesus. Even though He was going to be crucified as a malefactor and blasphemer, through his resurrection the world would know that He was a righteous man who had gone to the cross willingly. While the wicked would be punished, those who had followed Jesus would be protected and guided by the Holy Spirit. It was still hard for them to accept His coming death, and Jesus tried to encourage the disciples and reassure them:

Truly, truly, I say to you that you will weep and wail, and yet the world will rejoice; and you will be sad, but your sadness will be changed into gladness. When a woman is in travail, she is depressed because her day has arrived; but when she has given birth to a son, she no longer remembers her troubles because of the joy that a male child is born into the world. So you also are depressed; but I will see you again, and your heart will rejoice, and your joy no man will take away from you. In that day you will not ask me for anything. Truly, truly, I say to you that whatever you ask my Father in my name (my method), he will give it to you. (John 16:20–23)

Then He spoke candidly to them, trying to make them accept the fact that the prophecies about Him were soon to be fulfilled and that even they were to leave Him and flee for their lives:

For behold, the hour is coming, and it has now come, when you will be dispersed, every man to his own country, and you will leave me alone; and yet I am never alone because the Father is with me. These things I have said to you that in me you may have peace. In the world you will have tribulation; but have courage, I have conquered the world. (John 16:32–33)

His Father, for whose religion He was soon to suffer death on the cross, was not to forsake Him. He would be with Him to give Him strength in His hour of agony, and He would be with Him in the grave to raise Him up and confound His enemies, but His disciples, who were, after all, human, would be frightened and disillusioned, although they would later regain their courage.

One evening during Passover week, Simon the Leper, a Pharisee who had once suffered from leprosy, invited Jesus to dine with him at his house in Beth Ania. The term "leper" was used to distinguish Simon from the other men also with the same name. Easterners address men by their nicknames and the defects on their bodies, for example, they say Simon the Lame, Paul the Deaf, Joseph the Carpenter. We do not know why Simon the Leper extended his invitation to a man who had been denounced by the council and who was sought by the authorities, but a year before he had seen Jesus raise Lazarus from the dead, and he probably wanted to know more about this man from Galilee. Simon therefore gave a lavish banquet for Him and invited many friends and important figures. The sun had just set behind the lofty hills when thirteen sturdy and weather-beaten Galileans, dressed in coarse, provincial clothes and with woolen hats and turbans, emerged from the temple grounds and crossed the Brook of Kidron on their way to Beth Ania. When they reached the outskirts of the town, they were greeted by Simon and a number of dignitaries and escorted to the house. They were ushered to their places where they sat with their shoes removed but their hats on like the other guests. Easterners never remove their hats when they eat.

No episode in the Gospels is more misunderstood and misrepresented than that of Mary of Magdala. Magdala is a small village by the lake in Galilee and Mary, who had been a sinner, became a convert when Jesus had cast out the seven devils (seven bad habits) from her. Some writers who are unfamiliar with the customs and manners of the East, picture her as a prominent and wealthy woman who played a harlot with kings and who lived in a large palace in Jerusalem. We are told by some of these writers that she had hundreds of acres of land on which she raised flowers for the manufacture of perfume. But they do not know that a little alabaster container of precious nardin was the only valuable possession this woman had. It was an heirloom she had inherited from her mother.

Mary had come to the Holy City to celebrate the Passover and apparently stayed in Beth Ania because there was no more room in Jerusalem and the people of the small town were more friendly toward strangers. When she heard that Simon the Leper was giving a banquet in honor of Jesus, she could hardly believe it, for why should a Pharisee entertain a teacher of religion whose teachings had been openly repudiated by the religious leaders? She thought Simon was inviting Jesus to discredit Him or to denounce Him in public at the banquet, and she was greatly concerned, for she loved Him with a pure and spiritual love. No longer was she the sinner she had once been. She was now a sincere, repentant woman who had, since her conversion, dedicated her life to God. She felt she owed Jesus a debt for saving her, and she wanted to see Him once more before the rumors she had heard about His arrest and death came true.

With trepidation, she went to the house of Simon the Leper, carrying with her only the small alabaster flask of nardin. When she entered, the guests had just finished eating, and the little stools upon which the trays and dishes had been placed were removed. Simon was at the right hand of Jesus; at His left, another notable, probably the rabbi of Beth Ania or the mayor. Some of the women and children were standing and watching the guests while others were seated a few yards away from the men, as was the custom. Mary walked quickly toward Jesus and when she reached Him, she opened her precious flask of oil and poured some over His head. Gently she rubbed His hair until He was anointed with the oil. Then she knelt at His feet, and lifting them in her hand, anointed them as well. Jesus did not restrain her. She had started weeping bitterly, but He knew that her heart was filled with sorrow and that tears would give her relief. She was not weeping for herself, however, but for the coming agony and death of her Master, and she was preparing His body for burial.

When she was through anointing His feet, she wiped them with her long, beautiful hair. That hair which her lovers had once admired and had stroked was now serving as a towel to wipe the feet of her beloved Master. When her ministrations were finished, she went to where the other women were seated.

The guests were horrified by her actions. Some of them wondered why Jesus had allowed her to touch Him, for in their eyes she was still a sinful harlot. But Jesus had come to forgive sinners, and Mary was already forgiven and baptized with her own tears. Some of the disciples grumbled to each other, "Why this waste? For it [the

nardin] could have been sold for a great sum, and given
to the poor," but Jesus overheard them and said:

> Why are you troubling the woman? She has done a good
> work to me. For you always have the poor with you, but
> you will not have me always. But this one who poured the
> perfume on my body did it as for my burial. And truly I say
> to you, Wherever this my gospel is preached throughout the
> world, what she has done will also be told as a memorial to
> her. (Matthew 26:8–13)

The two men who were most displeased with Mary's
conduct were Simon the Leper and Judah of Iscariot.
Simon felt that Jesus should have known better and not
allowed the woman to perfume His head and feet, for
the Pharisees knew that the Mosaic Law did not tolerate
harlotry, and once a woman is a harlot, she is always a
harlot. Judah thought Jesus was acting like a wealthy
landlord by having his feet rubbed by a woman who
had once been a sinner.

Jesus knew what Simon was thinking, for He turned
to him and said:

> When I entered your house, you did not give me even
> water for my feet; but she has wet my feet with her tears and
> wiped them with her hair. You did not kiss me; but she, since
> she entered, has not ceased to kiss my feet. You did not
> anoint my head with oil; but she has anointed my feet with
> perfume. For this reason, I say to you, Her many sins are
> forgiven because she loved much; but he to whom little is
> forgiven, loves little. (Luke 7:44–47)

As for Judah, his faith in Jesus was shattered and he
could no longer hold his peace. He decided not only to

reject his Master, but to help His enemies capture Him, for he knew where Jesus and the other disciples were staying, and he could deliver Him easily into the hands of the authorities.

26

THE LAST SUPPER

Then the day of unleavened bread came, on which it was the custom to kill the passover lamb. So Jesus sent Peter and John, and said to them, Go and prepare the passover for us to eat. They said to him, Where do you wish us to prepare? He said to them, Behold, when you enter the city, you will meet a man carrying a waterskin; follow him. And wherever he enters, Say to the master of the house, Our Teacher says, Where is the guest room, where I may eat the passover with my disciples? And behold, he will show you an upper room, large and furnished; there make ready. (Luke 22:7-12)

IN BIBLICAL LANDS, HOTELS, motels and lodging houses such as we know them were unknown until recently, nor did streets have names or numbers. Most pilgrims and other travelers spent the night with relatives, friends or perhaps with pious men who saw them on the street and asked them in.

Jesus was well acquainted with the customs of Jerusalem, and He knew that the water carriers were always men who carried large jars on their shoulders or goatskins on their backs for the public houses where only males lodged. (Women carried water only for use in their homes.) When the two disciples whom Jesus had sent saw a man carrying a large goatskin filled with water, they followed him into the inn and told the proprietor that their Master wanted a room in which to celebrate Passover. All of the preparations for the meal were made according to the ancient ritual. The unleavened bread, wine, lamb and bitter herbs, similar to those that the Israelites' forefathers had eaten in Egypt centuries before, were ready on the trays that were placed upon stools.

When the sun had set over the Mediterranean, Jesus and the remaining disciples joined the two in the upper room. They sat on cushions around the meal, a jar of red wine and a large round earthen cup nearby. Jesus sat in the center with three of the disciples who had been closest to Him. The others sat according to their seniority. All were silent and sad, for they could still hear Jesus' words at the banquet concerning His burial. Judah was silent and moody; the silver he had received in payment of his betrayal was already in his purse. Jesus knew that Judah had betrayed Him for thirty pieces of silver. He knew that this was the last Passover He was to eat with His beloved disciples.

When the time came to eat the meal, He said to them sadly, "I have greatly desired to eat this Passover with you before I suffer; For I say to you that henceforth I

will not eat it until it is fulfilled in the kingdom of God."
And just as they were sitting down, a dispute arose
among them as to which was the most important. Jesus
rebuked them, saying:

> The kings of the Gentiles are also their lords, and those
> who rule over them are called benefactors; But not so with
> you; let him who is great among you be the least, and he
> who is a leader be like one who serves. For who is greater,
> he who sits down or he who serves? Is it not he who sits
> down? But I am among you as one who serves. (Luke 22:
> 25–27)

Later, as they were eating, Jesus said, "Truly I say to
you that one of you will betray me." The disciples were
upset and puzzled and asked Him who the betrayer was,
but all He would answer was, "He who dips his hand
with me in the dish will betray me. The Son of man is
going just as it is written concerning him; but woe to
the man by whose hand the Son of man is betrayed! It
would have been far better for that man never to have
been born." When he heard these words, Judah asked,
"Master, perhaps it is I?" and Jesus replied only, "You
say that."

Then He took the loaf of bread, the staff of life that is
symbolic of the Truth, and blessed it. Breaking it, He
gave the pieces to His disciples saying, "Take, eat; this
is my body." No longer was the bread symbolic of the
flesh of the lamb that had been slain as a memorial of
the Israelites. It became the symbol of Christ's body, of
the New Testament that was soon to be sealed by His
death.

He took the cup of wine and giving thanks, offered it
to them, saying, "Take, drink of it, all of you. This is

my blood of the new testament which is shed for many for the remission of sins." The wine became symbolic of the spiritual blood of Jesus, the blood of the New Covenant which was to be shed not only for the Jews, but for the whole world.

Then Jesus "Rose from supper and laid aside his robe; and he took a cloth and tied it around his loins. Then he poured water into a basin, and began to wash the feet of his disciples and to wipe them with the cloth which was tied around his loins." (John 13:4–5)

What Jesus did was contrary to the custom of the land. A woman who loved her family would wash the feet of her husband and children, or a slave would do it as part of his duties, but by washing the feet of His disciples, Jesus lowered Himself below the position of His disciples to illustrate that no one among them should make himself higher than the others.

When He came to Simon Peter, the disciple asked, "Are you, my Lord, going to wash my feet?" Jesus answered, "What I am doing, you do not know now, but later you will understand." Simon, horrified, argued back. "You will never wash my feet," but Jesus replied gently, "If I do not wash you, you have no part with me." (John 13:6–8) Then Simon understood that there was something holy in this new ritual, so he asked Jesus to wash not only his feet, but also his hands and head. Jesus, however, said to him, "He who has bathed does not need except to wash his feet only, for he is already all clean; so you are all clean, but not everyone of you," (John 13:10) for He knew that Judah's heart was unclean.

When Jesus had finished washing and wiping their feet, He sat down again and looking at the disciples said,

Do you know what I have done to you? You call me Teacher and Lord; and what you say is well, for I am. If

I then, your Lord and Teacher, have washed your feet, how much more should you wash one another's feet? For I have given you this as an example, so that just as I have done to you, you should also do. Truly, truly, I say to you, There is no servant who is greater than his master; and no apostle who is greater than he who sent him. (John 13:12–16)

Jesus' actions were His instructions for His followers. In the future, they were to accept His teaching, to become the example of a new order and a light to those who groped in the darkness. Now He was ready to reveal the identity of the one who was to betray Him. "Truly, truly, I say to you, one of you will betray me." John, probably the youngest of the disciples and the one closest of all to Jesus was very sad, and was leaning on the bosom of His Master. Jesus loved John as a son, and John felt certain He would reveal the secret to him, so he asked in a low voice, "My Lord, who is he?" Jesus replied, "The one for whom I dip bread and give it to him," and as He spoke, He dipped the bread and handed it to Judah, saying, "What you are going to do, do it soon." Since Judah was the man who purchased provisions for the group, the other disciples thought that Jesus meant that Judah should buy some of the supplies that would be needed the next day.

Then Jesus turned to the disciples and said sadly, "My sons, I am with you yet a little while, and you will seek me. And just as I said to the Jews, Where I go you cannot come; the same I now tell you also. A new commandment I give you, that you love one another; just as I have loved you, that you also love one another." (John 13:33–35) Simon Peter could not understand and asked Him where He was going. Jesus turned to him and looking into his eyes, replied, "Will you lay down your life for me? Truly, truly, I say to you, The cock shall not crow until you have denied me three times. Behold, the hour is coming, and it has now come, when you will be dispersed, everyone to his own country and you will leave me alone; and yet I am never alone, because the Father is with me."

The Old Covenant was closed; the Temple, the core of the Jewish faith, was soon to be demolished. The Lamb of God was ready to be offered for the remission of the sins of the world, a living offering which would abolish the animal sacrifices forever.

The last prayer of Jesus was different from that which He had taught His disciples two years before (The Lord's Prayer). His last prayer was emotional and supplicating—the prayer of a teacher of religion who had eaten the last Passover with His beloved disciples and was now ready to say farewell to them. He asked nothing for Himself. He had surrendered His human will to God's divine will, and He was sure that God would glorify Him and protect those whom He had entrusted with the divine and living truths.

Jesus prayed in such a way that His simple and illiterate disciples might understand His words and feel His emotions:

O my Father, the hour has come; glorify thy Son, so that thy Son may glorify thee. Since thou hast given him power over all flesh, so that to all whom thou hast given him, he may give life eternal. And this is life eternal, that they might know thee, that thou art the only true God, even the one who sent Jesus Christ. I have already glorified thee on the earth; for the work which thou hadst given to me to do, I have finished. (John 17:1–4)

He prayed to God His Father to exonerate Him before those who had condemned Him and those who
would crucify Him as a malefactor, and to raise Him from
the grave with glory and honor. His prayer was a peti-
tion made by Jesus, the man, to God His Father, and a
supplication on behalf of His disciples. He asked nothing
for the world. The princes of the world were already
condemned. By their own evil actions they had condemned themselves. The world was to pay for its evils.

What I request is for them; I make no request for the
world, but for those whom thou hast given to me; because
they are thine. And everything which is mine is thine; and
what is thine is mine; and I am glorified by them. Hereafter
I am not in the world, but these are in the world; and I am
coming to thee. O holy Father, protect them in thy name,
which thou hast given me, that they may be one, even
as we are. While I was with them in the world, I protected
them in thy name; those whom thou gavest me I protected,
and not one of them is lost except the son of perdition
(Judah), that the scripture might be fulfilled. (John 17:
9–12)

In a short time Jesus would leave His disciples and
appear to them in a spiritual body, the image and likeness of God, the true image in which God had created
man. Soon the hitherto doubtful disciples would transcend this physical world and start to live in a Spiritual
world. The world would hate them, imprison and kill
them, and Jesus wanted to see them protected. The hope
of a new and better world was in the Gospel which Jesus
had entrusted to them. They were to irrigate, cultivate
and nourish the seed which He had sown. Jesus was
leaving with faith and confidence that they would carry

on His Eternal Gospel to all corners of the world and that this Gospel would triumph. As Jesus had glorified God who had sent him, so His disciples would glorify their Lord Jesus Christ. As He was willing to die on the cross for the sake of the divine Truth, so they also would be willing to die for the Truth.

A few decades later hundreds of thousands of Jesus' followers died horrible deaths at the hands of their enemies during persecutions. But their deaths were not in vain. Thousands of other men and women were converted to Christ through their deaths and the testimony of the Living Christ.

27

BETRAYAL
AND
TRIAL

THE FEAST OF THE *peskha*,
Passover, was ended. The gray twilight had changed to
darkness and the narrow streets of Jerusalem, which during the day had been choked with humanity, were now
deserted. The city was silent, and some of the people
were preparing to leave. Immediately after the Last Supper, Judah had risen and hastily left the room. He had
gone to carry out his treacherous scheme of betrayal and
to offer his assistance in the arrest of Jesus.

After Judah's departure, Jesus and the other eleven
disciples returned to the Garden at Gethsemane where
they had been staying during the holy week. With no
room in the city for them, they had gone to the Garden
which was much like a park where travelers could sleep
out in the open under the olive trees. Gethsemane lies

at the foot of the Mount of Olives and is famous for its olive trees, some of which have been there since Abraham entered the town of Jerusalem two thousand years before. At that time, Jerusalem was known as *Shalem,* the Place of Peace.

Judah knew where his Master and the other disciples were sleeping, for he, too, had slept there many times before. Even though the April nights were chilly, Gethsemane was better than the crowded, dirty houses, for the air was pure and the brilliant stars were far better companions than the men who were conspiring to arrest Jesus. Furthermore, in case of danger it would be easier to flee from the Garden, for Jesus knew that His disciples would desert Him, and it would be easier for them to escape from the park than from the city itself.

Jesus and His disciples crossed the Brook of Kidron and entered the Garden during the night hours. They walked a few yards to the large olive trees and when they reached them, Jesus told the disciples to leave Him, for He wanted to pray, but He asked Simon Peter, James and John to accompany Him. These three men had been closer to Him than the others, and they understood Him, for they had been with Him longer.

As the four drew apart, Jesus turned to His companions and said, "My soul is sorrowful even to death; wait for me here and watch with me," for now He was to pour out His heart to God, and He had to weep for all His people whom He would soon be leaving. Then, moving apart from them a little farther, He began to pray aloud. "O my Father, if this cup cannot pass, and if I must drink it, let it be according to thy will."

The cup was symbolic of the conspiracy to have Him arrested. In the East, when men wish to do away with their enemies, they prepare a banquet and poison the

cup from which the victim is to drink, because of cour-
tesy he cannot refuse. Jesus did not have to drink the
cup of death. He could have fled with His disciples, but
He wanted to do the will of His Father and fulfill the
Scriptures.

After He had finished praying, He returned to His disciples, whom He found lying on the ground instead of
praying, for they were tired and frightened. At the Last
Supper, their Master had revealed to them that His betrayal would take place that very evening, and they
feared that because they had traveled with Him and were
therefore deeply implicated in His actions, they, too,
would be arrested even though they had heard Him
pray for their protection.

When Jesus saw them stretched out on the ground, He
said to them, "Awake and pray, that you may not enter
into temptation," for there were many temptations that
they were soon to meet—the temptation to resist, the
temptation to fight, the temptation to join Judah in
delivering their Master to His enemies thus exonerating
themselves. But Jesus faced even stronger temptation.
The man of flesh, the human side of Him, told Him to
flee to Jericho and thence to the desert, or to return
home and forget about reforming the world: *You know
well that all prophets who have walked this narrow and
thorny road have met with torture and death. Even
though you die for the sake of the world, the people will
not appreciate your sacrifice. Their forefathers did not
mourn when the prophets were slain; why should they
now mourn you? The world is not ready for your teachings. The people will forget you even as they have forgotten those who came before you.*

But Jesus once again emerged triumphant, for the
Spirit was stronger, and the flesh was conquered forever.

After a little while, He drew apart again and prayed a second time, "O my Father, if this cup cannot pass, and if I must drink it, let it be according to thy will," for even at this late hour, Jesus felt that He might not be arrested or that perhaps His enemies might at least have some compassion for Him. But this hope was faint, and if the arrest was to take place and if He was to be put to death, it should be in accordance with the divine will of His Father. Everything that had been written about Him was to be fulfilled according to the divine plan in the Scriptures.

Jesus returned to His disciples and found them dozing, so He went away again and prayed a third time, using the same words. Then He went back to the resting men and said, "Sleep from now on and get your rest; behold, the hour has come, and the Son of man will be delivered into the hands of sinners."

As He was speaking, a large group of men were descending toward the Brook of Kidron. They were Temple guards, servants of the High Priests and a few scribes and Pharisees, and many were armed with swords, lances or staves as though they had come to capture a dangerous criminal. In their eyes, the disciples were a bodyguard for Jesus and Galileans were known for their bravery and strength, so they expected a fight when they tried to take Jesus.

As the silence was broken by the approaching footsteps, the disciples awoke and realized at last that what their Master had told them concerning His arrest and death was soon to take place. They saw that the Scriptural prophecy was to be fulfilled: The Messiah was to go the way of the other prophets, and their dreams of an earthly kingdom vanished like vapor before the sun. What a dreadful hour of disappointment for men who for three years had dreamt of earthly rewards and who had expected to hold high positions in a newly established Jewish commonwealth!

"Arise, let us go; behold, he who is to betray me has arrived," Jesus said sadly. It was the hour for which He had waited all the night—all His life—a glorious hour, an hour of distress, but also an hour of triumph and victory over evil, an hour destined to change the course of religion and history, an hour for which He had come into the world.

The group of armed men surrounded Jesus and His companions, and from the group Judah of Iscariot stepped forward and with a sham smile said, "*Shalam,* Peace, Master," and kissed Jesus on the cheek. It was a prearranged signal which he and the captors had decided on. Many times before had he kissed his Master in greeting, but this time it was a kiss of betrayal, a kiss of death, an act of disloyalty and treachery.

With a faint smile, Jesus turned to him and asked, "Is it for this that you have come, my friend?" for Judah was still a friend in Jesus' heart and He knew there was still a chance for repentance despite his weakness, dishonesty and greed. But Judah showed no emotion. For a moment he felt he had done his job so well that Jesus, whom he felt had deceived him for three years, would be arrested immediately and he, Judah, would be rewarded and freed. Suddenly, Simon Peter drew a sword (machete) and cut off the ear of one of the men who had tried to approach Jesus. But Jesus felt pity for the servant who had only followed orders and taking the severed ear, put it back on the man's head and immediately it was healed. As He did so, He said to Peter, "Return the sword to its place; for all who take swords will die by swords. Or do you think that I cannot ask of my Father, and he will now raise up for me more than twelve legions of angels?"

Jesus from the beginning had decided not to resist His arrest, and he turned to the men who were to take Him and said, "Have you come out with swords and staves to arrest me like a bandit? I sat with you every day, teaching in the temple, and you did not arrest me." While He was speaking, His disciples, whom He had instructed not to fight for Him, turned and fled.

So Jesus was arrested, and the procession returned triumphantly to Jerusalem to the palace of the High Priest Hanan, the father-in-law of Caiaphas. Waiting at the door of the palace were the Pharisees, the scribes and the elders. The sturdy, strong and fearless Galilean prophet who had thrown the moneychangers out of the Temple and who had silenced them so many times and made them ridiculous in the eyes of their people, stood before them silent and helpless.

The priests had mapped their strategem carefully, for they did not want to lose any time. The false prophet had to be condemned as soon as possible during the night while the people were asleep so there would be no uprising. Accordingly, members of the Sanhedrin, the highest Jewish tribunal, were hastily summoned to the palace so the trial could begin. Jesus, His hands bound behind Him, was brought in before Hanan and the members of the Council. Hanan and Jesus had not seen each other before, although each had heard of the other. Everything that Jesus had done in Galilee and in Judea was reported to the High Priests, but all the questioning and the debates with Jesus had been carried on by the lesser priests, scribes and Pharisees.

Hanan sat in his high chair, dressed in his ecclesiastical robes, breastplate, hat and tire. Jesus was forced to stand in the middle of the chamber so that all might see the man considered a blasphemer. Hanan closed his eyes for a few moments as though he was sorry to see a man born and raised in the Jewish faith revolting against the religion of his fathers. Then he wryly looked at Jesus from under his heavy, drooping eyelids and tried hard to understand Him. He wondered how a man like Him could go so astray and cause others to turn against their old religion. The old man shook his head and stroked his long, white beard in false wonder and sympathy.

The first question Hanan addressed to Jesus was about His disciples and His teachings, for he wanted to know if all of the disciples were Galileans and also something about the new religion Jesus had expounded. But Jesus refused to answer, for He knew that no answer would satisfy the High Priest. Finally, after persistent questioning, He replied, "I have spoken openly to the people, and I have always taught in the synagogue and in the temple where all Jews assemble; and I have spoken nothing secretly. Why do you ask me? Ask those who heard what I have spoken to them; behold, they know everything which I said."

Jesus addressed the High Priest informally as though He were addressing an ordinary man in the street, for in His eyes here was seated in judgment the head of those who had made the holy Temple a den of thieves, the leader of the men whom He had accused of being corrupt and disloyal to the Jewish faith. But the answer was not befitting to a Jewish patriarch, and one of the guards standing near Him struck Him on His cheek and said to Him, "Is this how you answer the high priest?" Jesus, however, answered, "If I have spoken any evil, testify to the evil; but if it is good, why did you strike me?"

Jesus was not expounding any new philosophies or

advocating teachings contrary to the teachings of Judaism. All of His teaching was based on the Law and the prophets, and He taught openly in the synagogue and at the homes of the people. At some of the meetings, Pharisees, scribes and other religious leaders had been present, and even though they did not agree with Him on certain observances and ordinances, there had been no hard feelings on either side. Nothing had been concealed from the Jewish authorities. Even His denunciations were sometimes made in their presence. Now Jesus did not care to reply to the questioning of Hanan. The priest was too old and too faithful to rabbinical doctrines and Temple ordinances to understand Jesus' teaching. He would have to be born again in order to comprehend all that Jesus had said.

Finally, the hasty trial was over, but Hanan could find no fault with the prisoner who stood before him. He therefore sent Him to his rival and son-in-law, the High Priest Caiaphas, who knew more about Jesus and His teaching, who was versed in Jewish law and who could handle the Roman authorities. The High Priest Hanan had done his duty. He had conducted the preliminary trial and had given his approval to whatever Caiaphas and the Council should decide to do.

Now when Jesus had been arrested in Gethsemane, two of His disciples, Simon Peter and John, had bravely followed the procession to the palace, for they wanted to know what would happen to their Master. Apparently, John was known at the palace, for he was allowed inside, but Simon Peter stood with the servants and guards around a bonfire that had been built in the courtyard to ward off the chill of the April morning. Suddenly, some of the men asked him, "Are you also one of his disciples?" but Simon denied it vehemently, answering,

"I am not." Then one of the servants of the High Priest, a relative of the man whose ear Simon had severed in the Garden, said to him, "Did I not see you with him in the garden?" and again, Simon denied it. Then, an hour later another saw him and said, "Truly, you also are one of them, for even your speech proves it," and Simon, for a third time, denied knowing Jesus. And as he spoke, a cock crowed, and Jesus, as He passed him on His way to Caiaphas, turned and looked at him, and Simon remembered his Master's warning: "Truly I say to you that in this very night, before the cock crows, you will deny me three times." And Simon went aside and wept bitterly.

Caiaphas lived in the same palace as Hanan, his apartments on the other side of the spacious courtyard. When Jesus was brought in, His hands still bound behind Him, the Council was in full session. There sat the learned scribes with the Torah, the stanch Pharisees, the rabbis, the doctors of law dressed in their flowing robes—all ready to explain the prophecies and the Law. False witnesses had been hired to testify against Jesus, for the Council was anxious for a conviction so they could execute Him legally by stoning, the punishment for blasphemy. The first of the witnesses was called and testified, "This man says, I can tear down the temple of God and build it in three days." This was indeed blasphemy in the eyes of the ecclesiastical authorities, for the Temple was the most sacred institution in Judaism. But the witnesses themselves could not agree on the accusations they made, and the Jewish law says that a man can be convicted only on the testimony of two witnesses. Furthermore, even if the two witnesses had agreed, the High Priest could not have sentenced Jesus to death, for He was a

Galilean under the authority of King Herod Antiphas, and the authority of Caiaphas was limited only to Judea.

Other witnesses were brought forward, but Caiaphas had no use for them. He was well versed in both the Roman and the Jewish law and tried hard, though unsuccessfully, to make Jesus answer incriminating questions. Finally, in a rage he stood up and shouted at Jesus, "You are not answering anything. What is it that these men testify against you?" But Jesus was silent. He knew His answers would not be accepted and would only help to incriminate Him, and besides, He knew the purpose behind the questioning. Many of the members of the Council had heard Him, but they had never heard Him say anything that could be construed as blasphemy against God or against the Jewish religion. Finally, Caiaphas accepted the futility of his efforts and asked Him, "I adjure you by the living God, to tell us if you are the Christ, the Son of God?"

The question put Jesus in a difficult position, for He knew He had to answer. The High Priest had bound Him with a solemn oath, but how could they accept a poor provincial man who looked like a vagabond, who stood before them bound, as the mighty Messiah? He was from Galilee, a land inhabited by many descendants of the Gentiles, His doctrines suspected in the eyes of the religious authorities. Some inhabitants of Galilee were pagans and their concept of God was different from that of the Jews. Therefore, Jesus did not answer "yes" or "no." He had used the term "Son of God" so frequently that some of His enemies understood what He meant, but the High Priest did not, so Jesus, knowing what was in his mind, answered curtly, "You say that. But I say to you that from henceforth you will see the Son of Man sitting at the right hand of power and coming upon the clouds of the sky." In the eyes of the Jews, no human being would be worthy enought to sit at the right hand of God, so when the High Priest heard Jesus' reply, He said to the Council, "Behold, he is blaspheming; why therefore do we need witnesses? Behold, you have now heard his blasphemy. What else do you want?" and the answer came back, "He is guilty of death." Then to show their rejection and repudiation of His answer, they spat on His face, covered it with a cloth and struck Him, saying, "O Christ, prophesy to us; who struck you?"

The gray dawn had changed to full light. Caravans were leaving the city and the night silence was broken by the noise of merchants and laborers on their way to work. The High Priests and the members of the Sanhedrin had spent a sleepless night, but they were satisfied. They had captured their enemy peacefully, had tried Him and had successfully convicted Him of blasphemy. Now they took counsel on how to put Him to death. Any sentence had to be confirmed by the Roman Governor and carried out by Roman authorities, for He was a Galilean and could not be put to death by Caiaphas. So Jesus was delivered to Pilate, the Roman Governor.

Pilate had been governor of Judea for but a short time, but like other Roman governors and procurators, he knew a great deal about the Jewish people whom he was governing. We know little about his background. We do know he must have been a member of the aristocracy, for invariably, all the high offices in the Roman Empire were held by the wealthy classes, the landowners and noblemen. The Roman Empire was ruled by force and only those who were powerful ruled over those who were weak, and those who were rich ruled over those who were poor.

Pilate was an avowed enemy of the Jews, for he looked

on them as peculiar, fanatical, backward and suspicious —a people hard to understand who were reluctant to yield to government. Although he knew a great deal about them, he had no understanding of their regard for their sacred heritage nor about their call or their mission on earth. His sole interest in them was concerned with taxation, tributes and gifts to the emperor. He had his first unhappy encounter with the people when he spent Temple money to build an aqueduct to bring much-needed water to Jerusalem. The Jewish religious leaders were naturally infuriated by this impious act, for they looked on the money as dedicated to God. On another occasion, Pilate had planted the Roman insignia with the image of the emperor in front of the Temple, and again, the Jews protested vehemently until finally he had to give in and remove the hated flag.

Now the Jews wanted a favor from him. Only he could confirm the death sentence the Sanhedrin had passed on Jesus of Nazareth.

That Friday morning, in the East called Sad, or Suffering, Friday, Pilate was awakened by one of his servants who informed him that a Jewish delegation waited outside to see him. The Jews could not enter into the praetorium because it was holy week and they could not go where leavened bread was eaten, so they stood in front of the palace waiting for Pilate to come to them. Finally, he arrived and seeing the prisoner, asked why they had brought the man to him. Then the High Priest, Caiaphas, spoke and stated that the prisoner for a long time had been inciting the people of Galilee and other parts of Judea by telling them not to pay taxes to Caesar and that He Himself was the king of the Jews. Then Jesus was brought before Pilate and the governor, wasting no time, spoke to Him in Aramaic, the language Jesus spoke and which the Romans understood.

"Are you the King of the Jews?"

"Do you say this of yourself or have others told it to you concerning me," answered Jesus expressing surprise.

"Why, am I a Jew? Your own people and the high priests have delivered you to me; what have you done?"

Then Jesus explained to the governor that His Kingdom was not of this world, that if it were, His soldiers would have fought so that He would not have been delivered to the Temple guards in Gethsemane.

The governor, who believed in one life and one kingdom here on earth, had heard about the Messianic Kingdom, but he could not understand its spiritual meaning.

"Then are you a king?"

And Jesus replied, "You say that I am a king."

Then He vainly tried to explain His mission to the governor:

"For this I was born, and for this very thing I came to the world, that I may bear witness concerning the truth. Whoever is of the truth will hear my voice."

(The Aramaic word *ashid*, bear witness, means to die for the sake of truth. The noun of this verb is *sahdey*, which means "the martyr." Today, Western Christians believe that "bear witness" means to testify, but in Aramaic, it means "I am willing to die for Jesus.")

What Jesus meant was that He was born for this cause and was willing to die for it. The governor understood, but he wanted to know a little more about the doctrine, so he asked, "What is the truth?" for he thought Jesus had been preaching something alien to the teachings of Judaism, but Jesus answered simply, "If I were a king, I would not have been so easily arrested in the stillness of the night," and this answer was enough for Pilate. He saw that the whole affair was a frame up, that there was not a grain of truth in the accusations which the Sanhedrin had brought against Jesus. Pilate was so convinced of the innocence of the prisoner that he told His accusers that he had examined Him and could find no fault in Him. Had Jesus answered, "Yes, I am the King of the Jews," He would have confirmed the charge of treason against Him, but He had answered, "You say that I am a king; I have never claimed to be a political king on this earth."

Later at the trial before Pilate, when the governor wanted to save Jesus, he asked the Jewish leaders, "What shall I do with Jesus, who is called the Christ?" They replied, "Let Him be crucified." And when Pilate asked, "What evil has He done?" they cried again, "Let Him be crucified."

At last Pilate realized that once again he had been defeated by the Jewish religious authorities, and the voice of the Council prevailed, although it in no way represented the voice of the Jewish people. His back was to the wall, and had he refused the request of the Jewish leaders, he would have been disgraced and probably recalled for rejecting the demand of the leaders of the country under Caesar. There is not the slightest doubt that Pilate, despite his hatred of the Jewish leaders, was a good man, a man who believed in justice and truth, and who feared retribution for wronging others, but when the mob cried, "If you do not crucify Him, you are not a friend of Caesar," he had no choice.

The governor had exhausted all legal means to save Jesus, who stood before him badly beaten by the Temple guards. At that moment, his wife sent a message to him by one of the servants that the poor rabbi was a pious,

righteous man who should not be delivered to His enemies to be crucified: "Have nothing to do with that
righteous man; for today I have suffered a great deal in
my dream because of Him." The governor, therefore,
tried to persuade the adamant religious leaders to be satisfied with a less severe punishment. When he learned that
Jesus was from Galilee, he wanted to turn Him over to
Herod to save himself from having to condemn Him to
death.

Now King Herod happened to be in Jerusalem at that
time for the Passover celebration, and he was most eager
to see the Prophet from Nazareth. He expected to be
amused by a few miracles, but when the king tried to
question Him, Jesus was silent just as He had been silent
before the Sanhedrin. Finally, tiring of the sport, Herod
had Him clothed in the *klamis,* a red robe worn by kings
and emperors. Red symbolizes a king's dedication to the
cause of his people and his willingness to die in battle,
if need be, for them. (It is said that the klamis had belonged to the former Jewish kings of the Hashmonian
dynasty and had been kept in the Temple for a future
Jewish king, but this cannot be true. The High Priests
would never have allowed such a sacred robe to be
removed from the Temple and placed on a man who had
been convicted of blasphemy. I believe it was one of King
Herod's own discarded royal robes.) His servants placed
it upon Jesus as a mockery and to show the king's willingness to confirm the political charges brought against
Jesus by the Sanhedrin and to see Him crucified. Then
He was returned to the palace.

When Pilate saw the robe, he realized that the king
was on the side of the religious authorities, but nevertheless, he still hoped that he might free Jesus. During
the week of the Passover, it was the custom of the im-

perial government to release one prisoner in order to pacify the subjugated people. So Pilate asked the people who stood in front of the palace if they wanted Jesus released or if they wanted Bar-Abba, a criminal who had been imprisoned for sedition, and the crowd, who would settle for nothing less than death, cried out, "Not him, but Bar-Abba." When Pilate asked, "What shall I then do with Jesus who is called the Christ?" the answer came as though from one throat: "Crucify him, crucify him! We have no king but Caesar."

When Pilate saw that he was gaining nothing and that the confusion was increasing, he took water and washing his hands before the people, said, "I am innocent of the blood of this righteous man; do as you please," and the crowd of evil men answered, "Let his blood be on us and on our children."

Thus the governor released to the people Bar-Abba, a common criminal, and had Jesus scourged with whips and delivered to the soldiers to be crucified.

28

THE
CRUCIFIXION

IT WAS LATE MORNING AND the procession to Golgotha, the Hill of the Skull, was now ready. The soldiers had entertained themselves by dressing Jesus in a red robe and had woven a crown of thorns for His head. They placed a reed, symbolizing a royal scepter, in His hand, and kneeling before Him, mocked Him, saying, "Hail, King of the Jews!" Then they spat on His swollen face and taking the reed, struck Him with it. Jesus stood silently and proudly in their midst like a lion that is cornered by hunters. Finally, the soldiers tired of their sport and taking off the scarlet robe, dressed Him in His own clothes again and led Him forth to be crucified.

As the procession started, the sun was high in the blue

Palestinian sky and the air was sweetened by the fragrance of spring flowers. It was the month of *Hababey*, the month of flowers, the long-expected spring when nature adorns mother earth like a bride who is adorned with jewels. This was the month when the Israelites had freed themselves from Egyptian bondage. Jesus loved the beautiful countryside in the springtime, but now He was on His way to Golgotha, His cross upon His shoulders. It was the last time He would see the beauties of nature He loved so much.

Jesus was strong, but now His body had been weakened by the punishment inflicted on Him by the soldiers. He was without sleep, hungry and thirsty. Suddenly, as He labored under the burden of the heavy cross, He stumbled and fell. The soldiers accompanying Him tried vainly to raise Him, but He was helpless. Just then they saw a man name Simon Cyrenian who was coming across the fields. Quickly, they forced him to lift one end of the cross, probably the long end that dragged along the uneven pavement. Thus, with Simon Cyrenian carrying one end, Jesus rose and again took up His part of the cross.

Among the crowd that left the praetorium to follow the sad procession were some who were grief-stricken, some who simply, in their bloodthirsty curiosity, wanted to see the crucifixion, and a great many Jewish women from Galilee and Judea. These women were friends and followers of Jesus, who had been waiting in front of the governor's palace in the vain hope that their beloved Master would be spared. The air that had been filled with rejoicing before Passover now was filled with wailing and lamentations.

As He climbed the steep hill toward Golgotha, Jesus

looked upon these women with compassion and said to them:

> O daughters of Jerusalem, do not weep over me; but weep over yourselves and over your children. For behold, the days are coming in which they will say, Blessed are the barren and the wombs that never gave birth and the breasts that never gave suck. Then they will begin to say to the mountains, Fall on us; and to the hills, Cover us. For if they do these things with the green wood, what will be done with dry wood?" (Luke 23:28–31)

And as He spoke, warm tears flowed over the dry clots of blood on His face.

Jesus was symbolic of the green tree, the innocent man who was suffering at the hands of sinners. The dry tree was the sinful men who deserved punishment for their evil deeds. Jesus wanted these women to save their tears for the great days of tribulation that were to come when Jerusalem would be destroyed, the Temple erased, the day when the people would ask the mountains to fall on them, the impending days of reckoning and vengeance.

The hill of Golgotha, which is called *Karkapta* in Aramaic, is shaped exactly like a human skull. Two little caves above look like eyesockets and a larger below resembles a mouth. The hill was used as a cemetery for strangers who died in Jerusalem, for such men could not be buried in the Jewish cemetery on the other side of the Brook of Kidron near the Mount of Olives. Not long ago, Golgotha was a Moslem cemetery.

On the top of the hill as Jesus approached, men, among them some Roman soldiers, were digging holes in the ground for the crosses of Jesus and the two thieves who had also been condemned to death. There was little time to be wasted, for it was Friday and the bodies could not be left on the crosses after six o'clock in the evening. As soon as Jesus and His two unfortunate companions made the final ascent to the summit, the soldiers lifted the cross and put it into the hole which had been dug in the ground. Then they stripped Jesus of His upper garments and lifting Him up, nailed first His hands and then His feet. His robe and other garments were thrown to some soldiers who sat at the foot of the cross and who cast lots for their possession.

Now the little hill, usually deserted, was crowded with priests and scribes, Pharisees and Sadducees and other dignitaries. At one side of the cross stood some of the commanders of the Roman legions, captains and officials. All had come to see the greatest drama of all, one that would be repeated every year by unborn generations until the end of time. Another lamb was to be slaughtered, an unblemished lamb, the Lamb of God, who was destined to fulfill the Scriptures and save the world.

A soldier offered Jesus a drink of vinegar mixed with gall to lessen His suffering, but Jesus refused to drink, for He wanted to taste the complete suffering of humanity. Then the soldiers placed over His head a tablet that read:

THIS IS JESUS THE KING OF THE JEWS

It was written in three languages: Latin, the language of the Roman Empire; Greek, the most prevalent language in Europe; and Hebrew, that is, the Aramaic spoken by the Jews of Palestine, for the procurator wanted all to know the reason for His crucifixion. The term "king" was used sarcastically and was specifically aimed at those who had brought the false political accusations against Him.

It was the ninth hour, and the news was spreading rapidly. There was a great wailing on the hill. Jewish women were weaping, tearing their garments, beating their breasts and pulling their hair. The mourning was not only for Jesus, but for the two criminals who were being crucified with Him, for they had been sentenced to death for acts against the Romans, and their families had come to lament their fate. They had been driven to lawlessness by the oppression, high taxation and poverty thrust upon them by the Romans.

Then Jesus, His throat and lips dry, cried out, "O Father, forgive them, for they know not what they are doing." Even as death approached, instead of begging for mercy and thinking of His suffering, Jesus asked His Father to forgive His enemies, for they did not realize what they were doing. The soldiers did not understand the Jewish prophecies in the Scriptures, nor did they understand that Jesus was the Messiah. Now He was fulfilling that which He had taught and which was sealed in the New Covenant, not with the blood of dumb animals, but with the blood of the Son of God. It was the first time in the history of religion that a teacher had lived up to what he had preached and taught and had offered up his life for his beliefs.

The April day was warm. The sun shone on Golgotha and the birds sang, unconcerned with the great drama that was taking place.

Jesus' thoughts turned to His mother who had come to the Passover feast to try to persuade Him to return to Galilee. She had probably stayed with Martha and Mary at Beth Ania, and one of the disciples during the night had doubtless brought her the tragic news of the arrest of her son. She had hidden in the crowd before the governor's palace, hoping that Jesus would be released, and then she had followed the procession to Golgotha.

Now she was in the midst of the crowd with John, who was trying vainly to comfort her. But who can comfort a woman whose child is dying? Sobbing, she kept repeating the words David had uttered when he sang his lamentations over the death of his son Absalom: "I wish I could die instead of you. Oh, my son, my son. Let me die for you." Then she turned for a moment and gazed at His hands and feet from which the warm blood oozed. She was weeping, but the men and women around her did not know for whom she cried. The three crosses were close to each other, and many women were mourning for their loved ones.

But the sounds of crying were drowned out by jeers, curses and shouts of defiance as some of the men shouted at Jesus, challenging Him to prove that He was the Messiah and come down from the cross so that even the Romans would believe in Him.

Suddenly, Jesus opened His eyes and beheld His mournful mother standing there in her Galilean clothes with the veil He had often seen upon her shoulders. And when He saw her there with John at her side, He cried out, "Woman, behold your son!" Then He looked at John and said, "Behold your mother!" And from that minute, John became her son to care for her and comfort her.

It was afternoon, and still more people, eager to see the sight, jostled their way up the hill as others, disgusted, tried to leave.

Those who stood watching talked about Jesus. Some of them could remember the things He had told them during His visits to Jerusalem, some related the miracles He had performed—the dead He had raised, the restoring of sight to the blind, the lepers He had cleansed, the insane whom He had brought back to normalcy. Others shook their heads and said, "If He were the Messiah and all these things were true, He would not be on the cross. If He were able to raise the dead, why does He not help Himself, save His own life and come down from the cross? Why does He not perform a miracle right now?" Still others said scornfully, "He was a sorcerer and a dreamer. He did not perform any miracles, nor did He raise any dead. His disciples were duped into spreading stories. Why, they did not even try to save Him from arrest."

Then some of the men who stood near shouted, "You deceiver. Save yourself. Come down. Prove that you are the Messiah Christ," and the bandit on His left said to Him, "If you are the Christ, save yourself and save us also." But the one on the right rebuked him, saying, "Do you not fear even God, for you are also in the same judgment? And ours is just, for we are paid as we deserve and as we have done; but he has done nothing wrong."

Apparently, for a while the first criminal forgot his own agony in his enjoyment of the abuse that was being heaped on Jesus. But the other had been moved by Jesus' prayer, "O Father, forgive them, for they know not what they are doing." This sturdy young bandit had never heard such a tongue or such a prayer. He had never dreamed that a dying man would ever pray for those who were killing him. He had heard doomed men curse their slayers, but this was a new prayer from the heart of a righteous man, and he found hope in the living words which Jesus had uttered.

Opening his eyes, he said to Jesus, "Remember me, my Lord, when you come in your kingdom," and Jesus replied, "Truly I say to you today, you will be with me in Paradise." And the outlaw saw that there was life hereafter and a day of judgment. Jesus promised him that on that day he would be in His Kingdom, but even then, the bandit was already at peace in the Kingdom. His heaven began on the cross, for he was ready to die with the assurance that there is another life—a happier, eternal life. He knew the death of Jesus Christ was not in vain.

The malefactor was the last man Jesus converted while He was clothed in flesh. The cry of the bandit and his confession served as a rebuke to the arrogant Pharisees, scribes and others who did not know that Isaiah's prophecy of long ago was even then being fulfilled on the little hill of Golgotha.

Now it was the sixth hour, three o'clock in the afternoon. Darkness suddenly obliterated the sun that had been shining so brightly shortly before. Jerusalem was quiet, for the spectacle on the Hill overshadowed all the activities in the city. Death hovered over the ugly, bloodstained crosses. The three victims were in agony. They could hardly breathe and their bodies writhed with pain. At times they were delirious, for nature had mercy upon them, and their thoughts turned to the past when they were young and happy. But the fleeting moments vanished and they woke once again to the endless hours of torture.

The Prophet to whom the people from all walks of life had flocked was alone. All of His disciples except John, His mother Mary and a few other pious women had deserted Him. But God, His Father, who had permitted Him to drink from the cup of death to the last drop so that His love for His children might be revealed, was there to comfort Him. He had been with Him at the Garden of Gethsemane when Jesus had surrendered to His enemies. He had been with Him at the palace of Hanan and Caiaphas when He was branded a blasphemer. He had been with Him when Jesus stood before the Roman

governor, Pilate, and He had been there when He entered
Herod's palace. God had been with Him in all of His
trials, and now He was with Him on the cross. Men had
deserted Him, the world had turned against Him, but His
Father would never forsake Him. During all His trials,
Jesus had been guided by the Holy Scriptures and
strengthened by the Spirit of God which was upon Him.
What is human strength and endurance in such an hour
without faith in God and a triumphant victory over evil?

Suddenly, Jesus tried to speak. His chest heaved and
He cried out loudly, *"Eli, Eli, lemana shabakthani!"*
"My God, my God, for this I was spared (or left)!"

Those who stood near the bottom of the cross thought
He was crying for Elijah to come down to help Him.
That is why they said, "He is calling on Elijah. Let us
see if Elijah will come to His aid." (In Aramaic the same
word which means "My God," *Eli,* is written and pronounced like *Elia,* Elijah, which means "the Lord is my
God.")

The word *shabakthani* is one of the most difficult
words in Aramaic. It means to keep, to spare, to allow,
to leave, to forgive, and to separate. When used as "to
leave," it does not mean to forsake. The Aramaic words
for "forsake" are *taatani* and *nashatani.* Had Jesus meant
forsaken, His enemies would have said, "He has confessed that He is an impostor." Instead, they said, "He
has trust in God. Let us see if God will deliver Him."
Jesus was not quoting any Scripture, but, like thousands
of Aramaic-speaking people, confessing His destiny.

The cry of confidence in God came from the parched
lips of a dying man. The words were addressed to the
mournful, bereaved and bewildered women who stood
near the cross and to some of His distressed followers
who were in the large crowd. He was reminding them

that He had told them that He was to die on the cross and the cross was His destiny. The prophecies had to be fulfilled.

The Scriptures say, "God does not forsake the righteous nor those who trust in Him." The psalmist wrote, "I was born and I was reared and I never saw a righteous man forsaken." God does not forsake even the wicked.

The cry of Christ was not a cry of defeat, but a cry of triumph and victory over sinister death and the grave.

The agony of thirst was greater than the agony of His enemies' taunts. It was more painful than the wounds in His hands and feet, more painful than the swarms of insects around His face. Water is the most vital element for life, especially for a wounded man who loses blood. Man can live without food for a long time, but without water few can endure more than a short while.

The Hill of the Skull is some distance from the city of Jerusalem and even in the city itself, water is usually scarce. The last water Jesus had drunk was on the night of the Last Supper when both wine and water had been available. Since His arrest, He had had none. In His delirium, He seemed to return to the lake at Galilee and saw Himself kneeling at the water's edge, drinking deeply of the cool liquid. But then He would return to consciousness more thirsty than ever. How many times during those long hours did He wish He could put His mouth to one of the springs in Galilee or quench His thirst from the jar of a woman coming from the well in Nazareth.

The end was near. Jesus had lost much blood and craved water to cool His burning body, but there was no water available on the Hill. In this dark hour, who would dare to go to town to bring Him a cup of cold water? Besides, who would think of giving water to a dy-

ing man? In desperation, He cried out, "I thirst," and a
soldier who heard the cry took a sponge and dipped it
in vinegar and offered it to Him, and Jesus drank.

The people gazed at the sky. The sun, the lamp of the
universe, was clothed with darkness and some were anxious to leave, for they feared it would rain. But no rain
fell that day.

The victims' strength was ebbing fast, the blood no
longer ran down the crosses. The silence was broken oc-
casionally by their gasps or faint cries, but for the most
part, they were motionless. Suddenly, Jesus cried out,
"It is fulfilled," and all that the prophets had predicted
about Him came to pass.

Jesus had triumphed over death and the cross. He had
given life a new meaning and religion a new synthesis.
He had played courageously and well in the great drama
which would be played over and over by generations to
come. He had proved that those who take the sword perish by the sword. A new emblem was raised—the ugly
and fearsome cross which now had been sanctified with
Jesus' blood was to become the most holy symbol of the
new realm—a symbol which a few centuries later would
grace the crowns of kings throughout the world.

And He cried out again, loudly so that all on the Hill
might hear Him: "O my Father, into thy hands I commit my spirit."

Then His head dropped forward, and Jesus died.

Matthew tells us that an earthquake at that moment
shook the land, the veil of the Temple was torn in two,
graves were opened, and the dead rose up and were seen
by men.

When the centurian who was in charge of the crucifixion saw that the end had come at last, he ordered the
soldiers to break the legs of the dead men to prove their

death. When they came to Jesus, however, they found His body cold as ice and instead of breaking His legs, one of the soldiers thrust a spear through His side, and blood and water gushed out. The soldier had heard Jesus' last cry and confessed that Jesus was an innocent man.

It was near six o'clock and the Sabbath was about to begin. The bodies of the victims had to be removed from their crosses and since the Jews could not touch a body or blood, the Gentile soldiers did the distasteful job. The Hill was now quiet and almost deserted. Only the soldiers and a few followers of Jesus remained and witnessed the lowering of the bodies and the hasty burial of Jesus. A nobleman and secret follower of Jesus named Joseph of Ramtha (Arimathea is incorrect) went to the governor and claimed the Nazarene's body. It was hastily wrapped in a white cotton burial cloth and a napkin was tied over His face. The body was then placed in a new tomb that Joseph of Ramtha had prepared for himself, and a large stone was placed over the entrance. It was a temporary burial, for the complete burial ceremony was to take place early Sunday morning and the makeshift arrangements were all that could be done before the last rays of the sun disappeared and the Sabbath began. There had been some concern about Jesus' body, for the leaders of the Jews had heard that Jesus had said that He would rise up from the dead on the third day, and they feared that His disciples might steal the body and claim that He had risen. Accordingly, they went to Pilate and asked him to seal the tomb and to set a guard at the entrance, and Pilate grudgingly agreed to do as they requested.

The two malefactors were buried in the Strangers' Cemetery or in the Jewish cemetery across the Brook of Kidron, and the three hideous, blood-stained crosses stood deserted on the Hill of the Skull.

29

THE
RESURRECTION
AND
THE ASCENSION

WHEN THE SABBATH WAS over, Mary of Magdala and Mary, the mother of James and Salome, bought spices that they might go to the tomb of their beloved Lord to give Him a complete burial service, anoint Him and say farewell to Him. (In the East, people believe that the spirit of the dead man remains in his body for three days, and he can see and hear those who visit his tomb.)

They left the city at daybreak and started for the tomb. It was cold, and the women were dressed in their coarse, Galilean garments, their woolen shawls thrown over their heads to conceal their identity. They walked quickly, and as they hurried up the narrow path to the entrance of the tomb, they wondered who would roll aside the stone that had been placed over it. To their great surprise, however, when they reached the entrance, they found that the stone had already been rolled away, and when they hesitantly entered the tomb, they found a young man dressed in white sitting on the right. They were very much frightened, but the man, who was an angel of the Lord, said to them, "Do not be afraid. You seek Jesus the Nazarene, who was crucified; he has risen; he is not here; behold the place where he was laid. But go away and tell his disciples, and Peter, that he will be before you in Galilee; there you will see him, just as he has told you."

In her fear and not understanding what the angel had meant, Mary, the mother of James and Salome, turned and fled back to the city to tell the disciples what had happened. But Mary of Magdala remained behind, weeping, for she did not know where her Lord was and she feared His enemies might have stolen His body. Suddenly, she looked up and saw a man standing in a field. He was clad only in his undergarments and at first she mistook him for a gardener.

When the man asked her, "Woman, why do you weep? and whom do you want?" she replied, "My lord, if you are the one who has taken him away, tell me where you have laid him, and I will go and take him away." Then the man looked into her drawn face, and as he spoke her name gently, Mary recognized the Man whose head and feet she had anointed with precious perfume. She cried out in Hebrew, "Rabbuni!" (in Aramaic, *Rabbuli*), which means "My teacher," and overcome with joy, she tried to embrace Him. Jesus stopped her, however, saying, "Do not come near me; for I have not yet ascended to my Father; but go to my brethren and say to them, I am ascending to my Father and your Father, and my God and your God."

Mary did as she was bid, but still the disciples could not believe the good news. Peter and John had already run to the sepulcher and had seen it empty, but like the women before them, they thought enemies had stolen the body so it could not be found. When Mary insisted that she had seen the Lord, they decided she had had an hallucination, for they thought the news of a man who had conquered death was too good to be true.

Now on that same day, two of Jesus' followers were leaving Jerusalem on their way to Emmaus, a village about six miles from the Holy City. They walked slowly, talking quietly to each other about the crucifixion and the things Jesus had told them before His death. They were still not convinced that He was the Messiah Christ, for, after all, He *had* been killed, but nevertheless, they believed Him to be a good teacher or a prophet who had tried to help the people. Suddenly, they heard footsteps behind them, and a man fell into step beside them. For a while he listened to their conversation, and then he began to question them. Finally, one of the men, Cleopas, stopped and turning to him, asked, "Are you alone a stranger from Jerusalem, that you do not know what has happened in it in these days?" and the man replied, "What things?" "About Jesus of Nazareth, a man who was a prophet, mighty in word and deed before God and before all the people."

Then the stranger began to expound the prophecies about the suffering of the Messiah, explaining what Isaiah had written about the Man of Sorrows and proving that the Messiah Christ had to die in order to triumph over the evil forces and inaugurate the reign of justice and peace.

As the sun set, the three reached the village of Emmaus, and Cleopas and his friend urged the stranger to stay with them as Easterners do. Finally, he consented, and as they sat to eat their meal, he took bread and breaking it, blessed it, giving it to them as he had so many times in the past. Suddenly, their eyes were opened, and they recognized their Teacher and Lord, but almost immediately, He was taken away from them.

Without delay, the two men returned to Jerusalem to take the good news to the disciples, but by the time they arrived, Jesus had already appeared to Simon Peter.

The apostles remained silent as they listened to the story, for they thought that the two men, like the women, had seen a vision. All were tired and constantly thinking of Jesus. It would be easy to imagine they had seen Him. And why did He not appear to His enemies, or at least to His other disciples? Why did He appear only to those four? While they were discussing it and puzzling over it, the shadow of a figure appeared in the room and when they looked, it was their Blessed Lord. Jesus upbraided them for their doubts and disbelief, saying,

> Peace be with you; it is I; do not be afraid. Why do you tremble? and why do thoughts arise in your hearts? Look at my hands and my feet, that it is I; feel me and understand; for a spirit has no flesh and bones, as you see I have.

and He showed them the wounds in His hands and the spear wound in His side. Then He continued, "Just as my Father has sent me, so I send you," giving them courage and added, "Receive the Holy Spirit. If you forgive a man his sins, they shall be forgiven to him; and if you withhold forgiveness of a man's sins, they are kept."

The disciples were given powers greater than those given to the High Priests. They were empowered to forgive a man his sins without sacrifices and gifts, and it is this doctrine of forgiveness which makes Christianity supreme.

Now Thomas, one of the disciples, had not been in the room when Jesus had appeared to the others, and when they said to him, "We have seen our Lord," he refused to believe them. "Unless I see in his hands the marks of the nails, and put my fingers in them, and put my hand into his side, I will not believe." As far as he was concerned, Jesus was dead, and the whole affair was over. The Messiah he had expected was to be unconquerable. Jesus had been conquered, and His corpse had been laid in a tomb. The three years he had spent with Jesus had been wasted, and nobody could convince him that Jesus had risen but Jesus Himself.

Eight days later, when Thomas was with the other disciples, Jesus once more appeared to them when the doors were locked, and said to Thomas, "Put your finger here, and see my hands; and reach out your hand and put it into my side; and be not faithless but believing," and Thomas cried out, "O my Lord and my God!" Then Jesus said to him, "Now you believe because you have seen me? Blessed are those who have not seen me, and have believed."

Jesus appeared only to those who knew Him, were transformed and believed in Him, but not to those who did not, for they would not have understood His resurrection.

The disciples had returned to Galilee and to their fishing. They were destitute, for their Lord had gone and the people no longer came to them. One day He appeared to them again. A day and a night they had been fishing without success, and knowing of their toil, Jesus told them to throw the net on the right side. They did so and caught so many fish that they were amazed. When they came ashore, they found a fire burning and the fish they had caught cooking with Jesus tending them. But Simon could not believe his eyes and after watching him for a few minutes, Jesus said, "Simon, son of Jonah, do you love me more than these things [meaning the pile of fish]?" And Simon replied, "Yes, my Lord, you know that I love you." Jesus said to him, "Feed my lambs." And then He said a second time, "Simon, son of Jonah, do you love me?" and again, Simon replied, "Yes, my Lord, you know that I love you," and Jesus said, "Feed my sheep." A third time Jesus asked, "Simon, son of Jonah, do you love me?" and it grieved Simon Peter to be asked a third time because he felt that Jesus had forgotten the promises he had made to Him and was doubting his loyalty, so he answered with some consternation, "My Lord, you understand well everything, you know that I love you," and Jesus said, "Feed my ewes."

In the East, the sheep are divided into three groups and are fed by three shepherds. The most experienced shepherd is in charge of the feeding, and thus Simon Peter was to be the shepherd of the whole flock. Jesus had wanted to test Simon's faith and loyalty. Now He knew that the once rock-headed man who did not readily understand things was one of His most devout disciples and was ready indeed to be a fisher of men.

During the forty days after His resurrection, Jesus appeared to His disciples and followers eleven times in order to strengthen their faith. He had triumphed over death and evil forces and proved that it is the Spirit which gives life. The Spirit is the essence of life. Jesus had assured His followers that He would be with them forever and that whenever two or three were gathered in His name, He would be with them.

It was not for the disciples to know when the new Kingdom would come. This was a secret known only to God. Nevertheless, Jesus assured them of tremendous power, the power to speak in hitherto unknown tongues, the power to teach, preach and heal. In the East, when people are converted, their whole attitude toward the world changes and they express themselves in a different manner of speech. Instead of cursing others, they bless them, and people refer to them as being "newly born" and speaking in "new tongues." This is the power of the Holy Spirit:

When the Holy Spirit comes upon you, you shall receive power and you shall be witnesses to me both in Jerusalem and in all Judea, also in the province of Samaria and to the uttermost part of the earth.

And when he had spoken these things, he ascended while they were looking at him; a cloud received him and he was hidden from their sight. And while they looked steadfastly toward heaven as he went up, behold two men stood by them in white robes; And they said to them, Men of Galilee, why do you stand gazing up into heaven? This same Jesus who has ascended from you into heaven shall so come in like manner as you have seen him ascend into heaven. (Acts 1:9–11)